Exploring Core Competencies in Jungian Psychoanalysis

I0130806

Presented in five parts, this comprehensive collection offers an in-depth understanding of the core competencies in Jungian psychoanalysis.

It is aligned with the main task of analytical training and practice—that of integrating the unconscious aspects of experience and developing a living relationship with it—and defines a set of key resources and skills for recognizing the emergence of the unconscious and its multiple manifestations, while offering ways to relate to it that fit individual clients and encourage growth and healing.

Featuring contributions from renowned Jungian analysts from across the globe, the book sheds light on how Jungians integrate common therapeutic methods in their practices and how they utilize others that are unique to their personal experiences, making the book an essential read for Jungian professionals, trainees, and students.

Gražina Gudaitė, PhD, is a Professor of Psychology at Vilnius University. She is a Jungian psychoanalyst and works as chair of the Analyst Training program in Lithuania. Gudaitė is the author of several books and articles in analytical psychology. Since 2016 she is a member of the IAAP Executive Committee.

Tom Kelly is past president of the International Association for Analytical Psychology (2013–2016). He initiated and chaired the yearly meeting of the Directors of Training of the North American Societies of Jungian Analysts (CNASJA) for 20 years. From 2017 to 2020, Tom was co-editor-in-chief for the *Journal of Analytical Psychology*. He currently serves as Chair of the Ethics Committee of the IAAP.

Exploring Core Competencies in Jungian Psychoanalysis

Research, Practice, and Training

Edited by Gražina Gudaitė and Tom Kelly

Routledge
Taylor & Francis Group

LONDON AND NEW YORK

Cover image: Audrone Uzielaite

First published 2023
by Routledge
4 Park Square, Milton Park, Abingdon, Oxon OX14 4RN

and by Routledge
605 Third Avenue, New York, NY 10158

Routledge is an imprint of the Taylor & Francis Group, an informa business

© 2023 selection and editorial matter, Gražina Gudaitė and Tom Kelly;
individual chapters, the contributors

The right of Gražina Gudaitė and Tom Kelly to be identified as the authors
of the editorial material, and of the authors for their individual chapters,
has been asserted in accordance with sections 77 and 78 of the Copyright,
Designs and Patents Act 1988.

All rights reserved. No part of this book may be reprinted or reproduced or utilised
in any form or by any electronic, mechanical, or other means, now known or
hereafter invented, including photocopying and recording, or in any information
storage or retrieval system, without permission in writing from the publishers.

Trademark notice: Product or corporate names may be trademarks or registered trademarks,
and are used only for identification and explanation without intent to infringe.

British Library Cataloguing-in-Publication Data
A catalogue record for this book is available from the British Library

Library of Congress Cataloging-in-Publication Data
Names: Gudaitė, Gražina, editor. | Kelly, Tom, editor.
Title: Exploring core competencies in Jungian psychoanalysis : research,
practice, and training / edited by Gražina Gudaitė and Tom Kelly.
Description: Milton Park, Abingdon, Oxon ; New York, NY : Routledge, 2022. |
Includes bibliographical references and index. | (hardback) |
ISBN 9781032114378 (paperback) | ISBN 9781003219910 (ebook)
Subjects: LCSH: Jungian psychology. | Psychoanalysis. |
Jung, C. G. (Carl Gustav), 1875–1961.
Classification: LCC BF173.J85 E97 2022 |
DDC 150.19/54–dc23/eng/20220210
LC record available at https://lccn.loc.gov/2022006227

ISBN: 9781032114385 (hbk)
ISBN: 9781032114378 (pbk)
ISBN: 9781003219910 (ebk)

DOI: 10.4324/9781003219910

Typeset in Times New Roman
by Newgen Publishing UK

Contents

Contributors

Editors

Gražina Gudaitė, PhD, is a Professor of Psychology at Vilnius University and a Jungian psychoanalyst. She is a member of the Lithuanian Association for Analytical Psychology and has been a member of the IAAP Executive Committee since 2016. Dr. Gudaitė is the author of several books and articles in analytical psychology, and co-editor with Murray Stein of *Confronting Cultural Trauma: Jungian Approaches to Understanding and Healing.* She has a private practice in Vilnius and is the director of the Analyst Training program in Lithuania.

Contact information: g.gudait@gmail.com

Tom Kelly was president of the International Association for Analytical Psychology (IAAP) from 2013 to 2016. He is a senior training analyst, supervisor, and past president of the Inter-Regional Society of Jungian Analysts (IRSJA) and past president of the Council of North American Societies of Jungian Analysts (CNASJA). During his term of office with CNASJA, Tom initiated the yearly meeting of the Directors of Training of the North American Societies and chaired these meetings for 20 years. Tom was the North American Editor of the *Journal of Analytical Psychology* from 2017 to 2020. He also serves on the Advisory Committee of the Institute of Analytical Psychology and Psychodrama in Italy. Tom has been actively engaged in teaching and lecturing in Developing Groups of the IAAP in different parts of the world for many years.

Contact information: tom-kelly@sympatico.ca

Contributors

Astrid Berg, MB ChB, FCPsych (SA), PhD (Child & Adolescent Psychiatry), is a Psychiatrist, Child & Adolescent Psychiatrist as well as a Jungian analyst. She is an Emerita A/Professor at the University of Cape Town and A/Professor Extraordinary at Stellenbosch University. She was a member of the Executive Committee of the IAAP and Vice-President from 1997 to 2007. She organized and hosted the XVIIth Conference of the IAAP in Cape Town, South Africa. In 2010 she was invited to give the annual Faye Lectures in the A&M University in Texas, USA. Her book *Connecting with South Africa – Cultural Communication and Understanding* was subsequently published. She has numerous other publications in peer-reviewed journals and book chapters.

Contact information: zimi@iafrica.com

Misser Berg became an analyst in 1992, she is co-founder of the Danish Society for Analytical Psychology, served as President of DSAP (2000–2005) and Director of Training at the C. G. Jung Institute, Copenhagen (2005–2019). She was President of the Jung Society of Copenhagen (1994–2020), was a member of the Executive Committee of the IAAP from 2010 to 2013, worked as Honorary Secretary (2013–2016), was Vice-President of the IAAP from 2016 and President-Elect from 2019. Misser berg is Chair of the IAAP Education Committee and has a private practice north of Copenhagen. In addition, she teaches and examines in both Denmark and abroad. Her recent publications include When Symbols Create Meaning for a Soul in Pain (2004) in *Matrix, Northern Journal for Psychotherapy* (in Danish) and *Role Complexity at a Smaller Training Institute, Some Reflections on the Ethical Aspects* (2017, in Danish).

Contact information: misser.berg@mail.dk; www.misserberg.dk

Ieva Bieliauskienė, PhD, received her Master's degree in Clinical Psychology (1998) and PhD in Psychology at Vilnius University (2014), and she has participated in research work at the Center of Psychodynamic Psychology (2010–2016). She has worked as a Jungian analyst in Vilnius since 2007. Ieva is the author of several articles on analytical psychology in the Lithuanian language.

Contact information: ieva.bieliauskienė@gmail.com

Joseph Cambray, PhD, is the President and CEO of Pacifica Graduate Institute. He is a past president of the International Association for Analytical Psychology, has served as the US Editor for *The Journal of Analytical Psychology*, and is on various editorial boards He was a faculty member at Harvard Medical School in the Department of Psychiatry at Massachusetts General Hospital, Center for Psychoanalytic Studies, and former President of the C. G. Jung Institute of Boston. Dr. Cambray is a Jungian analyst now living in the Santa Barbara area of California. His numerous publications include the book based on his Fay Lectures: *Synchronicity: Nature and*

Psyche in an Interconnected Universe and several edited volumes: one with Leslie Sawin, *Research in Analytical Psychology – Volume 1: Applications from Scientific, Historical, and (Cross)-Cultural Research*, and an earlier one with Linda Carter, *Analytical Psychology: Contemporary Perspectives in Jungian Psychology.* He has published numerous papers in a range of international journals.

Contact information: cambrayj@earthlink.net

August Cwik, PhysD, is a clinical psychologist, hypnotherapist, and Jungian analyst in private practice in the Chicago area. He is a member of the Chicago Society of Jungian Analysts and the Interregional Society of Jungian Analysts. He is also an Assistant Editor of the *Journal of Analytical Psychology.* He was Co-Director of Training of the Analyst Training Program and Co-Director of the Clinical Training Program in Analytical Psychotherapy at the C. G. Jung Institute of Chicago. His recent publications include; Numinous Images of a New Ethic: A Jungian View of Kieslwski's *The Decalague* in *The Routledge International Handbook of Jungian Film Studies* and What Is a Jungian Analyst Dreaming When Myth Comes to Mind? Thirdness as an Aspect of the Anima Media Natura, in *Journal of Analytical Psychology* (presented as a plenary session in Kyoto, Japan on September 1, 2016 at the XXth International Congress for Analytical Psychology – Anima Mundi in Transition: Cultural, Clinical and Professional Challenges).

Contact information: guscwik@hotmail.com

Verena Kast, PhD, has been Lecturer at Zurich University since 1982. From 1995 to 1998 she was President of IAAP and from 1999 to 2020 she was a member of the Steering Committee of the Lindauer Psychotherapiewochen. From 2012 to 2020 she was a member of the Curatorium of the C. G. Jung Institute Zurich, Küsnacht and from 2014 to 2020 she was President of the Curatorium of the CGJIZ. She has lectured in Europe, the US, Japan, and South America. Since 1982 she has published more than 80 books (translated in 18 languages), and she has written many articles.

Contact information: kast@swissonline.ch

Marianne Müller is a graduate of the C. G. Jung Institute Zurich (1996) and of the University of Bern (Master of Law 1981, Clinical Psychology 1998). She was President of the Swiss Society for Analytical Psychology (SGAP) from 2004 to 2010, and she was President of the International Association for Analytical Psychology (IAAP) from 2016 to 2019. She is a training analyst and supervisor at the C. G. Jung Institute Zurich and Liaison Person for the IAAP Router Training in Greece. For many years she was the Regional Organizer for the IAAP Education Committee in Central

Europe and has been engaged in training at many places. She works in private practice as analyst and mediator in Bern and Zurich.

Contact information: maramueller@bluewin.ch

Dovilė Petronytė–Kvedarauskienė received her Master's degree in Clinical Psychology and PhD in Psychology at Vilnius University. She has been working as a clinical psychologist and psychotherapist since 2001 and as a Jungian analyst from 2013. Dovilė is a member of Lithuanian Association for Analytical Psychology (LAPA), International Association for Analytical Psychology (IAAP), and the Society for Psychotherapy Research (SPR). Her recent publications include Relationship with Authority in Narcissism in the *International Journal of Psychology: Biopsychosocial Approach*.

Contact information: dovilepk@yahoo.co.uk

Goda Rukšaitė received her Master's degree in Clinical Psychology at Vilnius University (1998), participated in research work at the Center of Psychodynamic Psychology (2010–2016). She has worked as a Jungian analyst in Vilnius from 2007, and she is President of the Lithuanian Association for Analytical Psychology. Goda is the author of several articles on analytical psychology in the Lithuanian language. Her recent publications include *Lithuanian Historical Heritage: Relationship with Authority and Psychological Well-being*.

Contact information: gruskait@gmail.com

Murray Stein, PhD is a graduate of the C. G. Jung Institute of Zurich (1973), Yale University (1965), Yale Divinity School (1969), and the University of Chicago (1985). He is a founding member of The Inter-Regional Society of Jungian Analysts and the Chicago Society of Jungian Analysts. He was President of the International Association for Analytical Psychology (IAAP) from 2001 to 2004 and President of The International School of Analytical Psychology Zurich from 2008 to 2012. He has lectured internationally and is the author of *In MidLife, Jung's Map of the Soul, Minding the Self, Soul – Retrieval and Treatment* and *Outside, Inside and All Around* (2017). He lives in Switzerland and is a Training and Supervising Analyst with ISAPZurich. He has a private practice in Zurich.

Contact information: Email: murraywstein@gmail.com

Jan Wiener is a training and supervising analyst for the Society of Analytical Psychology in London. She has recently completed a term of office as Director of Training at the SAP. She was Vice-President of the IAAP from 2010 to 2013 and during this time was Co-Chair of the Education Committee with special responsibility for Developing Groups and the IAAP Router Training in Eastern Europe. She teaches and supervises both in the UK and internationally. She is the author of papers and chapters on themes such as transference, training, supervision, and ethics. She is the author/editor of four books. The most recent, edited with Catherine Crowther, *From Tradition to Innovation: Jungian Analysts Working in Different Cultural Settings* was published in 2015 by Spring Journal Books.

Contact information: Email:jan@janwiener.co.uk

Mark Winborn is a Jungian psychoanalyst in private practice in Memphis, USA. He is a training analyst of the Inter-Regional Society of Jungian Analysts and the C. G. Jung Institute, Zurich, and author of several books on Jungian psychoanalysis. He lectures nationally and internationally on analytic technique and comparative psychoanalysis.

Ursula Wirtz, PhD, is a clinical and anthropological psychologist and a Jungian analyst with a doctorate in literature and philosophy, practicing in Zürich. She is a faculty member, training analyst, and supervisor at the International School of Analytical Psychology (ISAPZURICH) and actively engaged in the training of Jungian analysts in Eastern European countries and China. She has taught at various European universities and abroad. She has numerous publications on trauma, sexual abuse, and the interface of psychotherapy and spirituality in German, English, Russian, and Czech. Her recent book *Trauma and Beyond. The Mystery of Transformation* (Routledge 2020) has been published in Chinese, Russian, Polish and Czech.

Contact information: ursula@wirtz.ch

Mari Yoshikawa, PhD, is originally from Osaka, Japan, and was educated at Kyoto University. She is Professor of Gakushuin University in Tokyo, being engaged in training certified clinical psychologists in Japan. In 2008, she studied at ISAP in Zurich and got a diploma of AJAJ (Association of Jungian Analysts, Japan) in 2016. She managed the Yamanashi Hakoniwa Institute for practices with imagery. She recently published the Japanese textbooks *The Profession of Clinical Psychologist* (NHK Publication, 2020) and the *Understandable Personality Psychology* (Minerva Publications, 2020). Her publications in English are The Shadow of Modernization in Japan as Seen in Natsume Soseki's Ten Night's Dreams, in *Confronting Cultural Trauma-Jungian Approaches to Understanding and Healing*, edited by Gražina Gudaitė and Murray Stein (Spring Journal, 2014), and A Japanese Perspective on the Meaning of the Serpent in the Red Book, in *Jung's Red Book for Our Time* edited by Murray Stein and Thomas Arzt (Chiron Publications, 2019).

Contact information: mariyoshikawa@joy.ocn.ne.jp

Acknowledgments

When I think about the history of the emergence of this book, I want first of all to thank Marianne Müller, past president of the IAAP and colleague who supported the idea of research on core competencies and later the idea of this book. We spent many hours discussing how best to develop the idea of core competencies in the Jungian field. Our discussions and exchanges were inspiring and stimulating. My heartfelt thanks to you, Marianne, for sharing your ideas, for your support and for your encouragement to further the realization of this project.

I am particularly grateful to the co-editor of this book, Tom Kelly, for his careful work with the chapters that comprise the book we have now. Tom has much experience in discussions on issues of "what makes a Jungian" analyst. His assistance in realizing this book on core competencies was invaluable. Thank you, Tom, for all your work and for the numerous discussions we had together in developing the project.

A heartfelt thanks to each contributing author for your interest and generosity in sharing your reflections on what really works in Jungian analysis. Your interest in contributing to the book was the crucial condition in making this project come to life. I am grateful for your willingness to work together. The collaboration and communication with each of you has been a deeply motivating, inspiring, and enriching experience. My thanks for your kindness and care, for sharing your reflections. I am confident that many colleagues from the Jungian community and beyond will be grateful for your contribution and for your input in their professional development.

I also want to thank Toshio Kawai, President of the IAAP, Misser Berg, President-Elect, and the Officers of IAAP as well as members of Executive Committee of the IAAP. The multiple discussions on issues having to do with training and competencies, on the diversity of training models in the IAAP, on the influence of culture, on the Router program – each of these contributed to the development of the idea and eventual realization of this book. My thanks to each of you for your support and trust.

Last, but certainly not least, my appreciation and heartfelt thanks to the members of the Lithuanian Association for Analytical Psychology. My colleagues from LAAP did an outstanding job in their research on core competencies. Each member of our Group contributed to the success of this project in one way or another and in our numerous discussions on this topic. My thanks to each of you for your openness and willingness to participate in different projects of contemporary analytical psychology, and for your serious attitude towards developments in analytical training and practice. I know you will be among the first readers of that book …

With my heartfelt thanks and gratitude.

Preface

Tom Kelly

A book on the "core competencies of Jungian psychoanalysis" may seem somewhat anathema to many in the Jungian community. The very notion of core competencies awakens images and associations of techniques and methods that, in and of themselves, seem to go against the grain of what lies at the very heart of Jungian psychology, namely the process of individuation. The paradox of this serpentine process, unique to each individual, is that while the path for each person is indeed unique, the process itself is archetypal and rooted in the deepest layers of the collective unconscious. A precondition and essential element for this process to take root and come to life in what Erich Neumann referred to as the establishment of a functional ego-self axis. The groundwork for the establishment of an ego–self axis is what Henry Abramovitch, quoted by Ursula Wirtz in her chapter of this book, aptly refers to as the "ABCs" of the intricate and delicate process of establishing a relationship with the unconscious.

This book is less about technique per se but rather about the art of Jungian psychoanalysis; it is not about the "ABCs" and it does not offer any recipes. It does, however, open many pathways for thought and reflection. Each author has contributed their thoughts on possible avenues and pathways to establish and maintain a living relationship with the unconscious that can ultimately lead to growth, healing, and transformation.

I am indebted to each author for sharing their thoughts and insights so generously. It has been an honor and a pleasure to work with each of them on this project. I am especially grateful to Marianne Müller for breathing life into this project during her term of office as President of the IAAP. Without her support and that of the Executive Committee, this innovative project would not have been possible.

Last, but certainly not least, my heartfelt thanks and gratitude to Gražina Gudaitė for her thoughtful presence and guidance throughout this process. Her openness, sensitivity, sincerity, commitment, and work ethic have made the collaboration with her on this book a joy from start to finish. It has been not only a pleasure but also an honor to work with Gražina on this project.

Introduction

Gražina Gudaitė

How can an individual enable another person's healing, growth, or process of transformation? This is the most complicated and, at the same time, the most inspiring question for anyone interested in the field of psychotherapy. It is inspiring in that it posits the ultimate aim of our work and how it is dependent on establishing a meaningful relatedness with the other, but it is also complicated since we can never fully know if we will be successful in our efforts to assist the other. The element of the Unknown occupies an ever present and important place in psychotherapy. Understanding the unconscious, establishing and then maintaining and practicing a living relationship with it, is a central theme of analytical psychology as described by C. G. Jung. Though Jung himself never used terms such as "professional" or "competent analyst", he emphasized the fundamental role of the analyst in the analytical process.

> It seems to me, that the findings and experiences of analytical psychology can at least provide a foundation, for as soon as psychotherapy takes the doctor himself for its subject, it transcends its medical origins and ceases to be merely a method for treating the sick.
>
> (Jung 1933, para. 174)

Jung's ideas about psychotherapy and understanding of the importance of the psychotherapist, written 90 years ago, interestingly correlate with the findings of contemporary psychotherapy researchers who state that the role of the psychotherapist has until recently been undeservedly underestimated. To explore the role of the psychotherapist is a very complex task, as it depends on so many dynamic factors related to the psychic reality of both the psychotherapist and the client. There are many ways in which this can be done; the idea of defining and developing core competencies in the field of analytical psychology is one of them.

In general, psychotherapeutic competencies refer to a person's capacity to facilitate the other person's healing, self-regulation, or maturation processes. Some schools of psychotherapy have adopted this concept and included it in

DOI: 10.4324/9781003219910-1

their training programs or accreditation procedures. As a result, a number of studies on the topic of core competencies have been published in the last decade (Newman 2013; Sperry 2010; Barsness 2018). The very notion of exploring core competencies in the Jungian field, however, arouses controversial feelings: the theoretical construct "competence" by itself does not resonate with the spirit of analytical psychology, neither in theory nor in practice. The very term "competence" comes from the word "compete" and hence the theme of competition. The individual's effectiveness in the outer world is not the task of analytical practice, which in contrast is focused on an individual's inner development and Self-realization. Interestingly, the origin of the term "competence" is also related to the notion of "coming together". Knowledge and skills, the individual's attitudinal components and relational capacities, their ethical attitude – all these need to come together in a psychotherapeutic moment. Exploring the constellation of a particular combination of competencies in a particular moment of therapy is an extremely difficult and complicated task. In the first chapter of this book, "Exploring Core Competencies in the Field of Psychotherapy: Understanding, Research, and Development", we introduce general questions of core competencies in psychotherapy and provide moments of its constellation in the psychotherapeutic process.

The idea of core competencies in the Jungian field came to the fore in discussions concerning the Router program organized by the IAAP. I was among one of the very first Routers and I continue to be involved in organizing Router training in my function as Regional Organizer for Eastern Europe. The Router program proved to be an innovative and novel model of training that provided the only viable option for many professionals in post-soviet regions. The benefits of this project are more than evident: Russia, Lithuania, Estonia, and the Czech Republic now have their own independent analytical training programs and institutes. The need for the Router program remains pertinent in Eastern Europe as well as in several countries in Asia, Africa, and South America. In the chapter entitled, "How Can the IAAP Router Foster the Development of Core Competencies in Future Members of the IAAP?", Miser Berg provides a comprehensive overview of the history and current structure of the Router program and explores avenues to improve the training offered.

Though the Router program is recognized throughout the world, questions concerning the quality of training and evaluation remain pertinent among IAAP Group Members with Training Status as well. During her term of office as president of the IAAP, Marianne Müller provided the impetus for research to define and articulate more clearly the core competencies of analytical psychology. She stated clearly that her

administration set out as one of its central goals to place the theory of analytical psychology in relation to recent research, to continue promoting

psychotherapy research and building bridges between clinicians and academics as well as deepening the relationship between the two disciples.
(Müller 2017, p. 4)

As a result, the Research and Evaluation Working Group of IAAP initiated research on the core competencies in the Jungian field during her administration. In 2018–2019, five LAAP analysts, each of them actively engaged as a researcher at Vilnius University, carried out a research project on the subjective understanding of core competencies in the Jungian field. Semi-structured interview and Inductive Thematic Analysis were the main methods used in this study. In total, 60 participants from 12 countries took part in this research project. The analytic attitude, capacity for symbolic life, the analytical relationship, mediating processes of transformation, cultural awareness, and relatedness were clarified as the emergent themes most aptly describing the core competencies in Jungian psychoanalysis. The structure and results of this research project are presented in the chapter entitled, "A Study of Core Competencies in Jungian Psychoanalysis".

Not surprisingly, this project revealed that experienced analysts had a much deeper understanding of the competencies in the Jungian field than younger analysts or candidates in training. This result correlates with the view of psychotherapy researchers who suggest that exploring the reflections of senior psychotherapists is one of the ways to deepen understanding of psychotherapy effectiveness. Following up on this insight, experienced analysts were invited to write a paper, based on their reflections on a particular competence in Jungian psychoanalysis. The major themes that emerged from this study became a guide to the structure this book with a focus on a deeper understanding of the following: the analytic attitude; a living relationship with the unconscious; analytical training issues; and the importance of culture in the analytical process

On the Analytic Attitude

One of the basic themes in understanding core competencies in Jungian psychoanalysis is the analytic attitude. In general, psychological attitude is defined as a way of thinking, feeling, or acting towards a person or life situation. Psychotherapeutic attitude depends on theory and practice, on a person's life experience and capacity to integrate these into a philosophy of life. As the concept of individuation and respect for the variety of ways the Self can manifest is an essential part of an analytical perspective, it is, of course, not possible to extrapolate one single definition of what constitutes an analytic attitude understanding of the analytic attitude is inevitably multifaceted. In this book we focus on three aspects: the complexity of psychic manifestation, relatedness to the symbolic dimension, and spirituality.

A psychodynamic approach emphasizes that all psychic events are connected and that growing awareness about the unconscious reasons underlying life experiences yields a beneficial and healing effect for the individual. Developing a connection of the individual with their unconscious, which in and of itself is a multidimensional experience, is a central task of Jungian analysis. Psyche is a self-regulating system, which can be understood not only by the principle of causality but also by that of synchronicity as psychic manifestation. Analytic attitude includes the deepest respect for the autonomy of the psyche and attentiveness to emerging signs from the deepest layers of the unconscious. In his contribution entitled "Complexity and Transformation" Joseph Cambray explores the principle of synchronicity in the context of contemporary studies drawn from the field of complexity studies. He writes:

> Jung's experiences during his own creative crisis (…), ultimately lead him to propose a new cosmology in which causality was complimented by synchronicity … He expanded the associative methods of psychoanalysis, by moving beyond personal associations to collective ones. This method was deemed applicable when significant psychic energy remained unmetabolized during the work on material such as dreams, after the personal associations were exhausted. Then, cultural, historical parallels, often from mythology, but having a collective symbolic resonance, were brought forward to shed light on the unresolved material.
>
> (Cambray, Chapter 3 of this book)

Collective symbolic resonance and relatedness to the symbolic dimension of life is another essential part of an analytic attitude from a Jungian perspective. Murray Stein in his inspiring chapter, "The Symbolic Attitude: A Core Competency for Jungian Psychoanalysts", emphasizes the importance of relatedness to the symbolic world as the basis for an analytic attitude.

> Symbols guide us as analysts throughout the analytic process as we accompany our analysands on the journey through the labyrinthine pathways of the human psyche. …. The task of the analyst is to take careful note of them as they emerge in the therapeutic relationship, to lift them up and hold them in mind as the analysis proceeds, and to help the analysand to reflect on them and let them suggest the meanings they may convey to the conscious mind.
>
> (Stein, Chapter 4 of this book)

Attentiveness to emerging symbols is closely related to another aspect of an analytic attitude, that of attentiveness to the **spiritual** dimension of experience. Spirituality has always held an exceptional place in analytical psychology. The religious function and the deep respect for the Force that stands beyond the experience, the search for a deeper understanding of the phenomenology of numinous moments or experiences, the evolution of the God image – these and other themes have been explored by C. G. Jung as well as by more contemporary analysts. In a most inspiring chapter entitled, "The Heart of the Matter: Spiritual Dimensions in Jungian Practice", Ursula Wirtz explores how recognition of, openness to and respect for moments of an experience of a spiritual nature belong to the core competencies in analytical practice:

> A spiritual dimension can also be sensed in the analyst's attitude to the work, the opus magnum, in the spirit of letting be, of non-intentionality. This is a state of mind where the controlling, volitional ego retreats and becomes free from attachment and preconceptions.
>
> (Wirtz, Chapter 5 of this book)

On a Living Relationship with the Unconscious

Recognizing the reality of the Force that stands beyond the personal experience, is closely related to the next group of competencies which we entitled the ability to establish and then maintain a **living relationship with the unconscious**. Jung wrote that the relationship with the unconscious is:

> exactly as if a dialogue between two human beings with equal rights, each of whom gives the other credit for a valid argument and considers it worthwhile to modify the conflicting standpoints by means of thorough comparison and discussion or else to distinguish them clearly from one another.
>
> (Jung 1916, para. 186)

There are many ways to practice a relationship with the unconscious: active imagination and imaginal dialogue, exploring projections in the therapeutic relationship, analysing emerging symbols and dreams, interpreting unconscious manifestations – all these and many other ways can be actualized in analytical practice. Each psychoanalyst has the choice to decide which way they consider most appropriate in a particular analytic situation. Though the analyst has choices, they must have an ethically responsible attitude towards the Unknown.

> Only by taking the unconscious seriously, communicating with it often, and actually acting upon what was learned, will show the great respect – love and devotion – that is necessary and put energy back into the system. It is an alchemical imperative: keep the heat turned up and vessel well sealed in order to allow transformation.
>
> (Cwik 1995, p. 154)

In the chapter entitled "On Being Imaginative" Verena Kast describes a living relationship with the unconscious as the ability "to see with the inner eye, to hear with the inner ear, to feel with the inner sense of touch – to be in contact with all senses, without having corresponding objects in the outside world" (Kast, Chapter 6 of this book). She explores the multiple ways imagination can manifest and its crucial role in expanding consciousness.

> The whole therapeutic process is highly imaginative: we imagine the life of our analysands, their fantasies, but also the processes of transference and countertransference can be seen as imaginations. All the imaginations our patients produce also mirror the therapeutic relationship and the therapeutic process.
>
> (Kast, Chapter 6 of this book)

Psychotherapeutic work with images is closely related with the ability to explore the deeper meaning and significance of both inner and outer experience. From this perspective, interpretation as a core competence holds an exceptional place in analytical therapy. Some authors maintain that developing the competence of interpretation is the most complicated and demanding task in psychodynamic training because it depends on so many factors and variants, including the possibility that such an intervention is contra-indicated. Mark Winborn's chapter in this book, "Analytic Interpretation: an Illustration of Core Competencies in Jungian Psychoanalysis", explores the importance of analytic interpretation and offers practical examples of how an interpretation can not only help to understand the unconscious but can also act as an invitation for the patient to see their world in a new way.

Exploring projections and work with the transference and countertransference is recognized as a core competence in most schools of psychotherapy and is a basic competence for becoming a Jungian analyst as well. Understanding the alchemy of relationship can never be completed; it benefits from research in developmental psychology, studies on the phenomenology of the encounter with the other, and awareness of the importance of cultural awareness, etc. The psychotherapist's involvement is unquestionably an important condition for the therapy process; at the same time, it is a relationship of a particular nature that raises essential questions. How, for example, does one develop the quality of being deeply involved in a mutual exchange and at the same time maintain the asymmetry of a relationship in service to the healing processes of the client? In her stimulating chapter entitled, "On the Therapeutic Relationship", Marianne Müller explores the parallels between Jungian understanding of the therapeutic relationship, including transference and countertransference, and contemporary postulates of intersubjectivity theory.

Two subjective worlds meet and influence each other, but the analyst's participation and corresponding task is to serve the interests of the analysand. An empathic – introspective stance is basic for keeping the 'intersubjective perspective' ... that guides their clinical thought and action.

(Müller, Chapter 7 of this book)

An empathic–introspective stance is closely related to reflective practice. Developing the reflective function lies at the very base of many competencies in psychotherapy. How an analyst uses their knowledge and skills, as well as their integrated personal and professional experience, will define how they reflect on and mirror back the present psychotherapeutic situation. "After all, the most valuable gift for humanity may lie in its ability to be reflective – reflective about the self and the other." This quotation comes from the chapter written by Astrid Berg, "The Relevance of Reflective Practice in the Training of Jungian Analysts." She states:

Fundamental to reflective functioning is the awareness of the other and how I affect the other. It is this relational process that needs to be experienced – it cannot be taught. It can be thought about, it can be theorized about, but it also has to be 'felt' in a real life way. How this could be incorporated in a conscious way into a training program is a challenge.

(Chapter 9)

This question leads us to the next section of this book, which is focused on questions related to analytical training.

On Analytical Training

Understanding the importance of being actively engaged in and related to the experience of training, openness to the variety of ways to practice a living relationship with the unconscious, keeping a balance between cognitive and experiential aspects – all of these and other questions are discussed in this section. A deeper understanding of the role of the analyst as teacher and of the role of the candidate in the training process is another important theme of the training process. In general, there is agreement on the importance of developing a respectful relationship among all participants of the training process, but at the same time shadow aspects of this relationship need to be considered as well. Issues of power and authority belong to the shadow aspects of training. More than 50 years ago, Hans Dieckmann wrote about authority constellations in analysis and in training (Dieckmann 1977). Appropriate use of authority can be constructive in creating clearly defined structures and expectations. On the other hand, authority may also manifest as a complex. If the teacher or candidate denies the reality of an authority complex, such a stance can distort the relationship between the participants of the process. August Cwik in his chapter, "Training in Thirdness and Thirdness in Training", states:

> Training will always be asymmetrical in its hierarchical organization, but that should not preclude an attempt to be egalitarian and democratic in our process … We trainers—training analysts, colloquium facilitators, supervisors, and committee members—must keep in mind that we do not possess a necessarily healthier or superior view of just what makes a good analyst. We should be striving for our training process to be generative and able to produce 'good enough' analysts. Our training attitude should be one of reasonable devotion to and acceptance of thirdness principles.
>
> (Cwik, Chapter 10 of this book)

Growing awareness about issues of authority is especially important in countries that have been liberated from former authoritarian regimes, an issue already discussed in previous publications by Gudaitė (2021).

On Relatedness to Culture in Analytical Practice

Cultural awareness is recognized as an important factor in contemporary psychotherapy practice. Research shows that individual narratives and one's sense of identity, as well as the meaning-making-process can be shaped and influenced by the culture an individual lives in and that an analyst and their client may give different meanings to the same story. The understanding of psychological development, pathology and healing are also shaped and influenced by cultural narratives. Deeper understanding of cultural complexes, facing cultural otherness, awareness of cultural trauma and moving towards a multicultural approach are all themes of contemporary studies of psychotherapy.

Some of the basic questions analysts need to face in dealing with these issues in the contemporary world are the focus of the innovative and stimulating chapter by Tom Kelly and Jan Wiener "Cultural Otherness: Implications for the Analytic Attitude". The authors share their reflections and ask, "What does it mean to tend to the psyche in another cultural context; do we need to think of different ways to make space for the symbolic? How are transference projections and countertransference experiences influenced by the cultural context?" Both authors have a rich and wide-ranging experience in working with different cultures and seek answers to these questions both by sharing their experience in training and practice and by referencing ideas of other contemporary authors.

Exploration of the importance of the influence of culture in analysis continues in the next chapter with a contribution by Mari Yoshikawa entitled, "On Relatedness to Cultures: the Struggles with Cultures in the Case of C. G. Jung and H. Kawai". Meeting with people from other cultures, especially in an analytical context, can be a deep and transformative process. As the author points out:

> However, confronting different cultures is more than just acquiring knowledge. It is an encounter with another culture through the deep layers of the unconscious. It reaches a level of participation mystique, and through the struggle with it, true understanding of different cultures becomes possible.
>
> (Chapter 13)

Contact with individuals from other cultures is an inevitable part of our contemporary reality; consequently, analysts need to be ready to face this reality and to work within it. Meeting the Other can be a great challenge and it may be a great gift; it may influence shifts in our understanding of the analytical attitude, and it may open new perspectives on how to enter into relationship with the unconscious in an ever-changing world.

Understanding and reflecting on the core competencies in the Jungian field is a complex process. In this "Introduction" I have provided a brief outline of the ideas that are developed in our book. We are conscious that we have had to focus on a select number of core competencies in analytical practice and that there could, of course, be other ways of understanding the core competencies of Jungian analytic work. We nevertheless sincerely hope that this book will prove to be a helpful contribution in the continuing search for a deeper comprehension of what enables and enhances the process to facilitate a client's growth as well as, what core competencies need to be cultivated in order to assist in the healing of an individual and their individuation process.

References

Barsness, R E 2018, Core Competencies in Relational Psychoanalysis: A Qualitative Study, in *Core Competencies of Relational Psychoanalysis. A Guide to Practise, Study and Research*, New York: Routledge.

Cwik, A G 1995, Active Imagination: Synthesis in Analysis, in *Jungian Analysis* (Ed. M Stein), Chicago and LaSalle: Open Court.

Dieckmann, H 1977, Some Aspects of the Development of Authority, *Journal of Analytical Psychology*, vol. 22, no. 3, pp. 230–242.

Gudaitė, G 2021, Relationship with Authority: Moving from Helplessness towards Experience of Authorship, in *Political Passions and Jungian Psychology. Social and Political Activism* in Analysis, London: Routledge.

Jung, C G 1916, *The Transcendent Function, CW 8*, William McGuire (Ed.), R F C Hull (trans.), London: Routledge.

Jung, C G 1933, *Problems of Modern Psychotherapy, CW 16*, William McGuire (Ed.), Ralph Manheim and R F C Hull (trans.), Princeton: Princeton University Press.

Müller, M 2017, Joint Conferences IAAP/ University, in *IAAP Newsheet*, 12, p. 4.

Newman, C F 2013, *Core Competencies in Cognitive-Behavioral Therapy. Becoming a Highly Effective and Competent Cognitive-Behavioral Therapist*, London, New York: Routledge.

Sperry, L 2010, *Core Competencies in Counselling and Psychotherapy. Becoming a Highly Competent and Effective Therapist*, New York, London: Routledge.

Part I

Research on Core Competencies in Psychotherapy

Chapter 1

Exploring Core Competencies in the Field of Psychotherapy

Understanding, Research, and Development

Gražina Gudaitė

Introduction

What enables an individual's healing and growth processes? What competencies need to be cultivated to assist the psychotherapy of a person and the individuation process of that human being? Even though these universal questions are being raised in many schools of psychotherapy, the search for the answers depends on many conditions. Given the multiplicity of psychotherapy approaches in the contemporary world, it is important not only to reflect on common therapeutic factors, but also to clarify and differentiate the specific aspects of a particular approach leading to a deeper understanding of the possibilities for healing and transformation. Studies on the effectiveness of psychotherapy and reflections on training processes show the need for a deeper understanding of the role of the psychotherapist in these processes. In addition, some authors state that these questions have been undeservedly forgotten in psychotherapy studies (Wampold et al. 2017). Defining and developing the concept of core competencies can be one of the ways to elucidate the specifics of a particular approach that may serve as a background for the integration process.

The term "core competencies" was originally used working with organizations and was defined as a set of resources and skills ensuring a company's exceptional status and unique pathways to success. The search for these particular resources and skills has gradually become a universal theme observed not only in the theory of management, but also in medicine and in the field of education. The evaluation of competencies has become the starting point in accreditation of training programs with an emphasis laid on evaluating each individual's professional qualities and providing a license for practice.

According to some authors "competency" is the new buzzword in today's psychotherapy training and practise (Sperry 2010). Integrating a competency-based approach to the field of psychotherapy initiates new input in the development of psychotherapy and its recognition among other health care professions. On the other hand, it is a challenging task given the variety of psychotherapy models and the complexity of psychological influence. When

DOI: 10.4324/9781003219910-3

planning their studies in psychotherapy, researchers acknowledge being guided by four basic perspectives as alternative representatives of psychotherapy: (a) mental health treatment, (b) personal education, (c) a reform or correctional process, and (d) moral or spiritual redemption (Orlinsky 1989).

A number of studies on understanding the competencies in psychotherapy have been published in recent years. J. Binder (2004), L. Sperry (2010), F. Newman (2013), E. Farber (2010), N. Kazlow (2009), and many other authors have discussed the question of competencies in psychological consultation, in psychodynamic, cognitive or humanistic-existential psychotherapy. Competence in psychotherapy includes not only professional skills and theoretical knowledge but also relationship skills, components of personal attitude, as well as relationship with and sensitivity to cultural context (Anderson et al. 2015; Eleftheradou 2010). The development of the competence-based approach in psychotherapy includes several stages such as the description of competencies in psychotherapy, expert-based comprehensive differentiation of core competencies in a particular field, and finally the construct of core competence needs to be operationalized into an empirically implemented instrument that allows us "to investigate how the dynamics in therapy are affected by the therapists' use of these competencies and in what manner they impact the outcome of the treatment" (Parth and Loeffler-Stastka 2015, p. 2).

Description of Core Competencies

The articulation of foundational and functional competencies in psychotherapy practice is one of the ways to describe professional qualities of an individual and to develop a competency-based approach training. Foundational competencies refer to the knowledge, attitudes, and values that serve as a foundation for the functions a professional is expected to carry out. Functional competencies include a spectrum of skills that provide the basis for a psychotherapist to effectively perform the assessment and appropriate interventions in psychotherapy. For example, in describing core competencies of a psychodynamic model of psychotherapy Sarnat (2010) stated:

> I consider relationship, self-reflection, assessment and diagnosis, and intervention-from among the complete list of foundational competencies (reflective practice-self-assessment, scientific knowledge-methods, relationship, ethical-legal standards-policy, individual-cultural diversity, and interdisciplinary systems) and functional competencies (assessment, intervention, consultation, research-evaluation, supervision-teaching, and management-administration)—to be key for a psychodynamic model of psychotherapy.
>
> (p. 21)

Similar descriptions of core competencies were published in studies of integrative psychotherapy (Boswell, Nelson, Nordberg, Mcaleavey, and Castonguay 2010), of humanistic-existential psychotherapy (Farber 2010) and of cognitive behavioral psychotherapy (Newman 2013).

Taking into account that the number of publications on foundational and functional competencies in Jungian psychoanalysis is scarce, such differentiation could help to simplify the complexity of understanding the Jungian approach. The question of understanding the competences of Jungian analysts was discussed at numerous conferences and symposiums, as well as at meetings of Directors of Training. Several publications on that issue have been published in books edited by Stein (2010), Wiener (2007), and in the *Journal of Analytical Psychology.* In her article "Evaluating Progress in Training: Character or Competence", Wiener distinguishes the capacity of intuition, the capacity to understand unconscious processes at different levels, and an openness to authentic relationship as the main components required for analytic talent (p. 173). Kelly (2007) noted that despite different training models around the world the central competence of a Jungian analyst is "the capacity to work with the symbolic in a meaningful way" out of which could follow "a dynamic and living relationship with the unconscious as real, objective and as other" (p. 167). Overall, the authors agree on the need for further research into the development and integration of competencies in the various models of training.

Expert-based Comprehensive Differentiation

Expert-based comprehensive differentiation of core competencies in a particular field depends on the country and the state regulations of psychotherapy. We find numerous lists of competencies of a European psychotherapist or core competencies for psychoanalysis defined by the American Board for Accreditation in Psychoanalysis. Such descriptions serve as guidelines for the accreditation of training programs or for the creation of a formal system for certification of psychotherapists. For example, experts distinguish basic and specific competencies observed in psychoanalytic therapy. Knowledge of the basic principles of analytic approaches, engagement with the client in the analytic therapy, work with unconscious communications and exploration of unconscious dynamics that influence the relationship, the ability to work with both the client's internal and external realities are referred to as the basic competencies. Meanwhile, the ability to make interpretations, to work with and in the transference and countertransference, and to recognize and work with defenses are considered to be competencies specific to analysis. An expert-based differentiation of core competencies depends on the development of the psychotherapy approach as well as on the development of psychotherapy research into this particular field. The development of the research is closely related with the next theme – the question of methods to evaluate competencies in practice.

Evaluation of Core Competencies

The operationalization and assessment of core competencies is a complicated task that includes a whole spectrum of components. According to the researchers' understanding,

> competencies are interactive clusters of integrative knowledge of concepts and procedures, skills and abilities, behaviour and strategies, attitudes/ beliefs/values, dispositions and personal characteristics, self-perceptions, and motivations that enable a person to fully perform a task with a wide range of outcomes.
>
> (Kaslow et al. 2009, p. 2)

Keeping in mind such a complexity of phenomena, evaluation needs to be based on an integrative paradigm, which combines both the objective and subjective perspectives and focuses on the structural qualities as well as on the dynamic aspects of the process of competence integration into clinical practice. The researchers of the field name several methods most commonly used in the process of competence assessment. Self-evaluation and annual performance reports, peer review or supervision evaluation forms, case presentation reviews, standardized structural interviews, client process, and outcome data are referred to as the most suitable methods for competence assessment (Kaslow, Grus, Campbell, Fouad, Hatcher, and Rodolfa 2009). Even though all those methods provide valuable information on the development of competencies, the results obtained cannot guarantee a glowing result from the process of evaluation. Research into psychotherapy shows that even the evaluation of psychotherapy outcomes given by a therapist is different from that given by a client. Professionals have developed "an observing eye" and, of course, their evaluation is different from the clients' understanding; on the other hand, research shows that psychotherapists also tend to overestimate their abilities to assist the process. In this context, self-reflection reports and understanding of one's therapeutic capacities to assist in healing or growth can be rather subjective. The same problems emerge in using the client's outcome data as information to evaluate the therapist's competencies. Clients can be even more subjective than therapists. Standardized structural interviews perhaps are the most common method used for evaluating psychological issues in clinical practice. While this can be a useful tool for assessing some competencies of psychotherapists as well, it has limitations as it focuses on the evaluation of structural qualities rather than the dynamic ones.

While all methods have their strengths and their limitations, the usefulness of a particular method depends on both participants who take part in the evaluation procedure. Examiners and candidates, experts and those who apply for a psychotherapy license, researchers who evaluate psychotherapists' effectiveness – each participant in an evaluation needs to have an understanding of psychotherapy competencies and of the way one integrates them into practice. A comprehensive understanding of competency and of how this manifests is one of the ways to improve the evaluation procedures and to avoid an authoritarian one-sidedness. A deeper understanding of the requisites for integration of core competencies in psychotherapy can serve as guidelines for individuals in their training process and in the process of becoming a professional psychotherapist.

Later in this chapter, we will explore understanding of competencies in the analytical process with a special focus on the reflections of an analyst's experience. The examination of a variety of subjective experiences reveals the importance of an individual's way and awareness about his or her role in the moments of healing in the individuation process.

Constellation of Competencies in Psychotherapy Process

What knowledge, skill or attitude is needed in a meeting with a particular client at a particular moment is the most complicated question to explore due to the fact that the answer depends on so many factors related both to the quest of the client, to the psychotherapist's capacity to assist the process, and finally to the constellation that emerges when these two unique individuals meet. **Constellations** of a particular combination of several factors in a **particular moment** serve as the main focus in understanding the competence at work. A moment of healing or growth can be experienced as a moment of change, be it a moment of relief, an insight, or a shift in the psychic energy flow. Reflecting on the subjective experience and efforts to systemize this into the frame of a particular approach are especially valuable as a way to get a deeper understanding of the influence of the therapist in the constellation of a healing moment or of a moment of deeper and significant transformation. There are several very interesting studies that focus on the multidimensional experience of psychotherapists in the psychotherapy process. Tuckett's (2005) study on core competencies in psychodynamic therapy focused on a deeper understanding of the frames of experience that happen in a psychoanalytic process. The participant's observational, conceptual, and interventional frames are discussed as core themes of a psychoanalyst's capacities that need to be developed in analytical training. Barsness (2018) explored dozens of interviews with senior analysts and identified seven core competencies that contribute to healing and transformation in the therapeutic relationship: therapeutic intent, therapeutic stance/attitude, deep listening/affective attunement, relational dynamic: the "there and then" and the "here and now", patterning and linking, repetition and working through, courageous speech/disciplined spontaneity. Winborn (2019) in his study "Interpretation in Jungian Analysis" discusses the analytic process from the perspective of interpretation and distinguishes four steps in the interpretation cycle: confrontational observation, inferential clarification, interpretation, and construction. He mentions several stages of the process of interpretation: listening, attending, gathering information and experiences, conceptualization, generating a hypothesis, considering the frame of the interpretation, timing considerations, prioritizing what to interpret, crafting the language of the interpretation, offering the interpretation, and a return to listening and gathering. These and other studies show well the variations in the ways the analyst's participation can differ at different moments of the analytical process. Later we will discuss some of the constellations of competencies at a particular moment of the analytical process.

Before Entering the Process

There are many psychotherapy studies about personal qualities that can help predict a positive development of therapeutic capacities during training. Authenticity, a sincere interest in the other, flexibility, and openness to experience are all considered good predispositions for becoming a psychotherapist. In contrast, a rigid character, judgmental attitude, or latent hostility are accepted as contraindications for developing therapeutic qualities. On the other hand, with such a vast array of characteristics in psychotherapists, it is difficult to say which exact characteristics could predict or determine success in training. The development of one's potential strengths depends on an endless array of inner and outer conditions as well as changing life experiences. It is therefore hard to evaluate the potential to be developed in training or in a personal analysis. Regardless of the diversity of individual qualities however, there are still some basic values that loom ahead as important conditions for the development of psychotherapy competencies. Authentic interest in the relationship with the other is one of them. Competent analysts "are relentlessly curious about the mind/body experience and the dynamic between the patient and the therapist" (Barsness 2018, p. 18). It is important to be interested in other people as well as to be aware that psychotherapy is work for the benefit of others. It could be that motivation to become a therapist is deeply connected to a person's own difficulties or wounds and healing himself or herself could be part of the process of becoming a professional. C. G. Jung was the first who developed the idea of the *wounded healer* and the importance of this archetype for the analytical process (Jung 1985). He was also the first to insist that the therapist himself undergo analysis first as part of his training. Self-analysis and understanding the complexity of the experience of inner wounds needs to serve the healing process of the client who is the main focus of any therapy session. Last but not least is the quality of honesty. An analyst needs to be open and honest in terms of his/her participation in the therapy process, and the readiness to face difficult themes. We all have defense systems, we all wish to please the other, and we all have skills to escape unconformable truth or suffering. It is not easy to be honest, but nevertheless "the attempt to be emotionally honest is the wellspring of everything else that comes from analytical psychotherapy, and that cultivation that fosters progressive approximations of emotional honesty remains the central task of the therapist" (McWilliams 2018, p. 101).

Attending the Process

The analytical process starts from the moment when two individuals meet. All professionals agree on the importance of this moment, as it is kind of initial situation to understand the other, to develop a therapeutic alliance, to motivate the continuity of the process, etc. Tuckett (2005) distinguished a *participant observational frame*. Attentive listening, observing the nonverbal expressions, bearing uncertainty, deep listening and affective attunement, "waiting, but not too long", openness to holding projections and to being an object of transference, holding (Tuckett 2005; Jacoby 1984; Wiener 2007; Cwik 2010) – all these and even more categories can characterize the psychotherapist's stance in the initial meeting with the other person. The ability to be involved in the moment and the ability to contain the variety of experience that can emerge during the session is an important position which makes it possible for both participants to reflect on what is happening instead of reacting.

The main focus of this moment is attentiveness to the experience that emerges at the moment of interaction with the other. It may be that even the smallest moments of meeting provide the participants with contradictory information: for example, the words express different things than the body language or the verbally expressed thoughts contradict each other. Analysts need to observe these details and to see the duality of the moment. Winborn (2019) mentions the capacity for a *confrontational observation*.

> A confrontational observation is focused on something that is potentially observable to both the patient and the analyst but which the patient may not have consciously noticed or considered to be of significance. Ideally observations will be followed by clarifying inferences and interpretations that create a meaning, as well as providing the patient with the experience of being understood.
>
> (p.53)

The experience of being understood is fundamental for further development of the relationship with the other. Moments of empathic understanding, containing the heavy moments, even a confession with a catharsis in terms of C. G. Jung (1985), can shift the emotional state give rise to an experience of hope for change, as a hope for another way of being. Current authors state that already at this moment, important therapeutic changes may take place. Containing a patient's destructive impulses or phantasies means accepting the projected contents and transforming them to a more tolerable affect. "If the process of containment goes well, the patient can integrate the transformed sensations into his mind and that also gives a sense of relief and a sense of being understood" (Parth and Loeffler-Stastka 2015, p. 2).

Understanding the other and the experience of being understood is the basic theme of the entire psychotherapy process. Finding the right terms to describe this experience and formulating a concept that will capture its essence is another step in the therapy process.

Moment of Forming a Concept

The integrative knowledge of and theoretical assumptions concerning the personality's structure and dynamic, the personality's development and its interruptions, complexes, and their manifestation – all of these considerations and other theoretical perspectives can be relied on to conceptualize the particular moment of experience. The theory provides a basis for developing hypotheses about the deepest layers of what stands beyond the manifestation of behavior. A conceptual frame depends on theory and all psychodynamic authors agree that it is crucial to identify the transference and countertransference, resistance, or defenses to better understand and grasp the development and evolution of analytical processes. Jungian analysts will add knowledge and understanding of complexes and the development of archetypal themes, which highlight the symbolic meaning and as amplifications of the phenomenology of transformation.

A deeper understanding of the experience and conceptualization is related to the revelation of the latent meaning of material in the session and to how it connects with similar experiences from the past. Relational analysts highlight the importance of recurring themes and patterns and how these are linked to the past and are reflected in dreams and fantasies, thoughts, affects, and somatic experiences. In this context, conceptualization entails not only identifying and naming the unconscious themes that appear in the therapeutic relationship but also developing connections with their various manifestations in the human psyche, all of which leads to a deeper understanding and integration of personality. Integrating theory and knowledge, generating all the possible hypotheses about the meaning of a particular moment is intimately related to and dependent on the moment of interpretation.

Moment of Interpretation

Interpretation has always been accepted as a crucial core competence in a classical psychodynamic approach as it proposes the therapeutic transformation that results in lasting changes in the structures of patients. How interpretation is used depends on the conceptual frame and understanding of the analyst's theory of psychic change or transformation. In contemporary understanding, interpretation serves not only to further understanding of the unconscious, but also as an invitation for the patient to see their world in a new way. "Interpretation also provides **meaning** to what is being experienced; the experience having previously lacked meaning or for which meaning was distorted" (Winborn 2019, p. 16).

Authors acknowledge that this is the most difficult frame in the context of competence development. There are so many different ways to present an interpretation and sometimes, of course, an intervention is contra-indicated (Tuckett 2005). It depends on the situation. If the therapists' efforts are focused on support of the Ego and on adaptation of the individual to outer reality or to challenge the Ego to recognize the need for change, the interpretation will necessarily be very different. Even though C. G. Jung developed a lot of ways to make interpretations, he also highlighted the necessity of connection to reality as one of the tasks of the analytical process: "the fact remains that in many cases the most thorough elucidation leaves the patient an intelligent but still incapable child" (Jung 1985, p. 66).

Despite the warnings about the complexity of intervention, the capacity to interpret is one of the most important competencies of analysts and it is changing with our contemporary understanding of the psychotherapy process. The development of qualitative research and a deeper understanding of the meaning making process, as well as a recognition of the importance of intersubjectivity has opened up new ways to understand the role and significance of interpretation. According to Winborn (2019), the interpretative process works in much the same way as the scientific: experiential data are gathered by an analyst through observation, listening, and interpersonal experience with the patient; a hypothesis is generated based on the experiential data and the analytic theory; an interpretation is offered to the patient; the analyst returns to listening, observing and experiencing in an effort to discern the patient's response to the interpretation. Having clarity about analytical processes, working together with the client and developing an intersubjective understanding about the experience helps to reveal the truth that can serve the client's healing or growth processes.

Shifting the Positions of Participation

The analytical process is a sequence of moments; therefore it is quite possible that the ways of the analyst's participation, their conceptualization, or interventions might change several times even in one session. The possibility of being deeply involved in **here and now** and then shifting to **there and then**, (or, on the contrary, from "there and then" to "here and now") are two different ways of being with the other. It is important to focus on past experience, particularly on the episodes that reflect the patterns of relationship, developmental difficulties, and their manifestation in the patient's current life. All of this can give a deeper understanding of the way one participates in life. At the same time, contemporary analysts agree on the importance of the experience of the here and now and of a direct relationship with the analyst. True change becomes alive in the experience with the other rather than in the phantasies about that. An analytic dyad is the place where change can emerge and can be experienced.

Being close with the other and taking distance at the right time is another shift in the participation of an analyst that describes the sequence of moments in psychotherapy. Empathy and identification with the client leads to a deeper understanding of the psyche of the other; it is a necessary condition to help contain the experience and to return projections. A lot of studies have been published that show the importance of such an experience for the healing process. The moment of taking distance from the patient has not been so widely discussed, however it is an important aspect of the therapeutic process. Using the terms introduced by Perls, empathy and apathy are two positions of the same psychotherapist in the same psychotherapy process. Leaving a client at the right moment is necessary for him/her to find their own resources. It can be a frustrating experience, yet it is necessary to develop the client's self- support system (Perls 1973). Whether "apathy" is the accurate word to describe the opposite of empathy is open for discussion; however, taking distance from the other in a psychotherapy process is necessary for the analyst in order to connect with his/her own psyche and resources and thereby have a clearer perspective about the moment. Experiences of being met empathically and of meeting the other as different in the process of psychotherapy are crucial for the development of the client's identity and as opportunities to learn a variety of ways to relate with the other.

Being a participant observer and being a witness is another way to understand the shifts in the analyst's participation in the process. We have already noted how the capacity to quietly observe is intrinsically related to the richness of the moments of meeting of two individuals participating in the process. The capacity to witness is related to the belief that the secret Power participates in the process. Staying quiet and waiting for the signs of its manifestation is rooted in the deep trust that some processes take place by themselves, independent of, yet related to, the therapeutic process. And they really do happen! One can consider this as an expression of the deepest regulation of the Self, or as the autonomy of the unconscious, or as the participation of God. Witnessing numinous moments in the analytical process is an exceptional experience; it can lead to the deepest and most profound changes an individual. The analyst's role in such a moment is rather paradoxical. There are moments when an analyst needs to use all the competencies in order to get the work done responsibly, and there are moments when they simply needs to be silent and receptive to the emergence of the secret Power. It reminds me of an interview with a conductor who described her experience of conducting an opera by Philip Glass. She said that the most important thing in conducting the orchestra was the ability to remain calm and centered. It sounds like a real paradox, especially when we see the active movements of the conductor. Staying calm is an important inner state as it means leaving space for the participation of the bigger Creator than that of personal will. Such descriptions of experience reflect the deepest layer of the Ego–Self axis, which is one of the foundation stones of analytical psychology. The moment of being connected with some higher Power can be described as the vertical axis of the energy flow. Combining the vertical and the horizontal directions of movement of the psychic energy is one of the ways to study the process of psychological integration in the patient and of an analyst's participation in that process.

Engagement in the Creative Process

The analytical process is a creative process and the awareness of this is one of the themes that need to be developed in the process of becoming an analyst. Does the candidate experience the endless search for solutions as a privilege or as a deep frustration? Do they feel comfortable when shifting positions of authorship in the analytical process? Do they experience the work as creative? An analyst's engagement in the creative process can be described in different ways. The ability to catch the hints and to see the potential for development, providing assistance to search for the right way for a creative impulse to come to expression, patience to work on the right forms of Self manifestation – these and other moments of the analytical process are closely related to the creative process. Openness to the symbolic dimension of experience, searching for an amplification in order to get a deeper understanding of the symbols, and interpretation of these images is always related to improvisation. According to Winborn, an interpretation is kind of art.

> However, the interpretive process is where the creative aspect of analysis truly comes alive; when the analyst becomes the poet – carefully weighing words, sensing into the feeling of those words, imagining how the words will fit in with the emotional context of what has come before and what will come after. Ultimately, an interpretation is an attempt to capture in language and tone the essence of something only partially seen, still dancing behind a veil.
>
> (op. cit., p. 2)

Another aspect of creativity is related to developing the life narrative. Modern psychotherapy research states that the psychotherapy process is an endless process of re-authoring of life stories: "a sense of identity is both the product and the process of self- narrative construction" (Botella, Herrero, Pacheco, and Corbela 2004, p. 122). The narrative structure organizes and gives meaning to experiences; however, there are always feelings and lived experiences that are not fully represented by the dominant story. "Given the gaps between narrative structure and experience, therapy offers clients an opportunity to reauthor their life narratives by identifying individual personal events, feelings, intentions, and thoughts that currently fall outside the dominant narrative" (Bruner 2004, p. 249). Such a way of healing is especially important when we think about the healing consequences of a cultural trauma. It is important to remember and to fill in the gaps in the narrative of what was forgotten or never fully acknowledged. It is important to integrate the subjective reactions and feelings connected with the event. A reconstructed narrative can lead to creating a new understanding and meaning about the self and others.

The stories are not just an individual's self-manifestation, they are also part of our culture. An individual is part of the story, but at the same time he/she creates a story as well. Writing, recounting, listening, and reacting all help to recall what has been forgotten, ultimately helps to identify the important personal material that was not integrated in the dominant life stories. In this manner, creativity plays an important role not only in the process of healing the individual, but also in influencing the whole culture. On the one hand, psychotherapy depends on the culture an individual is surrounded by, lives in and is a part of, but at the same time one also needs to recognize and be aware that he/she creates culture as well.

Conclusion

Understanding the role of a psychotherapist in the psychotherapy process is an important theme, which contemporary studies are busy exploring. The development of a competence-based approach in psychotherapy is one of the ways to have guidelines for a deeper understanding of the essence of this work in order to assure the quality of a psychotherapist's work. Further discussions on a deeper understanding of core competencies of a particular approach is important in order to distil the specifics of each approach within the variety and richness of the field of psychotherapy.

The awareness of core competencies can be helpful in developing a sense of professional identity and creating connections to and relationships between professionals with other approaches as well. The focus of our study was the analysis of the constellation of particular competencies and the exploration of the sequences of their manifestation in the analytic process. Understanding the role of an analyst and the way to integrate these competencies into practice depends on experience, theory, practice, and the culture an individual lives in and is surrounded by. We understand that there may be other ways to understand the core competencies and other explanations of their constellations in healing and growth processes of an individual than those we have presented in this paper. This is a theme that clearly needs to be discussed further. We hope that the theme of core competencies in analytical psychology can be helpful in bringing analytical psychology in accordance with contemporary experience, research, and theoretical understanding.

References

Anderson, T, Crowley, M et al. 2015, Therapist facilitative interpersonal skill and training status: A randomized clinical trial on alliance and outcome, *Psychotherapy Research*, 26, 5, 1–19. DOI:10.1080/10503307.2015.1049671

Angus, L E, Lewin, J, Bouffard, B, Rotondi-Trevisan, D 2004, What's the story. working with narrative in experiential psychotherapy, in *The Handbook of Narrative and Psychotherapy. Practice, Theory and Research* (Eds. Angus L E, McLeod J), London: Thousand Oaks, Deli: Sage Publications.

Barsness, R E 2018, Core competencies in relational psychoanalysis: A qualitative study, in *Core Competencies of Relational Psychoanalysis. A Guide to Practice, Study and Research*, New York: Routledge.

Boswell, J F, Nelson, D L, Nordberg S S, Mcaleavey, A A, Castonguay, L G 2010, Competency in integrative psychotherapy: Perspectives on training and supervision, *Psychotherapy Theory, Research, Practice, Training*, 47, 1, 3–11.

Botella, L, Herrero, O, Pacheco, M, Segi, C 2004, Working with narrative in psychotherapy: A relational constructivist approach, in The Handbook of Narrative and Psychotherapy. *Practice, Theory and Research* (Eds. Angus L E, McLeod, J), Thousand Oaks, Deli: Sage Publications.

Braun, C 2020, *The Therapeutic Relationship in Analytical Psychology: Theory and Practice.* London: Routldege.

Bruner, J 2004, The narrative creation of Self, in *The Handbook of Narrative and Psychotherapy. Practice, Theory and Research* (Eds. Angus L E, McLeod J), Thousand Oaks, Deli: Sage Publications.

Cwik, A G 2010, From frame through holding to container, in *Jungian Psychoanalysis. Working in Spirit of C. G. Jung* (Ed. Stein, M), Chicago and LaSalle: Open Court.

Eleftheriadou, Z 2010, *Psychotherapy and Culture: Weaving Inner and Outer Worlds*, London: Karnac.

Farber, Eugene W 2010, Humanistic – Existential psychotherapy competencies and supervisory process, *Psychotherapy Theory, Research, Practice, Training*, 47, 1, 28–34.

Jacoby, M 1984, *The Analytic Encounter: Transference and Human Relationship.* Toronto: Inner City Books.

Jung C G 1933, *Problems of Modern Psychotherapy, CW 16* (Ed. William McGuire, trans. Ralph Manheim and R F C Hull), Princeton, NJ: Princeton University Press.

Jung C G 1985, *Memories, Dreams, Reflections.* New York: Vintage Books.

Kaslow, N J, Grus, C L, Campbell, L F, Fouad, N A, Hatcher, L R, Rodolfa, E R 2009, Competency assessment toolkit for professional psychology, *Training and Education in Professional Psychology*, 3, 4, S27–S45.

Kelly, T 2007, The making of an analyst: From 'ideal' to 'good-enough, *Journal of Analytical Psychology*, 52, 157–169.

McWilliams, N 2018, Core competence two: Therapeutic stance/attitude. Core competencies in relational psychoanalysis: A qualitative study, in *Core Competencies of Relational Psychoanalysis. A Guide to Practice, Study and Research*, New York: Routledge.

Newman, C F 2013, *Core Competencies in Cognitive-Behavioral Therapy. Becoming a Highly Effective and Competent Cognitive-Behavioral Therapist*, London, New York: Routledge.

Parth, K, Loeffler-Stastka, H 2015, Psychoanalytic core competence, *Frontiers in Psychology*, 2015. doi; 10.3389/fpsych.2015.00356.

Perls, F 1973, *The Gestalt Approach and Eye Witness to Therapy*, USA: Science and Behavior Books.

Orlinsky, D E 1989, Researcher's images of psychotherapy: Their origins and influence on research, *Clinical Psychology Review*, 9, 413–441.

Sarnat, J 2010, Key competences of the psychodynamic psychotherapist and how to teach them in supervision, *Psychotherapy Theory, Research, Practice, Training*, 47, 1, 20–27.

Sperry, L 2010, *Core Competencies in Counseling and Psychotherapy. Becoming a Highly Competent and Effective Therapist*, New York, London: Routledge.

Stein, M 2010, *Jungian Psychoanalysis. Working in the Spirit of C. G. Jung*, Chicago: Open Court.

Tuckett, D 2005, Does anything go? Towards a framework for more transparent assessment of psychoanalytic competence. *International Journal of Psychoanalysis*, 86, 31–49.

Wampold, B E, Baldwin S A, Holtforth M G 2017, What characterises effective therapists. How and why some therapists better than others?, in *Understanding Therapist Effects* (Eds. L G Castonguay and C E Hill), USA: American Psychological Association.

Wiener, J 2007, Evaluating progress in training: character or competence, *Journal of Analytical Psychology*, 52, 171–183.

Winborn, M 2019, *Interpretation in Jungian Analysis. Art and Technique.* London: Routledge.

Chapter 2

A Study of Core Competencies in Jungian Psychoanalysis

Gražina Gudaitė, Ieva Bieliauskienė, Dovilė Petronytė–Kvedarauskienė, and Goda Rukšaitė

Introduction

Exploring the core competencies in Jungian psychoanalysis is an important task for deeper understanding of the complexity of the healing process as well as for the process of becoming a professional Jungian analyst. Several authors have commented on how a psychotherapist's participation in the psychotherapy process was unreasonably forgotten in contemporary studies of psychotherapy (Wampold, Baldwin, and Holtforth 2017). Exploring the multidimensional picture of competency is one of the ways to fill this gap. In this context, competency in psychotherapy is defined as an ability to integrate knowledge and skills into practice in a way deeply connected to a psychotherapist's personality and attitude. The process of becoming a competent psychotherapist depends on the training process, on the theory on which a certain approach is based, on an individual's character, on his/her life experiences, and on the cultural context. In this chapter we would like to introduce a research project on subjective understanding core competencies in Jungian psychoanalysis. The study was initiated by the IAAP and executed by analysts from Lithuania, in 2018–2019.

Maintaining high quality of training and respect for cultural diversity and different models of training has always been important to the International Association for Analytical Psychology (Connolly 2015; Crowther and Wiener 2015; Kelly 2007; Merchant 2016; Stein 2010). The idea for our study came up during discussions about different aspects of the Router training programme organized by IAAP. The Router Programme is intended for individuals (and for groups of individuals) in countries where it is otherwise not possible to get analytical training. Experienced teachers, analysts, and supervisors worldwide have been involved in this programme and, as a result, many routers have become analysts. Subsequently, new training programmes and institutes in different cultural settings have emerged in the field of analytical psychology. Even though the Router Programme has already been recognized as successful, the question of how to ensure the high quality of this training remains open. Deeper understanding of the process of integrating knowledge, skills and

DOI: 10.4324/9781003219910-4

attitudinal components is important in order to create an alliance between teachers and candidates, to further develop research on effectiveness of psychotherapy, and to build bridges and connections with the academic field.

Having a better understanding of the core analytical competencies is important for candidates, too.

> I have read all what C. G. Jung has written, I know the methods and I work with my dreams and imagination but somehow that does not transfer into my work with clients, I lack something, but what is this 'something'?

The following is the reflection of a psychotherapist who came to the analytical training hoping to understand the mystery of "the Jungian 'something'": "I failed an exam during my Router training. I answered all the questions they asked, but still something was not right. Perhaps I do not have what they want. But I do not know what it is." This candidate also felt she had knowledge about the methodology and theory of analytical psychology but nevertheless something was lacking. Such reflections raise questions about how one integrates knowledge and skills and how one participates in the analytical process.

During the early stages of this study and then sharing its preliminary results we received a range of different responses from the analysts involved. Many professionals expressed their interest and liked the idea of such a research project. Others expressed their doubts about the search for core competencies in the Jungian field and opined that such research could contradict the importance of individuality and the very notion of individuation in general. R. Barsness (2019) noticed that among practitioners there is:

> believing that what we do is intuitive, automatic, and organic. Though this may be true, … it is also true that each analyst has their own internal guidelines – they simply are not articulated. For example, I think we 'know' we *listen* in a particular way different from other disciplines and we 'know' we *engage* our patients differently. The question is how do we do this?
>
> (p. 6)

This question "how" was a leading question in our study: how do Jungians understand their assistance to an individual in the contemporary world? How "to integrate knowledge, skills, and attitudes reflected in the quality of clinical practise that benefits others, which can be evaluated by professional standards and be developed and enhanced through professional training and reflection?" (Sperry 2010, p. 5).

The aim of our study was to explore the subjective understanding of the core competencies in Jungian analysis and their development in training and practise. Data was collected and analyzed using **qualitative methods** in order to reveal the diversity of subjective understanding of competencies and of the development of this understanding during the training process. Data were collected in the following manner: by conducting semi-structured interviews focused on competencies in Jungian analysis; or by asking participants to write their story of becoming an analyst or of making the choice to become an analyst.

Research Participants

Sixty participants took part in our research. There were two groups of candidates: 24 persons in the initial stage of training (8 male and 16 female, with an average age of 36.5 years); and 20 advanced candidates who had completed the propaedeutic level (4 male and 16 female, with an average age of 43 years). The third group consisted of 16 Jungian analysts teaching in the analyst training programme (4 male and 12 female, with average age of 54 years). In total, there were 16 male and 44 female participants of whom 35 were psychologists, 8 medical doctors, 7 social workers, 5 with a degree in arts, 2 in theology, and 3 in business.

The candidates were from Lithuania, Latvia, Russia, Belarus, and Estonia, and the analysts were from Germany, Switzerland, the United Kingdom, Lithuania, Russia and Estonia.

Procedure

Invitations to participate were sent out by email. Arrangements about time, place, and method of collecting the data (oral or written interview) were sent to those who gave a positive response. All data was collected during face-to-face meetings.

The interviews began with the following question:

- Could you tell your story of becoming an analyst as well as describe all the events and experiences which were of particular importance for you?

An additional question was subsequently asked:

- Could you highlight three key competencies of a Jungian analyst, which you consider the most helpful in your analytical practice?

Oral interviews lasted approximately 50 minutes; written responses took approximately 60 minutes. In total, 15 interviews were conducted orally and 45 in written form.

Data Analysis

Transcribed texts of the interviews were analysed according to the principles of **thematic analysis** (Braun and Clarke 2013; Boyatzis 1998). We combined *inductive* and *deductive approaches*. The inductive method derives codes and themes directly from data avoiding any theoretical premises. The deductive method rests upon theoretical knowledge that plays a role in the formulation of major themes, in this case, psychodynamic and analytical psychology. *Latent* and *semantic levels* of analysis were combined. The semantic codes reflect information directly reported by participants. The latent codes are formulated after researchers' interpretations of information provided by the participants verbally or nonverbally.

The principle of confidentiality was followed and respected throughout data presentation and publication, ensuring that all information that could reveal the identity of the participants was concealed.

The data was collected and analysed in 2018–2019 by five analysts from the Lithuanian Association of Analytical Psychology, all of them experienced in qualitative research and four holding a PhD.

Results

Willingness to Participate in the Study

Eighty percent (80%) of invited individuals responded positively to the invitation to participate in the study. Most of the participants (especially candidates and analysts from the new training societies) expressed their interest in the results of the study and requested discussion on these results after it was completed. A rather high rate of the participation in the study and an interest in its results show that deeper understanding of the analytical competencies and of the process of becoming a professional is an important subject, especially in the new training societies.

Primary Data: Describing the Competencies

A large diversity of understanding with regard to the competencies in Jungian analysis came up in the primary data analysis. We identified more than two hundred (200) different terms and expressions to describe a competent Jungian analyst. Seventy-four (74) codes were developed to describe the understanding of the competencies in Jungian work. The results showed that the understanding of these competencies became more differentiated as the training proceeded. Analysis of the distribution of the codes showed that although the group of beginners was the largest (24 participants), the number of codes in their answers was the smallest (28 codes). Meanwhile, the analysts, the smallest group (16 participants), produced the largest number of codes (75 codes to describe the subjective understanding of the competencies in Jungian psychoanalysis). The group of advanced candidates was somewhere in between (20 participants and 58 codes).

Figure 2.1 represents a summary of the five different axes that were identified in this study and the specific aspects of each axis.

Living relationship with the
unconscious
Attentiveness to the spiritual
dimension of experience
Search for meaning
Giving value to subjectivity

Creating an enabling space
Flexibility in participating
Observing and conceptualizing
Ability to intervene

ANALYTICAL ATTITUDE

ANALYTICAL RELATIONSHIP

CULTURE RELATEDNESS

RELATEDNESS TO THE SYMBOLIC

MEDIATING PROCESS OF TRANSFORMATION

Awareness of cultural context
Being sensitive to individual's
cultural identity
Being able to face painful
issues emerging from certain
cultural contexts

Interest in the symbolic
material
Understanding different
ways of working with
symbols
Capacity to live a
symbolic life

Ability to contain the opposites
Holding and navigating
„Experience of transformation can be
contagious"
On the role of analyst in transformation

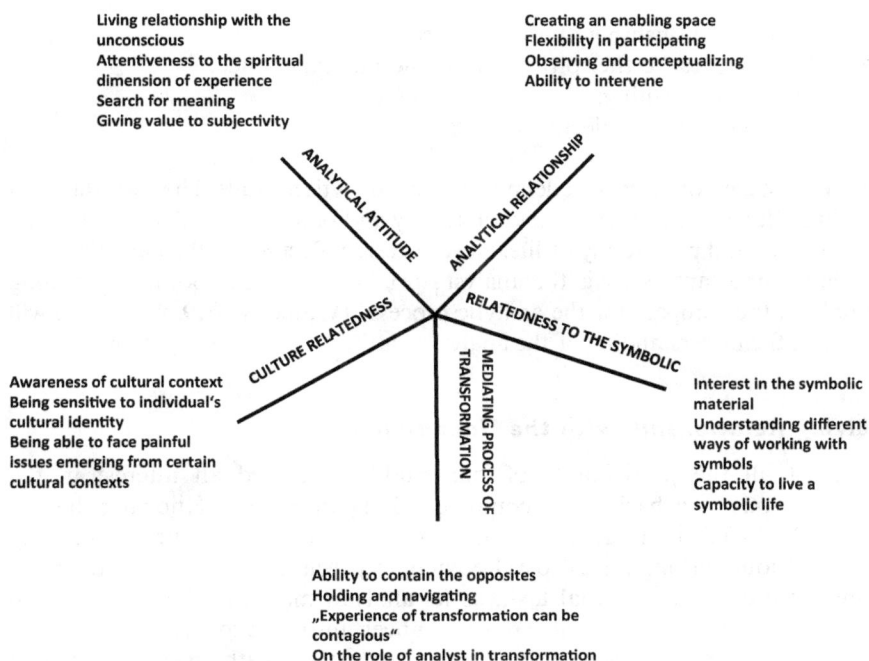

Figure 2.1 Overview of themes and subthemes

Part of the participants' descriptions of an analyst's competencies, and subsequently part of the codes do not refer specifically to the Jungian way of thinking, but they were mentioned as necessary conditions for conducting the analytical process. Reflections on the therapeutic relationship, the understanding of transformation, or of the analytic attitude included some qualities rather common in psychodynamic approaches and psychotherapeutic work in general. Such findings are realistic and illustrate the fact that the Jungian way is a rather open system and can serve as a good basis for the integrative processes in contemporary psychotherapy. At the same time no single approach can integrate everything, and the specific qualities of the Jungian approach need to be differentiated in order to better understand the variety of ways that can enable an individual's healing and growth.

Maintaining focus on clarifying the specific aspects and common qualities of the Jungian approach, we will further analyse the final themes that describe the participants' understanding of the core competencies in the Jungian field.

Analytical Attitude

- Living relationship with the unconscious;
- Attentiveness to the spiritual dimension of experience;
- Search for meaning;
- Giving value to subjectivity.

We do not have one clear-cut definition of an analytic attitude. There are different ways to describe it, which depend on theory and practise as well as on one's life experience and philosophy of life. Nevertheless, reflecting on the analytical attitude is important as it "is the analyst's primary orienting tool in conducting analysis, the compass for the analytic process" (Winborn 2019, p. 67). We will present the understanding of the analytical attitude as it came up in our study.

Living Relationship with the Unconscious

Almost all the participants of our study mentioned an interest in the unconscious as a basis for a competent Jungian analyst. Knowing that an individual's life is influenced by unconscious processes is one of the conceptual foundations for all psychodynamic psychology. Understanding the unconscious is an essential task, as its analysis makes healing and growth possible. "One needs to be able to stand uncertainty and to rely on the unconsciousness"; "one needs to be quiet and wait until something emerges"; "one needs to have a capacity to listen to the silence"; "to be open to the dialogue with the unconscious"; "to practise active imagination and dialogue with inner figures". These reflections shared by the participants of our study reflect the importance of the relationship to the unconscious. Not only *working* with the unconscious for its deeper understanding but also openness to *experiencing* it and developing a living relationship with it are mentioned as important competencies of an analyst. C. G. Jung writes about the autonomy of the psyche and describes the relation to the unconscious as:

> to a living psychic entity which, it seems, is relatively autonomous, behaving as if it were a personality with intentions of its own … The reaction of the unconscious is far from being merely passive; it takes the initiative in a creative way, and sometimes predominates over its customary reactivity.
> (Jung 1989, p. 621)

Developing a relationship with the Other and others is an integral part of the process of becoming a Jungian analyst.

Attentiveness to the Spiritual Dimension of Experience

A living relationship with the unconscious may manifest in different dimensions of experience and the spiritual dimension is one of them. Interest in the spiritual realm and openness to the spiritual experience were also mentioned in our study: "openness to the spiritual realm"; "an interest in spirituality"; "respect for the numinous qualities"; "an ability to experience awe". Facing the Numinous and experiencing humility or even awe are important categories for a deeper understanding of the phenomenology of the divine or archetypal powers. It involves the feeling of being very small in the presence of something majestic and powerful. The participants of our study shared different understandings of "being small". This was related to the complex of inferiority and also seen as part of a cultural complex rooted in cultural trauma. Helplessness, desperation, identifying with the victim are all parts of this experience. A competent analyst needs to be able to contain such painful experience, to differentiate the parts of the victim and of the aggressor, and to be attentive to projections and to the countertransference; all of these are necessary for the healing process. On the other hand, feeling small and being able to experience awe can be a part of a spiritual experience. Belief in the reality of a higher and unknown Power and openness to it gives a person a chance *to be moved*. Moments of being moved by such a higher Power are crucial for the analysis. If this happens in the analytical work, then the task of an analyst is to witness the reality of that Power and the reality of the emergence of the Self. The presence of such an attitude is important especially for the beginners, as their expectations are marked by the belief that a real professional is the main author of the psychotherapy process and is fully in charge of the analytical process as well. "The position of being a witness contrasts fundamentally with the instrumental, method oriented position in psychotherapy" (McWilliams 2018, p. 91). It is not action, but paradoxically it is action at the same time. It is action in search of the deeper meaning of that which has emerged in the analytical field.

Searching for Meaning

"What was my suffering in my youth has become gold for my work. I think it's my wounded soul that is helping me and sometimes I think it's too much but then I begin to stand and feel renewed". This quotation comes from the interview with a senior analyst who took part in our research. To accept the idea that suffering has meaning is perhaps the most challenging task for any individual. Many participants of our study spoke about trauma, injustice, the reality of destructive forces, and other shadow aspects that emerged in the analytical process. Knowing one's complexes and shadow, developing a hypothesis about their manifestations, even efforts to regulate one's emotions were mentioned as part of the analytical process. Searching for meaning and the capacity to take the hint of meaning even in the most unbelievable situations, openness to paradox as a path in searching for meaning all comprise the important abilities of a competent analyst as they build a bridge to a transformative experience. "The meanings that follow one another do not lie in things, but lie in you, who are subject to many changes, insofar as you take part in life" (Jung 2009, p. 262). Being an object of change and at the same time being the most important condition for this change sounds paradoxical and is closely related to our next subtheme: "Giving value to subjectivity".

Giving Value to Subjectivity

"I chose to study analytical psychology because of its serious attitude towards subjectivity": this quotation comes from an interview with a participant from the beginners group. Finding a balance between objectivity and subjectivity has always been a challenge in psychology. Being objective is considered equal to finding the real truth. We all feel the power of this principle in contemporary psychotherapy practice and research, but at the same time many voices speak in favor of a different position. "The assumption that subjectivity, far from being the enemy of the truth, can promote deeper understandings of psychological phenomena than objectivity alone – is one of the basis for analytical attitude" (McWilliams 2018, p. 95). "Serious attitude towards subjectivity"; "serving the individual's truth"; "interest in revealing true self"; these and other similar answers of the participants of our study resonate with Jung's idea of the importance of "truth which comes from inner things" (Jung 2009, p. 280). Developing the sense of inner truth and relatedness to the Self as the source of inner truth are the basic cornerstones on which an analytical attitude is built.

The other aspect of the valued subjectivity, especially in the contemporary understanding of the analytical process, is **intersubjectivity.** In his book *Interpretation in Jungian Analysis*, M. Winborn writes that:

> the interpretative focus has shifted from the model of the objective observer to a model in which the analyst is in the analytic soup with the patient – not in terms of mutual self-revelation – but as subjective co-participant, co-experiencer and co-creator of the analytic process.
>
> (op. cit., p. 68)

Our analysis of the stories of becoming an analyst showed that giving value to subjectivity and developing intersubjectivity can be a challenging experience. It takes time for the subjective truth to emerge and to be trusted; it takes time to establish a proper system of inner and outer relationships as well; and, it takes time to develop the sense of the Third emerging in the analytical process.

The concept of intersubjectivity is closely related to the next final theme of our study: "the analytical relationship".

Analytical Relationship

- Creating an enabling space;
- Flexibility in participating;

- Observing and conceptualizing;
- Ability to intervene.

Participants of our study thought that the ability to build therapeutic relationships was a basis for the analytical process. More than 80 percent of our participants mentioned the analytical relationship as the core competence of a Jungian analyst. Many participants thought it was self-evident and didn't need any explanation, while others explored some deeper aspects of the analytic relationship and tried to reveal specifics of it in the Jungian approach. The following four subthemes emerged in our study.

Creating an Enabling Space

The first subtheme of the analytical relationship is related to the notion of the **field** that is created by two people, in the majority of the cases with the analyst taking a leading role in this process. The participants used phrases such as "creating an enabling space", "creating a shelter", "a vessel for the process to happen", to define what was needed for the analyst to create a safe space and to contain various experiences that emerge. The importance of mutual exchange, moments of improvisation, and creativity were also emphasized, for example: "the analytic relationship is a special space for 'happenings'". "Happenings" are defined as a partly improvised or spontaneous piece of artistic performance, typically involving audience participation. The idea of "happenings" is rooted in the Fluxus movement, which tried to put together different forms of creative arts: visual art and poetry, music and design, theatre and architecture – all ways that might express the richness of a moment. In this context, the idea of a "happening" could be related to the variety of self-manifestations that reflect the deepest meaning of an analytical relationship and that may create a space in which a client's Self could emerge.

Flexibility in Participating

The second subtheme reflects the variety of ways in which an analyst can participate in the therapeutic relationship, which include the following abilities: "openness and involvement,"; "attentive listening"; "capacity for empathy"; "containing ambiguity and despair"; "being an object of transference"; "being close and keeping distance at the right time"; "awareness of one's own reactions". Identification with a client and dis-identification from them, immersion in the process and distancing oneself from it, waiting, and acting were all mentioned as patterns of an analyst's participation in the analytical process. Participation and awareness of the variety of ways of participating are closely related to our next subtheme, which we have entitled, "Observing and conceptualizing".

Observing and Conceptualizing

Attentively observing the process is a necessary condition for seeing the different layers of the analytical process. When a client speaks, they are using different modes of expression. Observing the variety of these expressions helps to answer the question of how the various modes are integrated. For example, are the verbal information and non-verbal language concordant and expressing the same message? Is the body saying something different than the words? Many participants of our study noted the importance of an analyst's ability to observe the manifestation of psychic events and to conceptualize it, for example, "observing repeated patterns and understanding the transference"; "developing a hypothesis about complexes"; "awareness of the countertransference"; "attentiveness to synchronicities"; "hypothesis of the emerging signs of Self". Finding the right names and structures and integrating the theory can open to a new understanding and to news ways of relating to it. The capacity to make appropriate interpretations is basic and has always been one of the key interventions of psychodynamic psychology.

Ability to Intervene

Giving an interpretation or sharing a hypothesis of the meaning of the real relationship is the main topic of our last subtheme entitled, "Ability to intervene". "An ability to interpret the transference"; "an ability to interpret the repeated patterns"; "sharing amplifications"; "sharing the meaning of the moment of the 'here and now'" were mentioned as important abilities of a competent analyst.

Building a trusting therapeutic relationship is considered essential by most schools of psychotherapy. All our participants also agreed that establishing a solid therapeutic relationship is one of the basic competencies in an analyst's work. The understanding of the transference level in a relationship was also considered very important. In addition, the awareness of a real relationship, of the meeting of "I and Thou" were considered important factors in the therapy process.

Deeper understanding of the relationship and of the "happenings" in the analytical field is closely related with our next and final theme, which we entitled "Relatedness to the symbolic".

Relatedness to the Symbolic

- Interest in the symbolic material;
- Understanding different ways of working with symbols;
- Capacity to live a symbolic life.

Deep understanding of the symbolic language takes an exceptional place in the Jungian approach. "To live with a symbol means to come back to it often and in this return, to renew its energy and to be renewed by its profound connection to the Source, the Self" (Stein 2009, p.vii). The word "symbol" was mentioned by every participant of our study.

Beginners considered **an interest in the symbolic** material to be one of the key words that attracted them to analytical psychology. Many participants spoke about their interest in dreams and their desire to understand their symbolic meaning. The advanced candidates thought it was important **to better understand how to work with symbolic material** effectively. *"An ability to find what was hidden or forgotten"*; *"an ability to regulate your emotions with the help of symbols"*; *"letting a symbol come and playing with it"* – each of these capture well the importance attributed to developing one's ability to work with symbolic material, an essential quality of a competent analyst. Developing one's ability **to live a symbolic life** is important for a Jungian analyst. An ability to reach and grasp the symbolic level can help to enter into a deeper dialogue with the Other. It may reveal new and unexpected meaning or significance and may become a life-changing experience. The following quotation from one interview illustrates this well:

> If you experience a symbol powerfully it will change your life … if you do that, you find that your patients … start changing, their attitudes start changing, their relationships start changing, they think differently about themselves, so a symbol is an agent of change.

This quotation is also closely related to our next theme: "Mediating processes of transformation".

Mediating Processes of Transformation

- Being able to contain the opposites;
- Holding and navigating;
- "Experience of transformation can be contagious";
- On the role of analyst in transformation.

Many participants of our study considered analytical psychology to be a process-oriented paradigm and "transformation" to be one of the key words in the Jungian understanding of psychoanalysis. Several requisites facilitating this process were mentioned in our study.

Being Able to Contain the Opposites

"Being able to see the opposites and to hold them" and "being able to contain what was suppressed" are comments that highlighted how our participants expressed what was important for them in the phenomenology of change. Helping a client to contain the shadow side of their experience is especially important when we are dealing with trauma or other dissociative experiences. The participants of our study repeatedly mentioned this when speaking about personal and cultural traumas, which are an important part of work especially in the post-Soviet regions. Though an ability to contain painful or shameful experience is an important part of being competent, it is not enough for the healing process. As one participant put it, "a navigation system needs to be developed too".

Holding and Navigating

"An ability to know when to hold back and when to move forward "; "knowing when to be there-and-then and when here-and-now" is an important part of navigating the analytical process. A navigation system includes having a map, or having a theory of the psyche together with some good instruments for observing the processes, be it careful observation of a client's reactions, a therapist's counter-transference, or attentiveness to synchronistic events and to the symbolic manifestation of the unconscious as well.

"Experience of Transformation Can Be Contagious"

The participants of our study shared their reflections on their motivation to become an analyst. Witnessing the reality of transformation in the other person was among the factors that helped them to make this choice: "I was surprised he really was different than before. That made me curious of what Jungian analysis was about." To witness somebody's renewal, somebody's strength and courage to confront crucial challenges and to move forward, has a powerful impact on the other. This in turn may work as a trigger for hope and willingness for renewal in dark or somber moments in the analytical process. "The contiguity of emotions works not only from an analysand to the analyst but also from us the analyst to the analysand ..." Awareness of one's own infection and of the antidotes against it is an important quality of an analyst who is mediating processes in analysis. Awareness of the mutuality of a projective identification and knowing that an analyst's projections or even projective identification with a client could be important for client's change were also listed among other analytical competencies.

On the Role of an Analyst in the Process of Transformation

It is interesting to notice that participants used different metaphors to describe an analyst's role in the process of transformation. They spoke about the roles of a mediator and a midwife, and some even mentioned an identity of a partisan or a stalker to express their understanding of an analyst's assistance in the process of transformation. Knowing how to be in between the two realms, between the conscious and the unconscious, and how to guide a client through the transitional space and how to assist them when new life and new energy come to life are important competencies in psychotherapy. The metaphors of being a partisan or a stalker are somewhat unusual and may be related to a certain historical–cultural context. Being a partisan in the Soviet era meant belonging to the movement of resistance against the enemy that destroys life, be it during times of war, such as the Second World War, or during periods of repressions after the war. Partisans were fighting for their land and for their rights in areas occupied by enemies. The ability to overcome defenses and to fight for one's truth and values carries important symbolic significance in analytical work, especially when we are dealing with cultural trauma or cultural complexes. Even under the harshest circumstances, be it in times of war or in periods of heightened tension in analysis, one needs to have patience and willpower to move further. One of our participants mentioned a film, *Stalker*, by Tarkovsky as depicting this tension well. In the film, an illegal guide (Stalker) leads people in their search of a mythical place known as the Room. Anyone who enters the Room will supposedly have all of their earthly desires fulfilled. The journey is full of dangers and apocalyptic images. It takes a long time and the end is rather different than what is expected. It could be that, in some cases, the analyst needs to have such patience and will to continue the process, even though the result is far from what was expected. Knowing one's culture, cultural wounds, and cultural treasures is yet another important theme of the analytical process.

Relatedness to Culture

• Awareness of the cultural context;
• Being sensitive to an individual's sense of cultural identity;
• Being able to face painful issues emerging from certain cultural context.

"We came to another country and we tried to teach what we had learned, but it did not work. We need to stand there and to look at their culture and their history." This quotation from one interview reflects the understanding that a competent analyst must be related to the cultural context. Research shows that individual narratives and a sense of identity can be shaped by the culture an individual lives in and that an analyst and their client may give different meanings to the same story, depending on their understanding, or misunderstanding, of a given culture. Even the understanding of development, of health, of pathology, and of healing can be shaped by cultural narratives. It is interesting to observe that almost 50 percent of our participants spoke about the importance of culture. Relatedness to cultural issues is not specific to the Jungian field but in our study the candidates coming from different stages of their training thought Jungian psychology was more culture-related than the other main schools of psychotherapy.

Culture seems to be especially important when the themes of oppression, discrimination, trauma, and cultural complex come into the therapeutic field. A competent analyst must have the courage and patience to stand there, sometimes with recognition and understanding of his/her limitations. Understanding the multifaceted conditions and mechanisms of an individual's development and individuation is a prerequisite in analytic work. This includes assisting in the natural processes of growth and serving the transformative process, which includes the social, cultural, and spiritual realm. Serving as a catalyst and creating a space for other transformative forces to come and being attentive to the manifestations of the Self as the centre of direction and regulation are all the important facets of the Jungian way of healing.

The whole picture of competencies in Jungian analysis may look rather complex and even complicated. However, if an analyst or a training analyst is honest, if they bring a loving attitude and sincere care to their work, it is also possible that their intuition allows them to meet the Other and for a new integration to begin. In addition, many of our participants mentioned honesty, love, intuition, and care as important personal qualities of a competent analyst. These, along with other qualities, are extremely important to facilitate the development of an analytical relationship and of an analytical attitude, to develop an ability and openness to live a symbolic life and to be in service to the process of individuation.

Conclusion

Our research brought to light **the diversity** in the subjective understanding of the competencies in Jungian psychoanalysis. Subjectivity is a valued part of the analytical attitude. Our study showed that training and life experience lead to a more complex and more differentiated understanding of what can transpire in Jungian psychoanalysis. The integration of theory and practise never ends. Relatedness to experience and the growing consciousness of the complexity of the process reveal new ways of deepening our understanding of theory and methodology in our work. The reflections of experienced analysts are especially important, as they offer a rich and multidimensional picture of the analytical competencies. Their unique and authentic way, based on a deep commitment to the theory and practise of analytical psychology, offers an important background to clarify the specifics of the core competencies in Jungian analysis.

Continuing to research and explore this field is important for our own professional identity, for communication with colleagues from other fields of psychotherapy or psychology, and for the development of our understanding of the process as well. As our study also confirmed, Jungians have a lot to say and to offer about the living relationship with the unconsciousness, about relatedness to the symbolic world and culture, and about the phenomenology of the deep dialogue between individuals. Continuing research on a deeper understanding of what enables the process of growth and healing of individual and on the main competencies for assisting the individuation process could be important for having an honoured place in the rich world of psychotherapy.

Reading the stories and exploring the narratives of becoming and being an analyst was an interesting and inspiring process. We want to thank everyone who agreed to participate and who shared their reflections, their ideas, and their stories.

References

Barsness, R E 2018, Core Competencies in Relational Psychoanalysis: A Qualitative Study, in *Core Competencies of Relational Psychoanalysis. A Guide to Practice, Study and Research*, London & New York: Routledge.

Boyatzis, R E 1998, *Transforming Qualitative Information: Thematic Analysis and Code Development*, London: Sage.

Braun, V and Clarke, V 2013, *Successful Qualitative Research: A Practical Guide for Beginners*. London: Sage.

Connolly, A 2015, The Delivery of Training: Personal Experience as a Trainer in Other Cultures, (Eds.) C Crowther and J Wiener, *From Tradition to Innovation: Jungian Analysts Working in Different Cultural Settings*. New Orleans, Louisiana: Spring Journal Books.

Crowther, C, Wiener, J 2015, From Tradition to Innovation: What Have We Learned?, (Eds.) C Crowter and J Wiener, *From Tradition to Innovation: Jungian Analysts Working in Different Cultural Setting*, New Orleans, Louisiana: Spring Journal Books.

Jung, C G 2009, *The Red Book. Liber Novus*, (Ed.) S Shamdasani, New York & London: W. W. Norton and Company.

Jung, C G 1989, Foreword to Neumann's "Depth Psychology and a New Ethic". *CW18*, Princeton, NJ: Princeton University Press.

Kelly, T 2007, The Making of an Analyst: From 'Ideal' to 'Good-enough', *Journal of Analytical Psychology*, 52, 2, 157–169.

McWilliams, N 2018, Core Competency Two: Therapeutic Stance/ Attitude, in *Core Competencies of Relational Psychoanalysis. A Guide to Practice, Study and Research*, (Ed.) R Barsness, London & New York: Routledge.

Merchant, J 2016, Research on Training: Findings from the Evaluation of the IAAP's International Router Training Programme, (Eds.) E Kiehl and M Klenck, *Anima Mundi in Transition: Cultural, Clinical and Professional Challenges, p. 1486 CD version,* Einsiedeln, Switzerland: Daimon Verlag.

Sperry, L 2010, Core Competencies in Counseling and Psychotherapy, *Becoming a Highly Competent and Effective Therapist*, London & New York: Routledge.

Stein, M (Ed.) 2010, *Jungian Psychoanalysis: Working in the Spirit of C. G. Jung.* Chicago and La Salle, Illinois: Open Court.

Wampold, B E, Baldwin, S A, Holtforth, M G 2017, What Characterises Effective Therapists. How and Why Some Therapists Are Better Than Others?, *Understanding Therapist Effects*, (Eds.) L G Castonguay and C E Hill, USA: American Psychological Association.

Winborn, M 2019, *Interpretation in Jungian Analysis*. London & New York: Routledge.

Part II

The Analytical Attitude

Multidimensionality of Psyche Manifestation

Chapter 3

Complexity and Transformation

Joseph Cambray

With the development of complexity science, we have been given new, sophisticated tools to explore the analytic experience of individuation. This chapter will begin with identifying the intuitive orientation towards complexity inherent in C. G. Jung's works, from the *Red Book* to his *Collected Works*. This includes his methods and practices as well as his theoretical understandings. Then we will proceed to recent advanced understandings of nature and psyche drawn from the field of complexity studies. The deepest levels of transformation require accessing aspects of the psyche that involve ecological and psychoid dimensions of experience that include aspects of both nature and culture. Examples will be used to facilitate comprehension and application.

Introduction

Throughout the twentieth century the term "complexity" gained increasing definition and utility through the developments in General Systems Theory (GST). While the roots of systemic thinking can be traced back to at least the ancient Greeks, including Aristotle's notion of the whole being more than the sum of the parts, it was Ludwig Von Bertalanffy who in the late 1920s first articulated the foundations for a more precise scientific vision of complexity, especially as applied to the biological world of organisms and environments (Von Bertalanffy 1972). Early on, however, it was recognized that this approach also offered new ways to consider holistic aspects of individuals (psychology) and of cultures (sociology).

In transcending the atomistic, reductionist paradigm of the sciences of the times, attention was paid to the creative tension between order and chaos. This was soon recognized as a pathway to increasing complexity in systems. Studying open dynamic systems (that is, systems evolving in open environments not constrained by the thermodynamic principles articulated for closed systems, near equilibrium described by nineteenth-century physics), brought the realization that they could spontaneously self-organize, creating

DOI: 10.4324/9781003219910-6

increased local order, at the expense of surrounding environment becoming more entropic. This, in fact, is an essential feature of all living organisms. The capacity for self-organization in turn led to the conception of emergence, the appearance of new holistic forms, non-reducible to their components, having properties in the aggregate not causally derived from the parts. A simple physical example is the wetness of water and its liquidity at room temperature. These features are due to the interactions between water molecules, the hydrogen bonding that interconnects them into a whole, and that cannot be derived from the properties of a single water molecule.

A graphic formulation is offered in Figure 3.1. Note that the emergent form exerts a reorganizing force on the components in an interactive, iterative manner. The process evolves in a circulatory fashion and remains dynamic. The duration of emergent forms can vary enormously, for example they can serve a momentary need, then dissipate, or they can become more permanent stable structures. In this chapter we will look at how they appear in psychotherapeutic practices associated with analytical psychology.

Applied to sentient beings, emergence offers a valuable perspective on the mind–body or psyche–soma problem. From an emergentist perspective the mind is neither reducible to being the result of physical processes (mind as epiphenomena), nor is it separate from the body (dualism). Rather the mind is an emergent property of our somatic, experiential realm in relationship with the environment (for humans this includes, at a minimum, the physical/natural, internal, imaginal, and socio-cultural worlds). Over time the aspects of

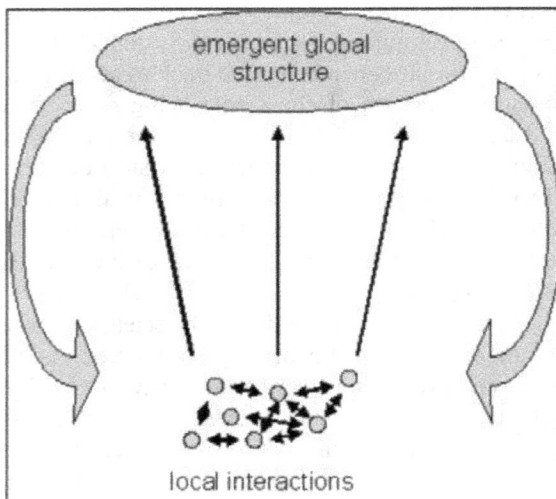

Figure 3.1 Self-organizing emergence in complex adaptive systems

mind associated with conscious perception of self tends to alter with experience and learning, though usually with an on-going sense of continuity across the lifespan. Thus, various levels of emergence are operating at differing time scales, maintaining continuity while underlying change occurs, up to a point.

This is where transformations can become important. In general terms transformations are changes resulting from inputs into a system, which alter structures and/or functioning of the system; these can be beneficial or detrimental. While the type and nature of these alterations can be highly variable, the focus here will be on valuable transformations related to Jungian-oriented psychotherapy, especially those that persist and even evolve beyond the therapeutic encounter. However, transformative possibilities often begin in crises or with trauma. Excessive or sustained trauma tends to be destructive and diminishing of most personalities over time, while traumas that can be metabolized and at least partially integrated into the personality tend to engender richer, more nuanced, and complex personalities over time. In other words, trauma that constellated fundamental changes in archetypal patterns can lead to valuable transformations if engaged with an appropriate therapeutic method.

Sustained deep psychological change requires holistic transformation, cognitive understanding alone is insufficient; affective, somatic, imaginal, and spiritual aspects must be involved. The broadest, far-reaching transformation of the individual is that leading to the process of individuation, becoming most fully who one is, the fullest expression of one's potential. This is not an achievable goal in the sense of a final, finished product, but is an on-going process, which if successful continues throughout the life of the individual.

As this model of psychological transformation was articulated by C. G. Jung throughout his writings, it may be helpful to understand its place in his own life. With the publication *The Red Book*, a fuller picture of the experiential base for Jung's idea has come to light and complements his scientific writings on the topic. In harmony with an analytic approach, turning to the origin story to find the metaphoric seeds of the future will serve as the portal to deeper understandings and appreciations.

Complexity and Transformation in *The Red Book*

The importance of *The Red Book* in contemporary Jungian studies is well documented (for a few cogent examples see: Murray Stein and Thomas Arzt who have edited four volumes on *Jung's Red Book For Our Time: Searching for Soul under Postmodern Conditions,* 2017, 2018, 2019, 2020 with another planned as well a conference in spring 2022; Kirsch and Hogenson 2014 edited a volume from a 2010 conference on *The Red Book*; Boechat 2017; Owens 2015; Hillman and Shamdasani 2013; Drob 2012). It documents transformations in Jung's inner life that were to inform the remainder of his psychological development as reflected in his personal life as well as his publications. The context for producing this work has been masterfully discussed by Sonu Shamdasani—see his Introduction to *The Red Book* (Jung 2009).

In the aftermath of the rupture of relations with Sigmund Freud (Freud and Jung 1974, p. 550), Jung had several "waking visions". Traveling by train from Zurich to Schaffhausen, where his in-laws lived, he fell into a reverie in which he saw Europe filling up with blood to the level of the Alps. Several weeks later he had a similar vision, each of these were of sustained duration. The visions shook Jung to the core; as a well-trained psychiatrist he worried he might be "doing a schizophrenia" (Shamdasani in Jung 2009, p. 232).

What was remarkable was Jung's response to the psychological shock of these visions. He clearly felt traumatized, but rather than try to seal this over, to encapsulate the psychotic process, he chose to explore it. Using auto-hypnotic techniques learned at the Salpêtrière under Pierre Janet, along with yogic techniques he had become familiar with, Jung deliberately engaged in actively entering his inner world—this is described to a limited extent in his biographical narrative, *Memories, Dreams, Reflections*, in chapter IV "Confrontation with the Unconscious" (Jung 1961, pp. 170–199). Jung describes how he would enter into a light trance, or altered state of consciousness, and observe and engage with the imagery self-presenting onto the screen of consciousness. For him this developed into the method of active imagination in which contents of the unconscious were engaged by the conscious personality—as I've noted previously, this forms a significant entry into the more general use of reverie in the analytic process (Cambray 2013). Jung felt he learned about the nature of psychic reality through this method; that the contents of the psyche were as real as the objective world but on a subjective level. Taking the imagery and affects that emerged as wholly real gave increased substance to this exploration of his inner world. Ultimately, a porosity between objective and subjective realities will become an important theoretical breakthrough, via the concept of synchronicity, as discussed below.

To assist in capturing and processing his experiences with inner imagery, Jung recorded his visions and the engagements, including dialogues with figures of the imagination, in an initial set of notebooks, the *Black Books* (only published in the autumn of 2020). He subsequently transcribed these along with paintings done in coordination with these experiences (though the paintings do not necessarily match the content of the text) in the form of a medieval illuminated manuscript, bound in red leather, hence *The Red Book*.

Following the sequence of the images, and the text, the reader is shown a set of transformations. One example is found by comparing the images in sequence (the pagination of *The Red Book* is also chronological, so viewing sequences of images also shows alterations over time, revealing emotional and psychological developments Jung was undergoing through this period, using this activity). Thus if one looks at the first book *Liber Primus* on folio iii (a very early image in the sequence) a blond hero (most easily associated with Jung's conscious ego state) is seen swimming desperately away from a pursuing black beetle, while a setting sun is being attacked by black snakes. Certainly the image gives the feeling of anxiety and fear of being overwhelmed by subterranean forces, and "going bugs". However, there are also rich symbolic aspects to the image, with parallels to the night sea journey in Egyptian mythology, where the first station of the underworld is associated with the god Khepri, the beetle-headed one. Going forward into *Liber Secundus* to page 55, the imagery is now of a solar barque moving through water carrying the sun on deck, while underneath a leviathan swims in concert with the boat, not in pursuit. The danger is no longer so immediate; there is a sense of orienting to and moving in tandem with these powerful dark forces. This would represent a profound realignment of consciousness with the energies of the depths.

Similarly, there is a sequence of imagery associated with the cosmic egg and solar disks. Several points on this trajectory include (pages from *The Red Book*, op. cit.):

Page 53: solar disk between animal horns;
Page 59: again a solar disk between horns, but now labeled explicitly by Jung as "hiranyagarbha", the Vedic Cosmic Egg;
Page 64: the opening of the cosmic egg as a fireball;
Page 80: the beginning of the mandala sequence with a figure Jung labels as "Phanes", who was the god inside the cosmic egg in Orphic myth;
Pages 81–97: a transformational process, culminating in a new, richer and more complex cosmic egg.

As I have discussed elsewhere (Cambray 2011a, 2018), Jung's experiences during his own creative crisis (Ellenberger 1970, *passim*), ultimately lead him to propose a new cosmology in which causality was complimented by synchronicity. To fully articulate this new vision his collaboration with the physicist Wolfgang Pauli will be required, which begins several years after stopping work on *The Red Book*. At the time of these paintings Jung was groping his way towards this new model of reality based on the symbolic meaning emerging from self-exploration of his crisis.

Early in *The Red Book* in a section "On the Service of the Soul", Jung's soul makes a remarkable prescient statement:

If you marry the ordered to the chaos you produce the divine child, the supreme meaning beyond meaning and meaningfulness.

(op. cit., p. 235)

This is a poetic statement on par with complexity science's own self-definition, as exemplified by one of the founders, M. Mitchell Waldrop, in the title of his book *Complexity: The Emerging Science at the Edge of Order and Chaos* (1992). Complex systems that can spontaneously self-organize and generate new, holistic emergent forms, which indeed seem like the birth of a "divine child", do so at the dynamic edge between order and chaos.

As I've discussed previously, this edge is a powerful descriptor of where psychotherapeutic transformations originate (Cambray 2002). While this is not a region one should expect to inhabit in an on-going fashion, its possibility is what permits deep structural change to take place through psychotherapy. Jung apparently was intuitively discovering this in his self-therapy experiences captured in *The Red Book*, though the language of complexity and emergence had not yet been formalized into a scientific perspective.

Jung's experiences, which led to *The Red Book*, began in late 1913, and by August 1914 when the First World War broke out, he had shifted from concerns of suffering a psychotic break, to anxiety about being a prophet. He was caught on the horns of a dilemma, how to see himself: descending into psychosis, or prophesizing world events, neither of which appealed to him. As I have demonstrated elsewhere (Cambray 2014), it took him about 16 years and a striking coincidence to find a new transcendent resolution to his dilemma.

In 1928 the sinologist Richard Wilhelm sent Jung his translation into German of an ancient Taoist alchemical manuscript, *The Secret of the Golden Flower*, with a request that Jung write a commentary. The frontispiece was of the Vajramandala, which stunned Jung with its similarity to the image he was in the process of painting (RB page 163—he even discusses this at the bottom of the page). This coincidence supplied him with the missing piece that allowed him to then set aside his work on *The Red Book* and, as Shamdansani notes in his introduction, "to return to the human side and to science" (op. cit., 219). Several months later he first formulates the notion of synchronicity in a private seminar (Cambray 2009, pp. 7–8). My interpretation of these events and Jung's reactions is that he had reached a new, novel understanding that avoided the collapse into either madness or prophecy, i.e., a universal, pattern-forming tendency of the universe that ultimately produces what humans identify as meaningful coincidences or synchronicities. It is a cosmological principle rather than an individual trait or fault.

I would agree that this brings a third perspective that transcends the tension of opposites that Jung had struggled mightily to overcome, but it still leaves open many questions. Rather than accept Jung's somewhat flawed energy argument (based on classical thermodynamics of equilibrium), I first applied complexity theory to show that clinical examples of synchronicity could be more productively viewed from the vantage of emergence within a complex system (Cambray 2002).

Several other aspects of Jung's *Red Book* period (1913–1930) are worth recalling at this point. This is the time in which he worked out his major methodological approaches to engaging unconscious materials and processes, and did his major study on psychological typology. In addition to active imagination, touched upon in this section, Jung also expanded the associative methods of psychoanalysis, by moving beyond personal associations to collective ones. This method was deemed applicable when significant psychic energy remained unmetabolized during the work on material such as dreams, after the personal associations were exhausted. Then, cultural, historical parallels, often from mythology, but having a collective symbolic resonance, were brought forward to shed light on the unresolved material. Jung referred to this method as "amplification".

By studying his use of amplification in the clinical setting several aspects become clear. First, this is not solely a cognitive exercise but emotional resonance is essential for an amplification to have any transformative potential. Second, the effectiveness of an amplification will also be tied to its ability to capture or bring to awareness an archetypal parallel that is currently at play in the therapy process. Amplification in this sense helps to make manifest what is implicitly present from the collective aspect of the psyche but may not be recognized otherwise. For example, a black dog in a dream may recall childhood traumas, such as fears of being bitten by a rabid animal, but in its role as threshold guardian of the underworld the canine figure may help a dreamer recognize the creative potential in a depressive state that is being avoided from fear of loss or grief.

Combing the methods of working with the unconscious in its various manifestations (from errors, omission, parapraxes, to dreams and synchronicities) with the development of the personality lead Jung to envision the deepest goal of psychological transformation, individuation. For Jung this was personally epitomized in his "Liverpool" dream of 1927:

> ... [t]he various quarters of the city were arranged radially around the square. In the center was a round pool, and in the middle of it a small island. While everything round about was obscured by rain, fog, smoke, and dimly lit darkness, the little island blazed with sunlight. On it stood a single tree, a magnolia, in a shower of reddish blossoms. It was as though the tree stood in the sunlight and were at the same time the source of light. My companions commented on the abominable weather, and obviously did not see the tree. They spoke of another Swiss who was living in Liverpool, and expressed surprise that he should have settled here. I was carried away by the beauty of the flowering tree and the sunlit island, and thought, 'I know very well why he has settled here'. Then I awoke.
>
> (Jung 1961, p. 198)

The dream came just before he received the manuscript from Wilhelm mentioned above. The psychological adventure he had been pursuing was reaching its denouement and Jung saw this dream as a key to the process he had been seeking. With the image of the tree of life standing upon the mandalic island in the pool of life (the liver), this was for him a vision of the realization of the Self (the collective, archetypal, transpersonal source of the personal self), which then became recognized as the true purpose of his psychological strivings. He spent the remaining 34 years of his life seeking to attain the realization in ever-deeper forms.

Over time Jung came to see this as an ontological instinct, the Self impelling the personality towards its fullest expression. As this culminated in his psychological development during mid-life, which the traumas initiated for him at age 38, lasting until about age 55, Jung emerged as the figure of *Jung*. His writing from this time forward are on topics of symbolism, alchemy, religious and spiritual practices, for which he is most generally known.

This was pioneering psychological work, on adult human development, on exploring the possibilities in engaging the interior world, on transforming trauma with the development of methods augmenting and expanding those already known to depth psychology. It validated the importance of psychospiritual work on one's own personality as a pathway to maturation as an individual. The achievements were remarkable and deserving of high praise. However, they should not be viewed as a final statement; there are limitations from the historical context of Jung's life and views, the extent of scientific knowledge of the time, including on genetics, neuroscience, social and cultural sciences, systems, and amongst others, the understanding of trauma and so forth. Not that the current era has complete answers either, just that knowledge has advanced on many fronts, and will continue to do so. Therefore, it may be best to appreciate the ground-breaking quality of Jung's work, yet revisit, examine, edit, and extend or modify the approach as befits contemporary knowledge and practice. The field is best served by ongoing modification based on critical inquiry and appraisal.

Juxtaposing the conceptualizing of synchronicity and individuation is worthy of a bit more reflection. The two ideas are often linked implicitly, e.g., popular views in which synchronicities are taken as originating in the Self and serving the individuation urge. We can now see that these ideas arose almost together as the products of working through a powerful set of traumas (including those that began in early childhood and erupting in the response to the ruptured relationship with Freud). As a result of Jung's efforts we have been moved towards an ecology of the psyche, in which the personal and the collective are deeply intertwined; we are always embedded in nature and in cultures with their own histories and developmental trajectories. Transformation can never be solely about the individual, though this may be the most apparent, even relevant locus of expression, yet it always affects the world in which it occurs. However, Jung's portrayal of his trans-formation, likes Freud's, is framed as an activity achieved in isolation, under the guise of the sole genius. In reality, many helped to contribute to both men's achievements, and many were positively impacted as well. The shift from individual intrapsychic to dyadic relational models of therapy has been a step towards acknowledging our deeper, inextricable connectivity. At this point in time we are poised to expand these views.

Eco-psychological Systems of Transformation

From a systems' perspective, for psychotherapy to be effective the participants form an interactive field with self-organizing capacities. In the psychoana-lytic community this approach grew out of Louis Sander's adaptation of Von Bertalanffy's models applied to psychotherapy. For a recent review of Sander's innovative approach and its impact on psychoanalysis see Seligman (2019). He was also a major influence on the paradigm shifting work of the Boston Process of Change Study Group, with their profoundly interactive model of transformation in psychotherapy (see their website for details and papers: www.changeprocess.org/). They evolved a dynamic model of thera-peutic change that involves the partners in the process of going through a set of affectively crescendoing encounters culminating in a "moment of meeting" in which anticipated responses (transferential anxieties) are met in new, fresh, and engaging ways that open up richer possibilities. This is, of course, not a single, pass-through model but a cyclic set of encounters that over time con-solidate and solidify positive change.

The formulation of the moment of meeting dynamics draws upon com-plex adaptive systems thinking, including the art of grasping the optimal timing of the meeting, the Kairos as the opportune moment. Jung's dyadic field model (Figure 3.2) is an early formulation of this general patterning, though without providing the explicit dynamics. However, his formulation of synchronicity and individuation provide a means to expand the moment of meeting model into a moments of complexity approach, as I began to envi-sion in a revision of therapeutic action from a Jungian perspective (Cambray 2011b).

The focus of all of these approaches is primarily on the individuals engaging in the immediate encounter. Nevertheless, the broader environment cannot be truly bracketed off, except as a convenience for attempting to iso-late the transmutative interventions. The appearance of therapeutically rele-vant synchronicities during the course of treatment renders this bracketing ineffective—something is missing from the description of therapeutic change limited to interactions solely between partners.

Obviously, the things said, done, focused on, or ignored are highly rele-vant to whether therapies are effective or not, they are just not sufficient to

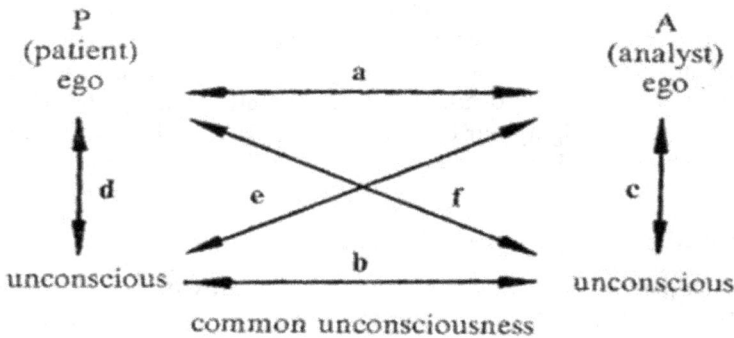

Figure 3.2 The interactive field in Jungian analysis

describe the whole story. Experiences with telecommunication therapy have shown that affective fields are non-causally interactive with the platforms (telecommunications therapies done over the internet often encounter difficulties, of connectivity, of pixilation, of frozen screens and so on, when highly charged affective encounters are emerging—Cambray 2017). These can be dismissed as irritating coincidences or considered for informational content not easily obtained elsewise. To include them in models of therapy, I believe we need a more ecologically based model of the psyche.

If the psyche is not restricted to the brain, or even constrained to the physical body but is emergent from the interactions of the body–mind with the environment, then, while it may be experienced as primarily "mine" and phenomenologically felt to be localized internally, in fact it has aspects that are distributed and non-local. These are immediate consequences of positing a transpersonal self involved in synchronistic phenomena. In other words, the conclusions Jung drew from his encounter with the unconscious ultimately demand we view the psyche in the wider sense as an ecological phenomenon. This is not a negation of previous models; they retain much utility in daily practice. However, it does open us to a significant paradigm shift in our conception of the psyche and of what it means to live in the world.

While the notion of an ecological aspect to the psyche is not new, especially in the Jungian community (see, for example, James Hillman's contributions to ecopsychology including on the Anima Mundi [1982], Susan Rowland on the Ecocritical Psyche [2012], the writings of Craig Chalquist, including most recently his work on Terrapsychological Inquiry [2020], as well as various other authors), the consequences for therapeutic practice have not been articulated in detail. While I have made some attempts, they have mostly been anecdotal, as the complexity involved is difficult to grasp in its totality.

The outlines of an ecological theory of the psyche can be found in nascent form in Jung's own writings. This can be most readily found in his comments about the psyche being like a rhizome:

> Life has always seemed to me like a plant that lives on its rhizome. Its true life is invisible, hidden in the rhizome. The part that appears above ground lasts only a single summer. Then it withers away—an ephemeral apparition. When we think of the unending growth and decay of life and civilizations, we cannot escape the impression of absolute nullity. Yet I have never lost a sense of something that lives and endures underneath the eternal flux. What we see is the blossom, which passes. The rhizome remains.
>
> (Jung 1961, p. 4)

By the end of his life the realization of connectedness with the world, especially of merging with nature at the expense of the individual self, seemed to be carrying him into finality and death. Speaking of old age, Jung says:

> [T]here is so much that fills me: plants, animals, clouds, day and night, and the eternal in man. The more uncertain I have felt about myself, the more there has grown up in me a feeling of kinship with all things. In fact it seems to me as if that alienation which so long separated me from the world has become transferred into my own inner world, and has revealed to me an unexpected unfamiliarity with myself.
>
> (ibid., p. 359)

Here individuation is transcending the life of the individual; perhaps the term itself needs to be reconsidered.

Clinical Implications

With this expanded model of the psyche, what are the implications for psychotherapy? Moments of meeting, open to include moments of complexity, which necessarily open the boundaries to what enters for consideration in the psychotherapy process. This does not mean boundary transgressions are to be simply embraced as transformational as most of them are deleterious to the process and often inhibit progress. Rather the frame itself is being expanded to the surrounding environment, at a minimum. This requires attention to not only communications (verbal and non-verbal) of client and therapist, but also what is occurring in the settings. Sensitivity to timing and place are key aspects to this addition to the interactive field.

A seemingly quotidian example: in a cross culture exploration of dreams during the COVID-19 pandemic, I raised the issue of decreased air travel and industrial slowdown mentioned in a *New York Times* article. One of the participants from a highly industrialized nation had a moment of deep insight from this. Noting a powerful feeling of nostalgia that had arisen surreptitiously on going outdoors a few days prior, this person was able now to articulate the stimulus for the feeling, the blueness of the sky, which had not had this particular, intense hue for more than 10 years. Sadness, with grief over environmental degradation followed, not only for the individual but for the entire group, ultimately proving to be a uniting force in the group dynamics.

With the pandemic, as the world has shifted to telecommunications for meetings, and videoconference therapy has exploded, there has been a huge demand to adapt to Zoom or related platforms. In the US, many insurance companies have begun to allow therapists to bill for "telehealth" consultation, something that was almost universally refused prior to the crisis. For those who had largely done therapy in person, this has been an enormous shift. The pivot to more online life has accelerated. With this are shadows, e.g., "Zoom-fatigue" being one of the first complaints arising from spending much of one's day in front of a computer screen, meeting with others, yet everyone in isolation. It may be helpful to consider what might be going on in this shift as we try to live locally and connect globally.

Then, there are the informational constraints: we usually see the other person as an upper body/talking head in a different room than the one we are in. Working across significant geographical distances, though simultaneous in appearance, in fact the partners are often in differing time zones, sometimes different days. The ambient light, especially if coming in from outside, is location specific as are background noises. We are in two places at once (for dyadic therapy and for other meetings such as group therapies this can be greatly compounded by multiple people in various windows), we see into the interior spaces of the other in ways not generally considered in classical psychotherapy. Our minds and psyches evolved under very different conditions and so we experience fatigue in trying to process an immense amount of information that is not naturally a part of our sensory world. And these concerns do not even touch the linguistic/language and cultural differences in working globally. I believe there is also a corresponding intensification of burden on the unconscious, the information overload is not restricted to conscious reflections.

The overloading of unconscious processes may be part of the activations mentioned briefly before, where more field and synchronistic phenomena emerge with media that collapses much of ordinary space and time. The associated clinical observations may be symptomatic of a transformation our species and our world are in the midst of, and being accelerated by the emergence of pathogens like the novel coronavirus.

Viruses are usually considered as molecular machines at the edge of biology and chemistry. Many of them can be purified and even crystalized (this was accomplished for the COVID-19 strain in late January 2020). In the crystalline state, viruses behave as if they were inanimate chemicals; the crystals can be stored for years without damage (i.e., suspended without energy input or discharge).

Existence hovering between life and inanimate matter, a twilight realm partaking of both, is conceptually familiar to Jungians as the realm of the **psychoid**: this describes behaviors where substances display psyche-like qualities as well as having properties generally associated with materials without any seeming psychological responsiveness. From Jung and Pauli we have learned that synchronistic phenomena are envisioned as involving activations of the psychoid level of archetypes. Thus, a viral pandemic at least suggests a profound archetypal activation and potential shift is occurring globally. Combined with the rise and rapid development of artificial intelligence, some believe we may be on the threshold of a post-human world (e.g., Harari 2017). While a fuller exploration of post-humanism is beyond the scope of this essay, it is a transformation with radically increasing complexity of the entities involved, i.e., who we are becoming.

From an ecological view, the emergence of a pathogen always occurs within an environmental context. Such pathogens including viruses are opportunistic and transgressive. Their appearance is in response to changing conditions; once a virus leaps across species, especially into the human world, it has the potential to endanger all who come in contact with it; hence viruses can be severe agents of change. Seen from this light their spread suggests disturbed ecologies, which manifest in biological and psychological ways. Our response can lead to positive transformation if we take a more holistic perspective and see the pandemic as part of an archetypal shift that challenges us to develop a new relationship with the world.

As a number of medical experts are pointing out there are numerous links between the emergence and spread of the novel coronavirus and the climate traumas our world is undergoing, e.g., see: www.hsph.harvard.edu/c-change/subtopics/coronavirus-and-climate-change/

As just one example, global warming and deforestation are propelling various species towards the poles to seek milder, cooler temperatures. In this process the migrating creatures are brought into contact with other species not normally encountered, increasing the likelihood of pathogen transmission across species.

If we are to pursue transformative responses, we will need to confront the psychotic defenses operating to inhibit our actions, especially denial, whether of climate change or the reality of the severity of the pandemic and the meaning of the changes we are witnessing. Collectively we need to attend to the messages coming from our world and take them seriously, rather than trying to contain them with placebo-like responses of the past.

The ecological world is not a passive partner to be exploited. It is communicating with us now, perhaps more loudly in this time of crises. Like Jung during his traumatic crises, we can either listen, learn, suffer, and hopefully engage the transformation, or struggle to silence the world, reinstate the status quo until the time that is no longer possible and the inevitable changes come with increasing devastation.

Turning Point and Conclusion

As the world has been going through a set of crises in 2020, which may escalate, we need to expand, revise, and reconsider our concepts and theories to make them more relevant and adaptive to the needed transformations seeking emergence. Let me conclude by hinting at some of the possibilities that I see on the horizon. First, to acknowledge the shift in culture from being based upon energy to a paradigm organized around information. There has been a subcurrent in scientific thought about the interchangeability of energy and information.

Dr. Melvin Vopson (2019) boldly offered a cosmological vision of the universe from an information perspective. To make this shift psychologically we might begin with a reconsideration of Jung's borrowing of energy theory from nineteenth-century physics to help construct his model of the psyche (I already discussed some of the limitations of this in my article on synchronicity and emergence, 2002). To reconsider libido and psychic energy more generally from an informational perspective would allow a radical revision, not only of our view of the conscious mind but the whole of the psyche. The way information is processed and even stored at different levels of consciousness could be investigated and reconsidered. The mechanisms of unconscious processes, larger metaphorized in energic terms, could be reconfigured more holistically from an informational lens.

Another area for reflection might be individuation applied to groups, in several ways. We might more deeply consider what psychological conditions foster the individuation of those who comprise groups, while differentiating this from the emergent individuation of the group or organization itself. In this we might ask if there are hybrid situations, for example, series of intermediate emergent states to involve co-emergence of the individuals and the organization though not in strict parallel or lockstep.

In this brief chapter I hope I have been able to show how the findings from complexity science may provide a means for contemporizing the Jungian approach. Historically this discipline has been marked by an intuitive attitude that when attended to, has kept its theoreticians and practitioners close to the cutting edge of cultural developments. The urgency of the present moment suggests it is time now to again invoke and embrace this tool for foresight, now within the context of a 21st century idiom.

References

Boechat, W 2017, *The Red Book of C. G. Jung: A Journey into Unknown Depths,* London: Karnac Books Ltd.

Cambray, J 2002, Synchronicity and emergence, *American Imago* 59 (4), 409–434.

    2009, *Synchronicity: Nature & Psyche in an Interconnected Universe*, (Fay Lecture Series), College Station, TX: Texas A & M University Press.

    2011a, Jung, science, and his legacy, in *International Journal of Jungian Studies*, 3 (2), 110–124.

    2011b, Moments of complexity and enigmatic action: a Jungian view of the therapeutic field, *Journal of Analytical Psychology*, 56 (2), 296–309.

    2013, The Red Book: Liber Novus, *The International Journal of Psychoanalysis*, 94 (2), 413–418, DOI: 10.1111/j.1745-8315.2012.00667.x

    2014, *The Red Book: Entrances and Exits, in The Red Book: Reflections on C. G. Jung's Liber Novus*, (Eds.) T Kirsch and G Hogenson, New York and London: Routledge.

    2017, Moments of complexity: Non-local aspects of moments of meeting, in *Moments of Meeting in Psychotherapy*, (Ed.) S Lord, London and New York: Routledge.

    2018, Neuroscientific studies of trauma applied to Jungian psychology, in *Research in Analytical Psychology – Volume 2: Empirical Research*, (Ed.) C Roesler, London and New York: Routledge.

Chalquist, C 2020, *Terrapsychological Inquiry: Restorying Our Relationship with Nature, Place, and Planet*, London and New York: Routledge.

Drob, S 2012, *Reading The Red Book: An Interpretive Guide to C. G. Jung's Liber Novus*, New Orleans: Spring Journal, Inc.

Ellenberger, H 1970, *The Discovery of the Unconscious*, New York: Basic Books.

Freud, S and Jung, C G 1974 *Freud-Jung Letters: Correspondence Between Sigmund Freud and C. G. Jung*. William McGuire, (Ed.), Ralph Manheim and R F C Hull, (trans.), Princeton: Princeton University Press.

Harari, Y N 2017, *Homo Deus: A Brief History of Tomorrow*, New York: Harper Collins.

Hillman, J 1982, Anima mundi: The return of the soul to the world, *Spring*, 71–93.

Hillman, J and Shamdasani, S 2013, *Lament for the Dead: Psychology After Jung's Red Book*, New York & London: Norton & Co.

Jung, C G 1961, *Memories, Dreams, Reflections*. Vintage Books: New York.

    2009, *The Red Book: Liber Novus*. Sonu Shamdasani, (Ed. trans.), Mark Kyburz, (trans.), John Peck, (trans.), New York: W. W. Norton and Company, Inc.

Kirsch, T and Hogenson G. (Eds.) 2014, *The Red Book: Reflections on C. G. Jung's Liber Novus*, London and New York: Routledge.

Owens, L 2015, *Jung in Love: The Mysterium in Liber Novus*, Los Angeles and Salt Lake City: Gnosis Archive Books.

Rowland, S 2012, *The Ecocritical Psyche: Literature, Evolutionary Complexity and Jung*, London and New York: Routledge.

Seligman, S 2019, Louis Sander and contemporary psychoanalysis: Nonlinear dynamic systems, developmental research, clinical process and the search for core principles, *Psychoanalytic Inquiry*, 39 (1), 15–21, DOI: 10.1080/07351690.2019.1549908

Stein, M and Arzt, T (Eds.) 2017, 2018, 2019, 2020, *Jung's Red Book For Our Time: Searching for Soul under Postmodern Condition,* Vols. (1, 2, 3, 4), Asheville, NC: Chiron Publications.

Von Bertalanffy, L 1972, The history and status of general systems theory, *The Academy of Management Journal*, 15 (4), 407–426.

Vopson, M. 2019, The mass-energy-information equivalence principle, *American Institute of Physics*, 9 (9), https://doi.org/10.1063/1.5123794.

Waldrop, M 1992 *Complexity: The Emerging Science at the Edge of Order and Chaos*, New York: Simon & Schuster, Inc.

Chapter 4

The Symbolic Attitude

A Core Competency for Jungian Psychoanalysts

Murray Stein

In habentibus symbolum facilis est transitur.
For those who have the symbol the passage is easy.

Mylius

Introduction

An adequate training of Jungian psychoanalysts must not only include, but directly focus upon and strongly emphasize, the art and craft of working with symbols in analysis. This is without question a core competency of the well-prepared Jungian clinician. Symbols guide us as analysts throughout the analytic process as we accompany our analysands on the journey through the labyrinthine pathways of the human psyche. Without symbols we are lost, while "for those who have the symbol the passage is easy" (1946/1966, para. 460, ftn.9) as Jung approvingly quotes Johann Daniel Mylius, the seventeenth-century German alchemist. Symbols are the key to discovering and unlocking the treasure chests of the unconscious. They provide direction for movement forward in time and in the individuation process, and they suggest meaning looking backward at one's personal and collective history. Symbols are like good pictures: one is worth a thousand words. Or they are like precious treasures wrapped in intricate packages that cry out to be opened. The task of the analyst is to take careful note of them as they emerge in the therapeutic relationship, to lift them up and hold them in mind as the analysis proceeds, and to help the analysand to reflect on them and let them suggest the meanings they may convey to the conscious mind. This essay will discuss the ways in which symbols and the symbolic attitude play an essential role in Jungian psychoanalysis and will argue for the importance of inclusion of this perspective in training programs.

Symbols and the Symbolic Attitude

Symbols appear from a multitude of sources and directions, inner and outer. They startle us when they catch our attention in a moment of synchronicity;

DOI: 10.4324/9781003219910-7

they impress us in big dreams; they may overwhelm us in visions; they move us profoundly in works of art and in the realms of interpersonal intimacy. They come to us as numinous experiences in the streets of daily life. We are surrounded by symbols. In analysis, we pay special attention to them. The question often arises, however: what exactly do they mean? And when they emerge within the clinical setting, what are we to do with them? Much thought has been given to these questions in the Jungian literature, first by Jung himself and them by the generations of Jungian psychoanalysts following in his practices. How symbols are to be worked with and understood in clinical work is not something that is obvious or falls into place like a ripe fruit from a tree of paradise. It is like surgery: some people have a gift for it, but all need careful preparation and training before taking the knife to a living body. In our case, the body is the psyche. And what we do to and with the psyche, we do to the soul. So, care and preparation are required. This essay will consider the problem of training students who are preparing to become Jungian psychoanalysts to work with symbols, whether as images or processes, in clinical practice.

To begin this reflection on training, it is useful to consider the important distinction that Jung made between sign and symbol:

> Every view which interprets the symbolic expression as an analogue or an abbreviated designation for a *known* thing is *semiotic*. A view which interprets the symbolic expression as the best possible formulation of a relatively unknown thing, which for that reason cannot be more clearly or characteristically represented, is *symbolic* ... An expression that stands for a known thing remains a mere sign and is never a symbol.
>
> (Jung 1921, para. 815–817)

To this he adds the observation:

> Whether a thing is a symbol or not depends chiefly on the attitude of the observing consciousness; for instance, on whether it regards a given fact not merely as such but also as an expression for something unknown. Hence it is quite possible for a man to establish a fact which does not appear in the least symbolic to himself, but is profoundly so to another consciousness. The converse is also true ... The attitude that takes a given phenomenon as symbolic can be called, for short, the *symbolic attitude.*
>
> (ibid., para. 818–819)

In discussing competency, we are therefore speaking about the ability to recognize symbols when they appear and about developing a symbolic attitude that will facilitate a symbol's meaning to become conscious. The question for analytic training is how to instill or cultivate this ability and attitude in candidates who wish to become analysts.

Jung briefly indicates what the symbolic attitude is in the quotation above. One can use the example of the image that the Starbucks Coffee company uses as their logo. It is a familiar image worldwide. This image can be read as a sign or as a symbol. If you are walking down a street and see this image of a circle with a female figure on a green background with a crown on her head and twin tails rising up from behind her, it can be read as a sign that says: "Here is a Starbucks Coffee Shop". But if you look at it as a symbol, you recognize the image of a Mermaid, an alluring anima figure of the sea who seduces sailors to a perilous adventure, and now the image says: "Something very attractive here: Come closer"! She calls you. Seeing the image as a symbol induces an emotional response and takes the mind to its fringes of awareness and directs attention to areas beyond the horizon of ego-consciousness. The activation of the symbolic attitude calls attention to the unconscious background of an image. We might be reminded that coffee is delicious but addictive, and the Starbucks logo now appears as a "siren's call" to passers-by to come inside and have an adventure, maybe even a numinous experience. Many people spend time in the Starbucks shops, reading books, chatting with strangers, attending to their emails, in other words expanding their horizons beyond simply drinking a cup of coffee. I have a friend who goes to the local Starbucks shop to flirt with the attractive young women who frequent it. He says it's the best place in town to meet cute strangers. This is the siren calling. The anima calls him to the coffee shop, and he could run into problems if he gets too caught up in this fascinating pastime. What the genius at Starbucks has done is create a sign that is also a symbol and one that therefore also appeals to the unconscious. When an image stimulates fantasy and emotion, we can treat it as a symbol.

The same distinction between sign and symbol can be applied to an image that appears in a dream. An analysand told me a dream that he had of traveling in a far-off foreign country and there he suddenly came upon a gigantic tree by the side of the train tracks. It was so large that he could scarcely see the top of it. The roots were gigantic and exposed, and the problem with the tree was that the roots on one side were poorly anchored and hollowed out, and this gave the tree an unstable grounding. The dreamer noted, however, that the tree had compensated this defect successfully and had grown to a magnificent size. He admired the resilience and ingenuity of the tree, even though it seemed unbalanced at the base.

The dreamer could easily associate his own life to the story of the tree: a traumatic childhood that was destabilizing and a lifelong compensating effort to rise ever higher in status within his social context despite the early debilitating handicap. He often felt unstable and anxious but continued to strive onward, and by this stage of his life he had become highly successful in worldly terms. Still, the uncertainty about stability prevailed, and fears of failure, poverty, and mental collapse haunted him in the wee hours of the morning.

As a sign, the tree tells the dreamer what he already knows, and it would function as a metaphor that captures in an image his conscious feelings about his fragility and achievements. It gives him a snapshot picture of his life's narrative as he knows it consciously. As a symbol, however, it takes on another dimension altogether. We often ask: if I already know this, why do I need to dream it? What does the dream add to consciousness that is not already there? And this inquiry leads into consideration of the image as a symbol. As a symbol, the dream tree is showing him something that is still largely unconscious but now on its way to consciousness since he can dream it. It is expressing this emerging insight as a symbol. As a symbol, the tree speaks of a mystery. This dream tree is discovered by surprise, and the dreamer is impressed by its size and height. He discovers this tree in a far-off foreign country, i.e., in the deeper layers of the unconscious. A tree of this impressive magnitude is an archetypal image, and it suggests meaning beyond the personal life story that is easily told in the narrative readily available to consciousness. What is this? And why is it something this dreamer might find important to take into account?

As I heard the dream and let it affect me in the analytic session, I could feel the awesome nature of this image, and also both its nobility and its fragility. The dreamer told me that this dream tree would make the giant redwoods of California look like saplings. This tree reached to the very heavens. Sometime after this session, a friend sent me a message that referred to Jung's discussion of the Christmas tree in a Swiss interview in 1958, where he says:

> The tree has a cosmic significance – it is the world-tree, the world-pillar, the world-axis. Only think of Yggdrasill, the world-ash of Nordic mythology, a majestic, ever-green tree growing at the center of the world. The tree, particularly its crown, is the abode of the gods. Hence the village tree in India and the German village linden tree round which the villagers gather in the evenings: they are sitting in the shadow of the gods ... These and many similar ideas are not invented, they simply came into men's heads in bygone times. It is sort of natural revelation.
>
> (Jung 1958, pp. 354–355)

Taking this into account, I came to the strong feeling that this dream image of my analysand's was telling him something far beyond the personal history that he was already so familiar with. This was a message from the collective unconscious and carried spiritual meaning. The dreamer had discovered a place within the psyche that is the dwelling place of the gods. This is a "natural revelation", to use Jung's words. A revelation is an opening to the meaning of mysteries beyond the grasp of ego-consciousness. And the tree's defect and potential fragility at one side of the root system, which is so clearly exposed in the dream, brings a chill to the mind. Is this a message of fragility in this time of collective anxiety about the very survival of the human species? It is a noble tree that has survived many seasons and crises, but the symbol speaks of danger and suggests caution. It is a world tree that hangs in the balance. This is a chilling reminder of a far larger risk than to the individual dreamer. I came away from this dream with a shudder, deeply impressed by the wisdom of the unconscious of which this dreamer had no earthly idea.

Why is this treatment of the image as symbol important for the analysand? In this particular case, the man who had the dream was excessively committed to his own position in the world of society. Social status and financial security were of paramount importance in his life, and other larger existential and spiritual concerns remained largely ignored. The gigantic tree puts all of this into perspective. The dreamer is tiny next to the tree. His life is short compared to the age of the tree. He needs to feel the spirit of the gods in the tree. The tree symbolizes the impersonal Self. This is a perspective he could never have reached and would never have thought of on his own. His consciousness was much too preoccupied with his own narcissistic personal concerns. The dream takes his consciousness to an entirely new level of awareness of the size and scope of the Self in relation to the ego. This is what the dreamer, who is now in his mid-60s, needs for the later years of his life. The question of life's meaning in the perspective of eternity is introduced by this dream. It will take years to digest the significance of this symbol. Analysis is the place where the reflection can begin.

For individuation purposes, treating psychological material such as dreams and fantasies as signs is sometimes unquestionably necessary and appropriate. It is personal and has the effect of grounding the analysand in the material world, in the time and space of personal life. For people who are lacking in stable identity and living in fantasies far off the ground, this is important. But for people who are suffering from the lack of a greater sense of meaning in their lives, the reductive interpretation of dreams will miss the opportunity for opening consciousness to a larger dimension of meaning. What a symbolic interpretation does is to expand consciousness, rather than to shrink it. It lifts the vision to levels beyond the already known and opens pathways to the depths of the unconscious that are otherwise inaccessible.

Dreams speak in the language of symbols. Every dream is a symbolic expression of an unconscious thought, and to begin to understand the meaning of the dream it is necessary to be familiar with the language of symbols. But this is not only a cognitive acquisition that one can acquire by studying similar images and associating them to one another. That would mean nothing more than linking signs to one another the way symbol dictionaries do. To treat the dream as a symbolic statement, the initial position is one of unknowing and wonder. The symbol calls for an attitude of openness to a multitude of possibilities. When these possibilities are exhausted, one can speak of approximate understanding even though a mystery remains for the time being. Perhaps other dreams will assist the interpretation; perhaps time will reveal an unfolding of meaning that is not possible in the present; perhaps synchronicity will offer insight. Some symbols can only be carried, and one never completely unpacks the unconscious meaning contained in them.

The symbolic attitude takes this approach even to images and thoughts that look obvious. For instance, a Stop sign appears in a dream. The analyst wonders: what does this suggest? The client says: it must mean that I should stop what I am doing or stop going where I am headed. That might be a beginning. Where are you going? the analyst might ask. And at this point many possibilities emerge. The client is studying to become a lawyer and wonders if this is a good choice. And further, the client is engaged to be married and feels some ambivalence. But Stop is a strong directive. The analyst reflects on the many meanings this might suggest in myth and fairytales. The associations multiply.

Symbolic Reality

There is a dramatic moment in *Liber Novus* in which Jung engages the prophet Elijah in a sharp exchange. After violently objecting to Salome's statement that she is his sister and Mary is their mother, he confronts Elijah:

JUNG: You are symbols and Mary is a symbol. I am simply too confused to see through you now.
ELIJAH: You may call us symbols for the same reason that you can also call your fellow men symbols, if you wish to. But we are just as real as your fellow men. You invalidate nothing and solve nothing by calling us symbols.
JUNG: You plunge me into a terrible confusion. Do you wish to be real?
ELIJAH: We are certainly what you call real. Here we are, and you have to accept us. The choice is yours.

(Jung 2009, p. 187)

Jung is challenged to accept the figures of his active imagination as "real". That is to say, to give them equal standing in "reality" with physical persons in his social world. They are "symbols" in that sense of the word: representations in our mind of realities that exist beyond or outside of ourselves, just as we take our perceptions of material objects as having reality beyond our mental images of them. This precise dialogue with the imaginal prophet Elijah would lead to Jung's argument for the reality of the psyche. Images make up the psyche, and whether they are derived from sense experience or imagination they are equally real.

Most people who enter training programs to become analysts come with the common conception that fantasy and imagination are the same identical type of psychic operations. On this, Jung makes a crucial distinction between true and fantastic imagination (Jung 1944, para. 219, ftn. 103). Fantastic imagination spins idle fantasies passively, whereas true imagination is an authentic feat of thought or ideation, which does not spin aimless and groundless fantasies 'into the blue' – does not … just play with its object, but tries to grasp the inner facts and portray them in images true to their nature. This activity is an *opus*, a work.

(ibid., para. 219)

In analytic practice, fantastic imagination, or daydreams, would generally be interpreted reductively and traced to wishes, fears, or complex discharges based on underlying complexes and traumata. The products of true imagination, on the other hand, are interpreted symbolically using amplification. They are considered to be accurate representations of unconscious psychic realities in the depths of the archetypal world. They tell a truth. The student is trained to read these as numinous symbols emerging from the collective unconscious. Reading the world's mythological systems, religions, fairytales, and imaginative literature of all kinds with a symbolic attitude is essential. This is a core feature of the education of Jungian psychoanalysts. It is more than academic learning; it is based on imagination as a cognitive function.

The Symbolic Life

The 18th volume of Jung's *Collected Works* is titled "The Symbolic Life", It is a collection of numerous forewords, interviews, and other miscellaneous pieces. The title of the volume is taken from a talk Jung gave in 1939 to the Guild of Pastoral Psychology in London. A number of distinguished clergy of several denominations were in the audience, and they asked him to speak about psychology and religious life in the contemporary world, collective and individual. In the course of the discussion, Jung spoke about what he called "the symbolic life". He said: "You see, man is in need of a symbolic life – badly in need. We only live banal, ordinary, rational, or irrational things … But we have no symbolic life. Where do we live symbolically?" (Jung 1939, para. 625). Asked why we so badly need a symbolic life, Jung answers:

Only the symbolic life can express the need of the soul – the daily need of the soul mind you! And because people have no such thing, they can never step out of this mill – this awful, grinding, banal life in which they are 'nothing but'. In the ritual they are near the Godhead; they are even divine.

(ibid., para. 627)

Jung's own personal experience of the symbolic life is expressed in his *Liber Novus,* the famous *Red Book*. There we see him in conversation with the anima figure, Soul, and with godlike figures such as Phanes and Philemon, as well as participating in a divinization ritual. Active imagination became for him and for Jungians after him the method for living the symbolic life within the context of secular modernity.

When Thomas Moore published his best-selling book, *Care of the Soul* (1994), it caught the attention of the public to such an extent that the author became an international radio and television celebrity. Obviously, Moore's work sparked such wide interest because it touched on the need that Jung spoke about in 1939 when he spoke about the need for a "symbolic life". This is the problem addressed already by Jung in 1933 in *Modern Man in Search of a Soul*, the title given to a collection of his earlier essays on his work as a psychotherapist. It was an issue that occupied Jung in his practice throughout his career as a mature psychotherapist. The German word for this is *Seelsorge* (lit. "soul care"), an activity associated with pastoral care. In Jung's case, the medical doctor and clinical psychiatrist joined forces with religious professionals who cared about the soul. Jungian psychology is a bridge between the mental health concerns of the clinically trained psychotherapist and the spiritual health concerns of the religious professional. An essential feature of this bridge is the centrality of the symbol for both depth psychotherapy and religion. Generally, it is considered that science" rules the one and "faith" rules the other. Jung objects in "The Symbolic Life" (Jung 1939) to the over-stated conflict between science and religion. On the point of the soul's well-being and health, there is no conflict. Symbols feed the soul whether they arise in the context of psychotherapeutic sessions or in the sacred halls of religious sanctuaries where religious rituals are conducted.

The training of Jungian psychoanalysts includes centrally an education in a variety of symbol systems from many disparate sources – world religions, myths, fairy tales, astrology, Tarot – with the intention of building a knowledge base that can be used in clinical work, especially with the interpretation of dreams, active imagination, and archetypal projections (as in the case of archetypal transference). This type of learning is augmented, however, by the equally important experience of the "symbolic life" as this arises out of the student's personal analysis and experiences with active imagination. Both cognitive and experiential learning are necessary. The former without the latter remains abstract and lifeless; the latter without the former remains too personal and specific to be of clinical usefulness. Together, they work in tandem to appreciate and understand the emergence of symbols and the possibility of a symbolic life for the analysand.

The symbolic life is characteristically an aspect of the individuation process as it proceeds in the second half of life once the ego has been well established in the world of everyday requirements for adaptation and functioning. Bereft of a symbolic life in the later stages of individuation in the second half of life, a person feels the "awful, grinding, banal life" that Jung speaks about. This is a life without living symbols in mind. As Verena Kast (1992) explains well in her work on fundamentals of the Jungian approach, *The Dynamics of Symbols*, the magic of Jungian psychoanalysis is that it makes a symbolic life possible without forfeiting one's personal life on the level of mundane needs and concerns. The symbolic life emerges spontaneously when a person opens consciousness to dreams and imagination, and equally importantly relates to these images as symbols. The task of the analyst is to open a space in the clinical dialogue for a symbolic attitude to enter, and this will be caught by the analysand as a spiritual resource.

The Symbol Paper

In the analyst training program at International School of Analytical Psychology (ISAP) in Zurich and in many other Jungian training institutes, students are required to write several 'symbol papers' in the course of their formation as analysts. These are essays in symbolic thinking and are regarded as a necessary exercise in learning to work with symbols in analysis. Basically, they are exercises in what we call the method of amplification. At ISAP, students receive the following Guidelines for writing symbol papers:

1. The basic task is to demonstrate the ability to understand an image or motif on the symbolic level and to distinguish between concrete and symbolic levels.
2. The paper should show familiarity with the methods of association, amplification (archetypal and cultural aspects) and interpretation.
3. Viewed psychologically, symbols further consciousness and transcend the rational. The paper should illustrate this with examples.
4. The paper should include personal experience of the symbol under discussion.

Writing such symbol papers is an exercise for working with dreams and products of active imagination in analysis. The emphasis is on articulating a symbolic perspective on the image rather than on interpreting it as a metaphor for states of mind that are already well known. Students find it challenging to resist reductive interpretations that read images as fanciful expressions of familiar moods and ideas but rather to expand them into polyvalent representations of what cannot be better said in discursive language. For this, eros must join logos to give a full account of symbolic meanings.

Jung himself offers many examples of such writing in his books and articles. Readers of his alchemical studies are often frustrated and baffled by the multitude of quotations, references, and associations he brings to a discussion of images such as, for example, the moon or salt (Jung 1955–56, para. 154–348). The text is an interweaving of references and quotations gleaned from his readings in alchemical writings, psychological reflections and interpretations, amplifications from world religions and imaginative literature, and clinical and personal experiences. The images are not reduced to single meanings but rather expanded upon to capture a multitude of facets that add up to a gemstone of symbolic features. As Jung declares in his famous Terry Lectures of 1937, titled "Psychology and Religion": "Interpenetrations of qualities and contents are typical ... of symbols" (Jung 1938, para. 126). Jung is arguing that the collection of qualities brought together in a symbol fuse with one another to create a specific complexity that we call "a symbol". This complexity gives symbols their polysemous quality. They draw on multiple references, and this diversity is difficult to package in a formula. Dogmatic statements such as "God is three in one" (i.e., a Trinity) attempt to do this, but they inevitably fail unless they simultaneously designate themselves as symbols, i.e., as mysteries. Nevertheless, this feature of complexity is what constitutes a symbol's power to move the heart and mind at the same time. We can witness this union dramatically in Dante's depiction of the Trinity in the third part of his *Divine Comedy*, "*Paradiso*". Or to cite another example, the symbol of the moon suggests a type of consciousness that has a number of specific interpenetrating qualities, but it requires art, music, and poetry to express the symbol adequately and to convey its essential meaning as a complex totality.

When we experience a symbol fully, we are usually left speechless. The impact cannot be conveyed in conversational language, much less in technical language such as is offered by psychology. What psychology can offer is a perspective on symbolic meaning using its vocabulary and conceptual tools, but these are inadequate to convey the experience of a symbol. That task must be left to art, religious ritual, and other forms of collective action such as initiations, ceremonies, sports events, military operations, etc. In clinical work we may experience a symbol in the temenos of an analyst's office or in the dialogue around a numinous dream. As always, a symbol cannot be explained, but it can be shared within the therapeutic relationship.

Conclusion

I hope I have made it clear that training in working with symbols in analysis is a prerequisite for students who wish to become competent Jungian psychoanalysts. To speak of a "core competence" in this field is to speak of fundamental skills in the practice of analysis. This means that anyone who wishes to train and to acquire the skills necessary to perform the work of analysis competently must have acquired the skill to work with symbols as they occur in the analytic process. For some aspiring analysts, this is quite easy; for others, it is arduous. A particular frame of mind is needed to think and work symbolically. It is a mind trained in archetypal images and their far-reaching significations. The vocation of analyst is similar to a religious vocation in the sense that one is drawn to this specific way of thinking about the meaning of images and experiences. A sensitivity to symbols is a key requisite for both. Both handle symbols respectfully and knowledgably, recognizing that they are handling the very stuff of soul.

References

Jung, C G 1921/1974, *Psychological Types, CW 6*, Princeton, NJ: Princeton University Press.

    1933/2005, *Modern Man in Search of a Soul*. London and New York: Routledge.

    1938, *Psychology and Religion*. New Haven, CT: Yale University Press.

    1939/1976, *The Symbolic Life, CW 18*, Princeton, NJ: Princeton University Press.

    1944/1970, *Psychology and Alchemy, CW 12*, Princeton, NJ: Princeton University Press.

    1946/1966, *The Psychology of the Transference, CW 16*, Princeton, NJ: Princeton University Press.

    1955–56/1970, *Mysterium Coniunctionis, CW 14*, Princeton, NJ: Princeton University Press.

    1958/1977, The Christmas Tree, *C. G. Jung Speaking: Interviews and Encounters*. Princeton, NJ: Princeton University Press.

    2009, *The Red Book: Liber Novus*, New York: Norton.

Kast, V 1992, *The Dynamics of Symbols: Fundamentals of Jungian Psychotherapy*, New York: Fromm International.

Moore, T 1994, *Care of the Soul*, New York: Harper Collins,

Chapter 5

The Heart of the Matter

Spiritual Dimensions in Jungian Practice

Ursula Wirtz

Analytical psychology has always been viewed as having a spiritual bent, particularly the Zurich school, sometimes ironically referred to as the 'grail' of Jungian psychology. I live and practice in Zürich, have served for many years on the admissions committee of ISAP, and worked with routers from different countries and cultures. I have learned that many of those who travel from abroad have chosen to train in Zürich exactly because of what they consider the spiritual underpinnings of analytical psychology. Arriving from the United States of America, China, Taiwan, Russia, the Czech Republic, or the Baltic countries, they want to nourish their soul and nurture it back into life. Many feel called to leave behind a spiritual wasteland, where "The gods have become diseases" (Jung 1929, para. 54). They yearn for a direct experience of the sacred and hope that the Jungian path will fill a spiritual vacuum and open a door to glimpses of transcendence. The notion that the soul is spiritual by nature speaks to them and they courageously set out on a journey into the depths, willing to surrender to the presence of the objective psyche, the transpersonal dimension of human existence.

The Spiritual Core of Jungian Psychology

In accordance with the recent "spiritual turn" in psychology, I have professionally witnessed an intrinsic desire for spiritual connection unrelated to any dogmatic religious doctrine, a yearning for what lies beyond our rigid ego, an intimation of a realm beyond space and time.

In my understanding, tending to the spiritual is a core competence of the Jungian path. Indeed, Jung considered religious experience as absolute, a great treasure and source of life, meaning, and beauty, that helps us to live (Jung 1938, para. 167). With the term "religion", he did not mean a creed, but what we now call spirituality, an experience based on the numinous that changes our consciousness (ibid., para. 9). Spirituality is the central meaning-making dimension of the human experience, a spiritual core that can be understood as the deepest center of a person, wherein ultimate reality can be experienced.

DOI: 10.4324/9781003219910-8

Jung has often been criticized for not having developed a sound theory of the treatment of neuroses, but he himself explained his stance:

> the main interest of my work is not concerned with the treatment of neuroses but rather with the approach to the numinous. But the fact is that the approach to the numinous is the real therapy and inasmuch as you attain to the numinous experiences you are released from the curse of pathology. Even the very disease takes on a numinous character.
>
> (Jung 1973, p. 377)

The unconscious is the transcendental realm from which spiritual and numinous experiences potentially emerge and to which we can relate to with awe and reverence. I often reflect upon a number of my patients who are struck by the emergence of numinous images and sacred symbols erupting from their psyche with great emotional intensity, transforming their behavior. According to Jung, the discovery of the unconscious entails "an enormous spiritual task, which must be accomplished if we wish to preserve our civilization" (Jung 1973, p. 537). Analysis can be viewed as our personal spiritual task to engage and make this world a wiser and better place in which to live. This, of course, does not mean navel gazing but may mean an ongoing commitment to social and political tasks of solidarity. Jung insisted that one's individuation included engagement with the issues of the world, a point candidates often overlook in their preoccupation with matters of interiority.

The Archetype of the Self

The Jungian concept of the Self, the core archetype of wholeness, belongs to a dimension beyond space and time. Wholeness as the basic principle of the universe is a kind of North Star to guide us on the path, although it is rationally inconceivable and can never be fully understood through our dualistic consciousness. However, Jung and the spiritual traditions treat the Self, or wholeness, as an empirically knowable reality. The Self is another very dazzling concept rooted in the Upanishadic phrase "Tat Tvam Asi"—Thou art that! "Tat Tvam Asi" means the Self is to be found everywhere. It resides in all of us as the source of our being human. This does not mean we have to think of the Self in terms of essentialism, or as a discrete entity, but in terms of Self as a process comparable to what in feminist theology is referred to as "Godding" (Hayward 1999, p. 20). "Godding" is the incarnation of God in our relationality, not as a personal figure but as the ground of our being. In similar ways we might think of a process of 'Selffing'—of incarnating the Self in the individuation process, a spiritual task of manifesting this eternal ground in our conscious living.

Originally, Jung viewed the Self as the *imago Dei* in our soul; however, later in his life he extended the definition of the archetype of the Self to include experiences of "'emptiness'" or "pure" consciousness. On his deathbed he read Charles Luk's book on Chan Buddhism, *Ch'an and Zen Teachings: First Series*, and exclaimed on reading it, that this understanding of self was exactly what he had always meant. It is the Buddhist idea of "no-self" that might have spoken to him (von Franz 1961).[1]

From my own spiritual practice in Zen tradition, I can see similarities of Jung's conceptualization of the unconscious with the metaphysical connotation of the unconscious in the Zen tradition. I have encountered many of our candidates with a great interest in meditation and Eastern wisdom traditions that resonate with analytical psychology.

The Gift of Paradox

In the Zen tradition of working with Koans, paradox is of extreme importance and in our Jungian practice there can be no talking about the Self without encountering paradox. For Jung, the Koans represent the inscrutable interrelations between ego and self. The incomprehensible, the "Unmoved Mover", cannot be expressed by our familiar rational discourse, as we cannot get beyond thought by means of thought itself. In analysis we can experience that the unconscious is, by its very nature, paradoxical and ambiguous. Self-contradictory behavior and entanglement in paradoxical knots are part of our human condition, yet I have often seen them magnified in working with trauma survivors.

The language of dreams, "God's Forgotten Language" (Sanford 1989), does not speak in terms of "either-or" but of "both-and"; two contradictory notions can be true at the same time, something is and is not, a "formless form", like the Self or what is called Buddha-nature in the Zen tradition. The process of analysis and our immersion in myths and fairytales can foster such an experience of life as paradoxical.

The paradoxical expression, "Become who you are", is an injunction to seek the Self concealed within. Everything being pre-existent, there is nothing to transcend. We need only to awaken to our true nature. Sometimes synchronistic events and their numinosity can alter the individual's conscious attitude and foster this awakening.

As an analyst I can witness those numinous moments when the unifying force of the spirit is experienced, the deep emotional resonance listening to the voice of the Self in a dream, or the encounter with a God-image in the active imagination of a client. It is very moving to accompany a patient in the process of awakening to the insight that the treasure is to be found within the psyche, a consciousness transforming process.

Jungian training emphasizes psychological experience followed by reflection, which is more than an act of thought. For Jung reflection is:

an *attitude* ... a spiritual act ... whereby we stop, call something to mind, form a picture, and take up a relation to and come to terms with what we have seen. It should, therefore, be understood as an act of *becoming conscious.*

(Jung 1942, para. 235, f. 100)

In Jungian understanding "man's worst sin is unconsciousness" (Jung 1945, para. 455) and analytic work is meant "to kindle a light in the darkness of mere being" (Jung 1989, p. 326) thus enabling one to become self-reflective. Self-reflection nourishes self-knowledge, affirming the Delphic injunction "Know thyself".

Shakespeare's "To thy own self be true", and the words of the apocryphal St. Thomas Gospel: "If you bring forth what is within you, what you have will save you. If you do not have that within you, what you do not have within you will kill you" (Miller 1992, #70)—form the background for Jung's understanding of individuation. Fidelity to one's own being and the recognition of one's personal life pattern as an ethical obligation can be understood as a kind of categorical spiritual imperative.

Analysis places great emphasis on relating towards a reality beyond our limited ego consciousness, a process that bears similarity with a spiritual quest and not merely a secular pursuit of self-actualization. Working with the core concept of Individuation implies a transformation of consciousness, a purification process of rather arduous inner work to come to terms with one's nature, make sense out of life, and manifest its meaning in the way one lives, loves, and works.

I have often been struck by experiences of synchronicities in the analytic space, when outer events correspond to inner movements of the soul, when shared somatic phenomena point to the underlying field of interdependencies. This principle of meaningful connection between natural events and the patterns of arrangements of said events emanate from the archetypal realm and have the power to convey meaning and destination to patient and analyst alike. Synchronistic events in the analytic dyad alert us to a hidden meaning that we were unable to see before, had not the unconscious paved the way to deeper insights.

The Mystical Core in Analytic Psychology

A spiritual dimension can also be sensed in the analyst's attitude to the work, the *opus magnum*, in the spirit of *letting be*, of non-intentionality. This is a state of mind where the controlling, volitional ego retreats and becomes free from attachment and preconceptions. Only with such "empty mind" can we be receptive to the voices from within.

For Jung, Meister Eckhart's way of letting things happen, of acting by non-acting, became the key that unlocked the door to the way. The relinquishing of ego consciousness, or a kenotic self-emptying, is found in many spiritual traditions and in conjunction with the paradoxical Taoist *wu wei* principle this analytic stance increases the analyst's presence. *Wei wu wei*, the action of non-action, the soft yielding in which the being is the doing, creates an energy field that reveals the spirit of the unconscious calling us to a deeper level of existence.

In discussions with students at the university I have often been asked if Jung was a mystic rather than a psychologist or scientist. There is undoubtedly a mystical core in analytical psychology, apparent not only from his references to Meister Eckhart and Jakob Böhme.

In my perception, Jung's conviction that the goal of all spiritual striving is the relationship with the "eternal ground", where modern man "stands before the Nothing out of which All may grow" (Jung 1928, para. 150) evokes mystical, non-dual experience.

Jung's own confrontation with the unconscious leaves us with encouragement to discover in turmoil the experience of something enduringly sacred and unifying. The *Red Book* is a manifestation of embodied spirituality. I subscribe to Leon Schlamm's radical thesis that Jung was "a secular (post-religious) Western visionary mystic" (Schlamm 2007, p. 1) as well as a scientist. I too believe we can place Jung in the mystical tradition and identify his active imagination as a visionary spiritual practice—as the publication of the *Red Book* undoubtedly testifies.

Shared with mysticism is the openness to the penetration of the divine into the human heart and a shifting of the center of gravity from the ego to the self, from the part to the whole.

The task in analysis lies in reconnecting the ego with the archetypal energy of the Self, "the window on eternity" (Jung 2009, p. 159), thus creating a reliable bond between Ego and Self, the doorway through which Divinity can enter the psyche: "*Vocatus atque non vocatus Deus aderit*".[2]

For Jung, the divine is intrinsically interwoven into the fabric of the human sphere; there is a dialectical relationship between the human and the divine. It is important to note to non- believers that when Jung refers to God, he has a specific meaning in mind:

> It [God] is an apt name given to all overpowering emotions in my own psychic system, subduing my conscious will and usurping control over myself. This is the name by which I designate all things which cross my willful path violently and recklessly, all things which upset my subjective views, plans and intentions and change the course of my life for better or worse.
>
> (Jung 1976, p. 525)

Analysts are acutely aware that modern man has lost all the metaphysical certainties of the past; our collective neurosis is self-alienation and we need to search for meaning to counter our uprootedness. Modernity suffers from transcendental homelessness and millions of refugees have literally lost their homeland and with it a sense of inner home, orientation and meaning. We are collectively in need of a *spiritus* that can contain broken nations and broken cultures.

> Only when all props and crutches are broken, and no cover from the rear offers even the slightest hope of security, does it become possible for us to experience an archetype that up till then had lain hidden [....] This is the archetype of meaning [...]
>
> (Jung 1934, para. 66)

As a psychotraumatologist I can testify that in fatal illness, torture, and existential nausea meaning can make the unendurable, endurable. We might even be "condemned to meaning-making" (Merleau-Ponty 1958, p. xxii) where once split off psychic contents become more dominant pushing for renewal.

Jung's advice is to 'religiously' tend to the messages of the unconscious and to listen carefully to the dreams and numinous symbols derived from the archetypal level of the psyche. Paying "religious" attention to our experience, to consider or carefully observe all that presents itself within the psyche is believed to be the most appropriate means of expanding consciousness. This non-judgmental openness and undivided attention to everything that reveals itself has a close affinity with the spiritual practice of mindfulness and meditation fostering a reflective stance toward internal states thus mediating the powerful energy erupting from the unconscious. I always remember Jung confessing: "I wanted the proof of a living spirit and I got it. Don't ask me at what price" (Jung 1973, p. 492).

Being open to everything that reveals itself means having an open eye to what is happening in the outside world, to engage in the social and political realm and to ask ourselves how we can creatively serve the world in which we live. Clinical and political work can go hand in hand as both become part of healing a system.

Students of analytic psychology often perceive their training as offering a healing fiction to endure life's tribulations, a life orientation to something transcendent, providing a framework through which to live in close relationship with themselves, their physical and social environment, and the Infinite. According to Jung:

> The decisive question for man is: Is he related to something infinite or not? That is the telling question of his life ... In the final analysis, we count for something only because of the essential we embody, and if we do not embody that, life is wasted.
>
> (Jung 1989, p. 325)

The Transformative Power of Love

Training analysis becomes a quest to embody the essential, the spiritual values of hope, trust, love, and compassion, while at the same time bearing with uncertainty, doubt, and the blackness of the *nigredo*. As in the alchemical dictum *Ars requiret totum hominem* (art requires the whole person), the art of therapy requires trust in the indwelling healer and faith in the soul's entelechy. In the valuing of *eros*, the relational function, I see a deeply spiritual component to healing the wounds of one's estrangement from the self. I believe without Eros there is no analysis, no serving the life of the soul.

I consider love, the erotic affective connection, as a matrix for a spiritual transformation that calls into being a force to reawaken and bring to the fore what has been entombed or distorted by early wounding or receded out of defense and self-protection. The Jewish poet Hilde Domin (1995) beautifully captured in her poem "Es gibt Dich" (You Exist), an experience I relate to analysis and to the archetypal yearning of being seen and understood:

> Where eyes meet, you come into being … you exist because eyes want you, eyes look upon you and affirm that you exist.
>
> (p. 75, author's translation)

Transformative healing processes are deeply connected with the power of love. Without love and a culture of compassion the fragility of human identity in the face of death and the reality of evil might not be meaningfully encountered. Analysis, like love, is a process of ripening, a task Rilke has described so beautifully as a great demanding task "to strive to mature in the inner self "(Rilke 2000, pp. 63–64). Rilke knew about love being difficult and the ultimate test and claim for the individual to ripen. I totally agree with the alchemist's belief, that beyond intellectual knowledge and studies, beyond meditation and patience, love is needed for the opus, even though the paradoxes of love remain a koan to be chewed on just as Jung admitted:

> I falter before the task of finding the language which might adequately express the incalculable paradoxes of love … I have again and again been faced with the mystery of love, and never been able to explain what it is.
>
> (Jung 1989, p. 353)

Love and compassion are needed for the individual to heal and are also needed to humanize our societies and help build a world that overcomes the wounding of our culture at large and the general indifference to human and environmental destruction. Love's labor on the collective level can be considered as tending to and restoring the jeweled net of Indra, a beautiful Hindu metaphor for the interconnectedness of all beings. Jung said it very distinctly:

Still nothing is possible without love, not even the processes of alchemy, for love puts one in a mood to risk everything and not to withhold important elements.

(Jung 1977, p. 402)

Analysis possesses the means of opening doors "otherwise tightly closed" (Jung 1928, para. 544), the door to an understanding of the interconnectedness of the universe, that we are ultimately One in our wretched human condition. The analytic process offers the potential to contemplate the ultimate mystery of the psyche and connect to a sacred place within that gives meaning and beauty to life. Energies of spiritual transformation are also activated through an alert attention to the telos of our dreams and visions that help us to come into being. I see analytical psychology in accordance with Teilhard de Chardin's conviction, that we are basically spiritual beings who to awaken and become conscious, need the energy of love. "Driven by the forces of love, the fragments of the world seek each other so that the world may come into being" (de Chardin 2008, p. 264).

Die and Become: the Spiritual Imperative of Individuation

This becomes the spiritual imperative of the individuation process, to responsibly fulfil my proper place in the greater whole by integrating the conscious and unconscious dimension of my being and coming into "selfhood" and become who I am meant to be, according to Jung,

Individuation is a philosophical, spiritual, and mystical experience (Jung 1938, para. 448). There is a spiritual libido driving us to become what we are ordained to be, an idea that can be found already in Nietzsche's work: *Ecce Homo. How One Becomes What One Is* (Nietzsche 1908).

The temenos of analysis can become the "sacred Cauldron" (Corbett 2015) where analyst and patient are held within a larger presence that seizes and changes both of them. The concept of a dynamic relational field and its subtle body manifestations deepens our understanding of archetypal transference as an individuating force and reminds us of the spiritual roots of our profession. Presence implies openness to the emergence of archetypal manifestations; it is a quality of being grounded, centered, and fully there, a state rooted in the spiritual realm and comparable to the "empty mind" of the Zen practitioner. When we learn to quiet ourselves and embody presence, we allow a healing energy to pulse through the therapeutic space because one is aligned with the Self, the transcendent core. These are the spiritually charged moments when both therapist and patient experience themselves as part of a single, all embracing reality.

In analysis we can witness the inner experience of archetypal numinous Self-images and how they impact and possibly transform the person. The process of stepping over the ego-threshold is often a bewildering experience, as the ego feels threatened by the archetypal force pushing up from the unconscious. The dissolution of the ego, the shattering of long-held convictions about oneself requires heart-wrenching shadow work. Trying to integrate facets of the Self in our conscious personality is a lifelong process of incarnation. Serving the Self and doing inner work can come with the price of tremendous psychic pain, an experience of dying and becoming. This Phoenix experience in analysis also reminds me of Nietzsche's dictum in Thus Spoke Zarathustra: "you must wish to consume yourself in your own flame: how could you wish to become new unless you had first become ashes!" (Nietzsche 1968, p. 64).

The Value of Inner Experience

Reflecting on the training of Jungian analysts I find it important to convey that in Jungian epistemology experience and inner knowing are held sacred and considered a legitimate mode of exploring reality and gaining knowledge. Jungian practice resonates with the insight of the medieval theologian John Duns Scotus: '*Expertus infallibiliter novit*'—'He who has had an experience has infallible knowledge' (Duns Scotus 1891).

Only experience leads to real knowledge, which is obvious in Jung's provocative answer to John Freeman's question in the 1959 Face to Face BBC interview: "Do you still believe in God today?" Jung replied after a pause: "Today? Hard to answer. I do not need to believe. I *know*". I understand this "I know" as an experiential wisdom that has the character of evidence for him. Analytic psychology – like the mystics and wisdom traditions – stresses the importance and effectiveness of inner experience that transcends thinking and provides a more intuitive insight into the nature of things. This perception of truth as a view of the essence is anchored in the mystical and gnostic realm. Without doubt, Jung represents the value of inner experience as a legitimate access to an absolute, transcendent reality whose validity for him was unquestionable. His challenging antinomy of faith and knowledge does not mean knowledge as an accumulation of theoretical insights but rather experiential knowledge, knowledge of the whole that transforms. This knowledge, that I would call wisdom, is concerned with deciphering the invisible in the visible, a task an analyst tries to do when listening with the third ear or seeing with the third eye.

A paradigm shift in the human sciences is necessary so that spiritual experiential insights of an ultimate reality that transcends the ego can be integrated into our therapeutic practice because the psyche cannot be treated without "touching the whole and thus the last and deepest" (Jung 1943, para. 175). For Jung it was his lifelong concern to develop a scientific psychology based on direct experience and phenomenological description as seen in his Augustinian advice: "Go not outside, return into thyself: truth dwells in the inner man" (Jung 1973, p. 467).

Inflation and 'Spiritual Bypassing'

An adage from earlier times is well worth remembering: "If God is present, the devil is not far behind". Spirituality is not only a gold mine; it can also turn into a minefield. A close look at our culture reveals how the meaning of spirituality has been emptied out, morphed to a cultural trope, exploited and instrumentalized by mainstream corporate interests, mass leaders, and fascist movements. In my practice I have often witnessed the damage done by therapists, self-made gurus, and spiritual teachers who were locked in a fantasy of narcissistic grandiosity and who fell victim to their own disowned psychic material.

A strong inflated ego ideal always constellates a huge shadow just as the spiritual traditions teach us, that the greatest danger for the Saint is his holiness.

If we as analysts are too convinced we know about the ways of the Self, too certain we understand the dream's message, even believing that God is using us to facilitate the transformation process in the client, we might do more harm than good. I recall the advice: It's best to remain an analyst and to let God be God. As I reflect on this, a Jungian joke comes to mind: "What is the difference between God and Jung?" And I smile at the answer: "God knows that he is not Jung".

My colleague and friend Henry Abramovitch from Jerusalem told me that the Jungian reputation in Israel is: "they know how to dance with archetypes but miss the ABCs of therapy". As much as we in Zürich might be inclined to the dance, a grounded way of working is required when there is too much Self and too little ego.

To the analytic process we must bring our recognition, acknowledgement, and trust in the cycle of disintegration/reintegration. In other words, we bring in addition to our own solid, robust egos—egos that can bow to the forces usurping conscious will, while also holding the oppositions of spiritual experience and material reality.

Where it lacks in our clients, we must constantly remind ourselves of the task to strengthen and consolidate the ego and to foster reality adaptation in cases of severe threatening inflation. We must avoid the seductive trap of diving into the products of the unconscious by amplifying symbols to no end—or tracking the archetype, while losing sight of our client, the person, in whom it is active.

I find it helpful in my work to surrender and be guided by the gifts of Apollo. From his shrine of Delphi, the oracle spoke: "know thyself", "nothing in extreme," "observe the limits", "hate hubris"! Embodying these jewels of wisdom will protect us in our Jungian practice. Be alert to spiritual narcissism and spiritual bypassing, to practices which avoid dealing with the personal mud and the suffering of our unresolved wounds and which engage instead in rigorous meditation, constructing a spiritual persona of specialness with grandiose spiritual insights. I find it alarming to observe in some of our candidates the passionate embarking on the lonely quest for the philosopher's stone, while missing the royal road of relatedness as a spiritual value.

I have encountered spiritual bypassing as a defensive maneuver to avoid the pain of working through trauma, a flight from an unbearable reality. I particularly recall a patient who had been sexually exploited by her father in childhood and in an attempt to distance herself from this shaming, crippling experience, she renounced the world, chose asceticism, and entered a cloister in search of refuge. She forced herself to forgive her father but the striking psychosomatic symptoms she developed made it clear to her that there was no escape from facing the trauma with all its repercussions. Becoming gradually aware of her spiritual bypassing, she finally left the order and began living a more embodied existence, eventually getting married.[3]

It is well known that the perils of the spiritual path can serve the personal defenses and often compensate for underlying developmental deficiencies. The personal work on one's own shadow material cannot be bypassed and has to be dealt with. I have observed this Icarus flight in meditation retreats but also in the analysis of candidates where an archetypal approach is used as a spiritual bypass. This is particularly dangerous when the ego structure is too weak and fragile, tends to inflation and gets easily overwhelmed and possessed by archetypal material. As analysts we are obligated to help discern what belongs to the ego and what belongs to the objective psyche. Otherwise, our clients may display "the puffed-up attitude of inflation", when the archetype seizes hold and "loss of free will, delusion, and enthusiasm in good and evil alike". In our work we must guard against fostering inflation, which "is always egocentric and conscious of nothing but its own existence" (Jung 1944, para. 563).

As analysts we must pay attention to the lack of grounding when there is too much yearning for transcendence and an embodied spirituality is missing. I find it important to ask: "Can we use creative tools to channel and transform energies that override the ego and threaten dissolution?" How do we respond to the fascination that we and our candidates might experience when facing Icarus-like flight in our clients? Are we grounded enough to help clients free themselves from archetypal possession? Can we assist in differentiating an individuation process from a fateful fall into psychopathology, discerning visionary mystical experiences that are growth promoting from inflated, psychotic manifestations that lead to severe impairment of thinking, feeling and reality testing? Can we guide others from the stormy ocean of the unconscious to conscious relatedness to the emerging images?

Though in the analytic temenos we are often confronted with manifold individual and cultural disenchantments and fragmentations, in my long life as an analyst I have also witnessed the emergence of a kind of "resacralization" (Davie 2010) in our society, a noticeable transformation in what is considered meaningful and sacred. The deep concern with our planet earth, the growing sense of care and awareness for all that is marginalized in our *Zeitgeist* belongs to this societal change just as the growing importance of "the spiritual" in our Jungian training and practice.

Notes

1   "He expressly asked his secretary to write to tell the author that 'He was enthusiastic …When he read what Hsu Yun said, he sometimes felt as if he himself could have said exactly this! It was just it!"
    Unpublished letter from Dr. Marie-Louis von Franz to Charles Luk dated September 12, 1961. Extracted from back cover of *Ch'an and Zen Teaching: First Series* by Charles Luk.
2   Jung carved this inscription above the door of his home in Küsnacht. In English it reads: Called or uncalled, God is present. Jung, C. G. 1946, On Creative Achievement, in C. G. Jung *Speaking: Interviews and Encounters.* ed. by R.F.C. Hull, *Princeton, Princeton University Press 1977*, p. 164.
3   A case vignette is contained in Wirtz, U 2020, *Trauma and Beyond. The Mystery of Transformation* (pp. 270–277), London: Routledge.

References

Corbett, L 2015, *The Sacred Cauldron: Psychotherapy as a Spiritual Practice*, Asheville, NC: Chiron Publications.

Davie, G 2010, Resacralization, (Ed.) Turner, B, *The New Blackwell Companion to the Sociology of Religion*, Hoboken: John Wiley & Sons.

Domin, H 1995, Es gibt Dich, in *Ich will Dich: Gedichte*, Frankfurt am Main: Fischer.

Duns Scotus, J 2015, in Walach, H, Secular Spirituality. *The Next Step Towards Enlightenment*, New York & Heidelberg: Springer International.

Heyward, C 1999, *Saving Jesus from Those Who Are Right: Rethinking What It Means to Be Christian,* Minneapolis, MN: Augsburg Fortress.

Jung, C G 1928, *The Spiritual Problem of Modern Man, CW10*, Princeton, NJ: Princeton University Press.

Jung, C G 1929, *The Aims of Psychotherapy, CW 16*, London: Routledge.

Jung, C G 1934, *Archetypes of the Collective Unconscious, CW 9.1*, Princeton, NJ: Princeton University Press.

1938, *Psychology and Religion, CW 11*, Princeton, NJ: Princeton University Press.

1942, *A Psychological Approach to the Dogma of Trinity, CW 11*, Princeton, NJ: Princeton University Press.

1943, *Psychotherapy and World View, CW 16*, Princeton, NJ: Princeton University Press.

1944, *Epilogue, CW 12*, Princeton, NJ: Princeton University Press.

1945, *The Phenomenology of the Spirit in Fairytales, CW 9/1*, Princeton, NJ: Princeton University Press.

1973, *C. G. Jung: Letters, Vol. 1: 1906–1950*, (trans.) Hull, R F C, Princeton, NJ: Princeton University Press.

1976, *C. G. Jung Letters, Vol. 2: 1951-1961,* (trans.) Hull, R F C, Princeton, NJ: Princeton University Press.

1977, *C. G. Jung Speaking, Interviews and Encounters* (Ed.) McGuire, W and Hull, R F C, Princeton, NJ: Princeton University Press.

1989, *Memories, Dreams, Reflections,* (Ed.) Jaffé, A, (trans.) Winston, Richard and Clara), London: Vintage Books.

2009, *The Red Book: Liber Novus,* (Ed.) Shamdasani, S, New York: W. W. Norton.

Merleau-Ponty, M 1958, *Phenomenology of Perception,* (trans.) Smith, Colin, London: Routledge Classics.

Miller, J (Ed.) 1992, *The Complete Gospels: Annotated Scholars Version,* Westar Institute: Polebridge Press.

Nietzsche, F 1968, *Thus Spoke Zarathustra,* (trans.) Kaufmann, W, London: Penguin Books.

2005, *Ecce Homo: How One Becomes What One Is,* (trans.) Hollingdale, R J, London: Penguin Books.

Rilke, R M 2000, *Letters to a Young Poet,* (trans.) Burnham, J M, Novato, CA: New World Library.

Sanford, J A 1989, *Dreams: God's Forgotten Language,* San Francisco: Harper Collins.

Schlamm, L 2007, C. G. Jung's Visionary Mysticism, (Ed.) Voss, A H, *The Imaginal Cosmos: Astrology, Divination and the Sacred,* Canterbury: University of Kent.

Teilhard de Chardin, P 2008, *The Phenomenon of Man,* (trans.) Wall, B, New York: Harper Perennial Modern Classics.

Walach, H 2015, *Secular Spirituality. The Next Step Towards Enlightenment,* New York & Heidelberg: Springer International.

Part III

The Analytical Process

A Living Relationship with the Unconscious in Practice

Chapter 6

On Being Imaginative

Verena Kast

"We live immediately only in the world of images", C. G. Jung

I do not contest the relative validity either of the realistic standpoint, the *esse in re*, or of the idealistic standpoint, the *esse in intellectu solo*, I would only like to unite these extreme opposites by an *esse in anima*, which is the psychological standpoint. We live immediately only in the world of images.

(Jung 1960/1972, para. 624)

We live in a transitional space according to Jung, and by imagining we shape this space.

Imagination is the reproductive or creative activity of the mind in general. It is not a special faculty, since it can come into play in all the basic forms of psychic activity … Fantasy as imaginative activity is … simply the direct expression of psychic life or psychic energy which cannot appear in consciousness except in the form of images or contents …

(Jung 1921/1990, para. 722)

To be imaginative is not special – it is how psychic life shows itself and develops itself.

Imagination: A Perception without an Object of Perception

Being imaginative means to see with the inner eye, to hear with the inner ear, to feel with the inner sense of touch – to be in contact with all senses, without having corresponding objects in the outside world. Imaginations and mental images can be experienced in all sensory modalities, and they can be understood as primarily sensory–perceptual representations. "The brain areas activated during imagery overlap very considerably in processing

DOI: 10.4324/9781003219910-10

the equivalent sensory and perceptual events" (Holmes and Mathews 2010, p. 351). However, imaginations have a shorter duration and change faster than perceptions.

The View of C. G. Jung

> This autonomous activity of the psyche, which can be explained neither as a reflex action to sensory stimuli nor as the executive organ of eternal ideas, is, as every vital process, a continually creative act. The psyche creates reality every day. The only expression I can use for this activity is *fantasy.*
>
> (Jung 1921/1990, para. 78)

For Jung, being in touch with the imagination meant being "alive", becoming more and more alive. "Soul is the living thing in man, that which lives on itself and causes life" (Jung 1934/1980, para. 56). To be in contact with fantasies corresponds to being in contact with the living, but it also means that the everyday things of life become "alive". How deeply Jung values imagination is reflected in the following quotation:

> Every good idea and all creative work are the offspring of imagination. ... The dept we owe to the play of imagination is incalculable.
>
> (Jung 1921/1990, para. 93)

We should, however, add that unfortunately we also owe all destructive ideas to the imagination as well.

The quotations presented here make it clear that for C. G. Jung imagination is the basic function of the psychic; therefore the work with imagination is fundamental for Jungian psychology.

Various Models of Technique of Imagination

Jung's notion of "Active Imagination" covers first of all giving form to the symbol: seen as visualisation of a symbol but also the representations in all modalities of perception.

Imagination is understood as playing with or engaging the inner figures the followed by illustrations of everything that has been experienced, in pictures, drawings, sculptures, or in written texts. It is also possible to start from an image – without any connection to a previous imagination – and to keep track of changes in the image while painting. C. G. Jung also understood the expression of the inner situation via dance as imagination.

Each of these techniques is then followed by a process of reflection on what was experienced. It is important to keep in mind that this broad perspective was what Jung had in mind concerning active imagination. Over time, only the active interaction with and development of the image in a waking state and the active dialectical interaction with it came to be understood as "Active Imagination". This kind of Active Imagination was understood by Jung and his followers as a kind of meditation whose goal was to become independent of your analyst.

For me, Active Imagination is what happens when we concentrate on fantasies, when we let them flow and observe what happens; we capture the fantasy and then reflect on and contemplate it. This can occur in different ways. In the strictest sense, to speak about Active Imagination is to talk about inner dialogues.

Methodological Notes

> One concentrates one's attention on an impressive but incomprehensible dream image or on a spontaneous visual impression and observes which changes take place in the image. Of course, all criticism must be eliminated and with absolute objectivity the occurrence observed and recorded ... under these conditions long and often very dramatic fantasy series are created. The advantage of this method is that it brings to light a lot of content of the unconscious. One can also use drawing, painting and modelling for the same purpose. Visual series, when they become dramatic, easily cross over into the auditory-linguistic field, from which dialogues and the like are created.
>
> (Jung 1941/1980, paras. 319, 320)

If the fantasies are flowing, a hint from Jung in dealing with active imagination, is helpful: In a letter written in 1947, Jung briefly describes what he understands by "Active Imagination":

> The point is that you start with any image ... Contemplate it and carefully observe how the picture begins to unfold or to change ... Note all these changes and eventually step into the picture yourself and, if it is a speaking figure at all, then say what you have to say to that figure and listen to what he, she [or it] has to say ... therewith you gradually create the unity of conscious and unconscious without which there is no individuation at all.
>
> (Jung 1947, letter II, p. 76)

Key in this quote is to "say what you have to say". In the imaginations we can experience destructive images, images of hatred and violence, or images of mistrust, such as in conspiracy theories. A strong, reflective ego is needed that can oppose these images and assume responsibility for which images one wants to cultivate and which images one wants to change for the better once one has understood them.

This methodological instruction on imagination by C. G. Jung is funda-mental to all varieties of imagination. The imagination begins with an image that occupies us, or with a dominant emotion. We concentrate on the experi-ence and "we let it flow". To let the fantasies flow means to give up control, to have so much trust in the processes that fear does not take over. Fear blocks the imaginations. Therefore, it is helpful to work with imaginations within the therapeutic process, because in this way the analyst can reduce the fear of the imaginer.[1]

Imagination and Narrative

To imagine and then to share what is experienced in the imagination with someone belong together. Recounting the imagination belongs to the imagin-ation and clarifies what has been experienced. Imaginations are often a bit vague; by recounting them they get a greater clarity, the emotions associated with them can be experienced more clearly, they get more real. In this con-text I find a quote from C. G. Jung from the Zarathustra Seminar extremely important. He says:

> Our unconscious contents are potentialities that may be but are not yet, because they have no definiteness ... Definiteness only appears when matter appears ... To give body to one's thoughts means that one can speak them, paint them, show them, make them appear clearly before the eyes of everybody ...
>
> (Jarrett 1988, p. 194)

Imaginations already give a certain definiteness to our unconscious contents, but this is much more the case when we talk about imaginations, write them down or paint them. When we tell each other our memories, and if we imagine them, we are then in a common imaginary space, which is also a space of transformation.

Imagination: The Basis for Various Techniques in Jungian Psychotherapy

Because images are so fundamental to our experience, imaginations can be described from a variety of perspectives. We can differentiate between autono-mous, spontaneous, unconscious imaginations, stimulus-induced imagin-ations, guided imaginations, and deliberate imaginations. Episodic memories are imaginations and they can be easily linked to future plans. Imaginations can be pleasant, meaningful, full of fantastic sceneries, or disturbing. Imaginations connected to the future can facilitate creativity (Zedelius et al. 2020). In connection with mental disorder, imaginations can be repetitive, distressing, and boring. They can be an expression of complex episodes whose ruminative imaginations can be used to work on respective complex episodes. The whole therapeutic process is a highly imaginative endeavour. We imagine the life of our analysands, their fantasies; in fact, the processes of transference and countertransference can also be seen as imaginations. All the imaginations our patients produce also mirror the therapeutic relationship and the therapeutic process (Kast 2012; Schaverien 2008).

For therapists, imaginations are therapeutic techniques, which require knowledge of and concentration on all kind of symbols: symbols that spring to mind unbidden, symbols in dreams and symbols in narratives like fairy tales and myths. Conversely, we can also concentrate on an important emotion and expect images to emerge as a result. Working with images and imagination touches on our fundamental conviction that the symbolic is an inherent part of human constitution, that everything that exists also has a meaning, an inner equivalent, and that the inner world and the outer world always merge into one, if we want to feel alive. Our imagination is not only about our personal memories and plans, it also includes nature, our cultural memory and our cultural visions. In our imaginations, in our daydreams, in our dreams of the night, we experience ourselves in resonance with images of nature, images of art, images that arise in connection with listening to music, with reading stories, with hearing thoughts from others, seeing films and much more. If they appeal to us emotionally, they touch us, they activate our "inner world". Through this being in-resonance, our imaginations are enriched, placed in a larger human context; we feel much more alive and experience meaning. It depends on what we deal with in our lives and how we deal with this. Many fantasies, imaginations, and dreams arise automatically from our life story and from the current demands of life. But also here questions arise: do we want to repeat over and over again the scenarios in which we are victims of life, or do we want to recall situations of contentment, of success and of harmonious human relations? We also have an area of life in which we can freely choose to turn to life: Do we want to watch a destructive film, or do we want to read an interesting story, a poem, a myth that has always interested us? Do we want to follow stories of mistrust or do we want to explore stories of trust?

Imagination is fundamentally important when it comes to activating universal basic emotions, to establishing an emotional equilibrium, to playing with images, to perceiving emotions associated with them, but also to perceiving the body's feelings. The perception of a state of being in the body can be an emotional starting point for imaginations. We know that Jung valued imaginations highly in dealing with emotions.

> To the extent that I managed to translate the emotions into images, that is to find the images which were concealed in the emotions, inwardly calmed and reassured. ... I learned how helpful it can be, from the therapeutic point of view, to find the particular images which lie behind emotions.
>
> (Jung 1961, p. 201)

Imagination and Neuroscience

We Jungians are aware of the importance of imagination in the regulation of emotions, which includes dealing with daily problems and mental disorders but also includes dealing with dreams, expressions of creativity in the sciences and in the arts, in personal development and in experiencing meaning.

Langwieler highlighted that there is a discrepancy between a great wealth of experience with imaginative material in therapeutic and artistic contexts and its embedding in recognized psychological and neurobiological theories (Langwieler 2014, p. 262). This is not the case anymore. Emily A Holmes, professor of clinical neuroscience at the Karolinska institute in Sweden did a lot of research on imagery. In a fundamental article entitled "Mental Imagery in Depression" (Holmes et al. 2016), she mentions that psychological treatment techniques have long been associated with mental imagery, mentioning Pierre Janet and C. G. Jung. There is a lot of research done in the last years about mind – wandering, self – generating thoughts and imagery. This is all about imagination in a broad sense and is in accordance with Jung's idea that we live immediately in the world of images.

Research about Self-generated Thinking

Self-generated thinking is understood by neuroscientists (Fox and Koroma 2018) to be mental content that forms a stream of thoughts largely independent of the external environment; it is about memories, future plans, daydreams, fantasies, simulated social interactions but also about ruminating and dreaming. These self-generated thoughts, images, and emotions are largely independent of external, sensory stimuli; they can be spontaneous or deliberately induced, even automatically through affective patterns. Self-generated thinking consists of uncontrolled forms of cognition, such as dreaming, thought wandering, creative thinking, but also of automatic and ingrained forms of thinking, such as compulsive thinking, ruminating, or brooding (Fox, Christoff, and Dixon 2018 b).

The spectrum of these spontaneous thoughts ranges from mental content that is not controlled, even appearing confused, as in a psychosis, to focused attention on the other side of the spectrum, for example when taking an exam. Fox sees dreaming, daydreaming, and creative thinking approximately in the middle of this spectrum (Fox and Koroma 2018 a). Spontaneous thoughts can be unintentionally imposed, but can also be intentionally sought. Fox has evidence that most daydreaming occurs unconsciously, at least below the threshold of conscious awareness (Fox and Koroma a). In the imaginations there is a high prevalence and wide variability of affects. Emotions, feelings, moods belong indispensably to self-generated thoughts. The mood in the daydreams seems to depend on the modality in which the daydreams occur: "for instance negative affect correlates with increased narrative /verbal/

auditory) thought, whereas positive affect correlates with thoughts that are more visual in nature" (Fox et al. 2018 b, p. 6). They deal with what currently occupies us most emotionally and are therefore also related to social situations.

These affects in mind wandering can be related to an experience with the external world, but they can also be triggered intrinsically.

> Indeed many powerful experiences (such as grief, anger or joy) can occur in the absence of any direct external referent. These subjective driven emotional and cognitive states that are unrelated to events in the here and now are a core element of the human condition: They make up half of our waking thought.
>
> (Tusche et al. 2014, p.107)

Their research suggests, that the MOFC (Medial Orbitofrontal Cortex) is activated in both situations, meaning that affects from the unconscious directly activate the brain (Tusche et al. 2014, p. 114).

Dreaming Below the Threshold of Consciousness: Fox and C. G. Jung

Fox (Fox and Koroma 2018a) sees these processes of self-generated thinking as taking place continuously below the threshold of consciousness, competing with other input or signals in the brain that demand attention. These processes can be turned to consciously, but they also demand our attention when we do not want it. These thoughts can be highly emotional, elated, or disturbing.

C. G. Jung has described this phenomenon in a similar way.

> Imagination is actually the soul's self-activity, which breaks through wherever the inhibition by consciousness weakens or even stops altogether as in sleep. In sleep, fantasy appears as a dream. In addition, in the waking we dream further under the consciousness threshold and this completely particularly by virtue of repressed or otherwise unconscious complexes.
>
> (Jung 1929/1971a, para. 125)

For Jung, fantasy appears as a dream during sleep, but he is of the opinion that we continue to dream even while awake below the threshold of consciousness and that these "daydreams" occasionally become accessible to us (ibid.). Jung sees the reason for this in the complexes, in generalized dysfunctional emotionally stressed relationship experiences. These cause dreams; that is, emotional problems trigger the dreams, but they are also "dreamed away" in the dreams and the associated relationship patterns are gradually changed, not least because the complexes offer imaginations which, to follow, "sets his life in motion again" (Jung 1929/1971a, para. 86). "Complexes are the actors of our dreams" (Jung 1960/1972, para. 202).

Already in 1916, Jung pointed to the emotionally charged contents, the complexes, as starting points for imagination (fantasies, series of images), and as a starting point for the formation of symbols. Complexes are seen as centres of energy, grouping them around a strong intrinsic emotional core and called forth whenever the individual has a painful encounter with an outer demand or an event in their environment that overwhelms them. Each experience with a similar topic or a similar emotion is identified and understood; we react in the structure of the complex and therefore reinforce the complex (Jung 1971/1985, paras. 77–196). Complexes show the vulnerable parts in the psyche, but as energy centres they have a certain activity – expressed in the inherent emotion of the complex – that creates psychic life.

Complexes hinder the individual in developing in the area of the main complexes, but in the complexes are also seeds of new life possibilities (Jung 1960/1972, para. 63). These creative seeds can be found and nourished if we accept the complexes and if we let show it in fantasies, if we work on it with imagination. The idea that in the affective disorder lies the energy that the suffering human needs for his emotional self-regulation, also for forthcoming developmental steps, is a theoretical basis for various techniques such as imagination, painting, performing games, sand play, and other techniques that are used in Jungian therapy to make complexes more conscious and to enable creative change. To work with the unconscious, to be attentive to the to the creative in the psyche, was a basic idea and contribution of Jung, which applies to therapy as well as to everyday life.

That we can identify a continuum between imagination and dreams encourages us to work on dreams with imagination and to expand dreams with imaginative techniques. This makes the connection to the emotionally important stimuli of the dream more visible and can thereby be linked to the current imagination space, the life themes that are activated and the creative ideas associated with them (Kast 2019).

The Past and the Future

In the light of depth psychology, imagination is related to memory and perception as well as to emotion. In this form of remembering when we visualize past situations, the memories of past experiences become current and can thus also be newly reflected and integrated into the whole of life. Since remembering is also dependent on the respective prevailing emotions, and thus also connected to the current life situation, what we consider to be the facts can be remembered enriched with new perspectives (Kast 2010). Many of our fantasies are fear fantasies. If we did not want to perceive them, then, according to Schacter and Buckner, we would also be inhibited in the fantasies that reach into the future (2007). But just by facing these fear fantasies, by looking at them, new perspectives can be experienced and new spaces can open up.

But imagination is also about productive imagination, a spontaneous form of imagination as an aspect of creativity that we associate with freedom, emotionally with anticipation, and with interest. What we long for and wish for we first find in our imagination; if we let ourselves go there. All theories of change, but especially creativity research, are based on the imagination. The space of the imagination is the space of freedom and possibilities – a space in which boundaries are crossed in a completely natural way, space and time are relativized, possibilities that we do not yet have become tangible. It is a space in which people can play, can test themselves in play, find solutions to problems, and also develop new visions for the future.

On Being Imaginative: Some Clinical Notes

Working in the psychotherapeutic field and very explicitly in supervision, means working with imagination: everything is imagination. We are in resonance with another person, we imagine how he or she feels, we hear life stories and dreams that we can only imagine

To become aware of particular memories out of the many possible memories and imaginations depends on the mood you are in and also on the people with whom you share these memories (Markowitsch 2002). If we are in a joyful mood, we are more likely to have joyful memories. If we are bitter and grumpy, then experiences come to mind that encourage us in this bad mood. If we are angry, we remember more and more experiences that annoyed us, and everything that might still be good in this world, in this life, is then flooded and darkened by anger. The emotion, the mood in which we find ourselves, lets us choose stories to remember and tell, or to colour the stories we have always told. If we are depressed, we might tell a different story than when we feel inspired, or we might tell this otherwise inspired and also inspiring story with a melancholic undertone.

According to research of Holmes – depressives not only have many negative imaginations but also suffer from an impoverishment of positive imaginations. They can fantasize about bad positive experiences and positive future expectations. But they have self-defining positive memories of important situations in their lives. If you ask for them (Holmes et al. 2016, p. 256). "Repeated imagery of positive scenarios (versus just listening to the same scenarios) over one week resulted in decreased depressive symptoms and reduced negative interpretive bias in participants with depression". These are the findings of Torkan (cited in Holmes et al. 2016, p. 260). This is one of the reasons why memories of situations when you were happy, when you were filled with great interest, are so helpful and make people feel better. Making generalized statements is insufficient, they have to engage imaginatively in positive scenarios.

In this context, anticipation of joy also is an important emotion. Anticipation of joy arises from a positively toned imagination of the future and also draws energy from past surprising, joyful experiences (Kast 1991).

Emotional Contagion and Countertransference

We can catch the emotions of other people, and this not only in the analytical process. For example, we are in a concert, people are enthusiastic – and as the crowd gets increasingly more enthusiastic, so do we.

In the analytical process we can be trapped in the emotion of the patient and it is difficult to understand what is going on in the patient and in the therapeutic relationship.

The contagion of emotions is understood as a consequence of the unconscious and of the conscious and the unconscious perception of facial expression, voice, body movements, and more. This is also the basis for empathy and sympathy and the basis for the understanding of countertransference.

Research carried out by Hatfield shows that the fact we humans automatically adopt or mimic expressions, postures, movements, and vocalizations from each other makes it possible to read the emotions of other people (Hatfield et al. 1993, p. 96ff.).

Emotional contagion is the basis for counter-transference in the analytical situation. We concentrate on a feeling or an impression – in connection with the patient, of course – and perceive which image is created. We then reflect on the significance of this image for the analysand and for the therapeutic process.

In an article about this, Joy Schaverien described this as a Jungian way of understanding countertransference: "the idea is to reframe countertransference generated imagery as active imagination and to explore its impact on the symbolic function in the analysand" (Schaverien 2008, p. 148).

In practice, we concentrate on a feeling or an impression in connection with the patient, of course, and perceive which image is created. We then reflect on the significance of this image for the analysand and the therapeutic process.

Example

In a session with a 30-year-old man, I get increasingly bored. I start to concentrate on my emotions. What I perceive: a grey feeling, grey hangs over everything, boredom spreads, there is a paralyzing atmosphere. Silence. I concentrate on this atmosphere. I see the image of a very steep mountain climb, where you get out of breath, it is autumn. Beautiful autumn colours. I see a person on this path who resembles my patient. He stands still and doesn't move. Should he? Shall he not?

I share my emotions and my imagination with my patient, as well as the change of emotions. He responds: "Now that you say it – yes, these are my feelings – paralyzing. Your imagination would indeed be very very exhausting."

ME: But the emotion is not so paralyzing anymore; there is fresh air, there are colours, there would be a good view.
HE: Yes, but it is exhausting! Lately I've been thinking about finally getting my degree at the university after all, but that would be exhausting.
ME: Could it be that an exhausting topic should be dealt with in therapy – and we are both not so sure whether we want to take it on or not?

I know this ascent, which I have imagined, in reality and I know that it is a great effort, which is rewarded by a wonderful view and broad perspective. But what does he see? He: "I see the ascent to Mount Everest". I tell him the name of the mountain I have seen in my imagination, a mountain he also knows well, and we both start to laugh. It is in no way comparable to an ascent to Mount Everest, more like a weekend trip. Does he expect to have to climb Mount Everest? Does he think that I expect him to have to reach such an achievement? Is that the reason he would rather do nothing?

By concentrating on the emotional contagion, an imagination arose which provided an important insight for the therapeutic process.

Active Imagination in the Strictest Sense[2]

Consciously, it was a major concern of Jung to get into contact with dissociated parts of the psyche by the technique of "Active Imagination". The numerous imaginations of Jung himself portrayed in the *Red Book* (Jung 2012) are basically attempts to embed numerous inner figures in imagination and to give to their energy, their emotionality, and their topics access to consciousness. Jung's experiences provided evidence that dissociations and split off complexes can be connected to consciousness in a symbolic way, especially through imagination. Seen more fundamentally, our dissociated, disjointed human brokenness (Zerrissenheit) can be cured through work with symbols. In my view this is of great significance for Jungian psychology nowadays. The prerequisite for *repairing* dissociations is to *become aware of* and give up identification with the split off parts and to get into relationship with them. However, it is important to note that inner dialogues do not necessarily qualify as being "Active Imagination"; more often they are the expression of a complex, very similar to fruitless soliloquies. If these kinds of imaginations are endlessly repeated, mostly without any change because too much anxiety hinders the flow of images, new symbols and new possibilities of behaviour will not be found. On the contrary, the dissociations are maintained and old patterns of behaviour are perpetuated and become cemented. It can also be observed that, to compensate the original complex–episode, imaginations with somewhat comforting inner figures are realized. This might be appeasing and important for a period of time but if nothing changes, everything remains at a standstill.

This is where we meet the boundaries and limits of the "Active Imagination" method that follows the principle of the creative process and the formation of symbols. This method requires a well-structured ego as a dialogue partner to the unconscious. We can't expect a well-structured ego in every person in every life situation. This is the reason why I developed ways concerning how different kinds of imagination can also be used, especially about how the analyst can reinforce the analysand's ego function in the imaginative process. Through a learning process, the analysand can take over helpful ideas of the analyst, become more courageous in the imaginations, and thereby enabled to dialogue with inner figures. The structure of the ego can be strengthened and imaginations become possible without the analyst's guidance.

"Active Imagination" needs practice in imagination in a general way. Through practice it does not lose its aspect of freedom and autonomy. On the contrary, having been trained to develop the inner pictures as vividly as possible with all the modalities of our senses, having developed strategies in dealing with delicate situations, we are able to let these inner images unfold in a quiet way, and we do not have to control or to correct it prematurely. We can trust that we will not be carried away by these imaginative processes but rather that we can work on them and with them.

In addition, we can also come into contact again and again with imaginations and images that fulfil us, such as those of social situations that take hold of us deeply and also link us to other people in a new emotional way. Here we encounter the social meaning of imagination, which opens up onto an additional wide and exciting field.

Notes

1   For aspects on the development of Active Imagination according to C. G. Jung, see Kast V (2014) Complexes and imagination, in *Journal of Analytical Ppsychology*, 59, 5, 680–694.
2   Further literature: Kast, V 2021, Complexes and their compensation. Impulses from neuroscience, in Carpani, S (Ed.), *The New Ancestors, Anthology of Contemporary Theoretical Classics in Analytical Psychology*, London: Routledge.

References

Fox, K C R, Koroma, M 2018, Wandering along the spectrum of spontaneous thinking: dreaming, meditation, mind-wandering, and well-being, an interview with Kieran Fox, *ALIUS Bulletin* 2, 1–15.

Fox, KC R, Christoff, K, Dixon, M L 2018, Affective neuroscience of self-generated thought, in *Annals of the New York Academy of Sciences*, May 2018.

Hatfield, E, Cacioppo, J T, and Rapson, R L 1993, Emotional contagion, Current Directions in Psychological Science, *2*, 96–99.

Holmes, E A, and Mathews, A 2010, Mental imagery in emotion and emotional disorders, *Clinical Psychology Review*, 30, 349–362.

Holmes, E A, Blackwell, S, Burnett Heyes, S, Renner, F, Raes, F 2016, Mental imagery in depression: Phenomenology, potential mechanisms, and treatment implications, *Annual Review of Clinical Psychology*, 12, 249–280.

Jarrett, J L 1988, *Nietzsche's Zarathustra. Notes on the Seminar given in 1934–1939 by C. G. Jung*, Bollingen Series. Princeton, NJ: Princeton University Press.

Jung, C G 1921/1990, *Psychological Types, CW 6*, London: Routledge.

Jung, C G 1929/1971a, *The Aims of Psychotherapy, CW 16*, London: Routledge.

Jung, C G 1934/1980, *Archetypes of the Collective Unconscious, CW 9*, London: Routledge.

Jung, C G 1941/1980, *Zum psychologischen Aspekt der Kore Figur, CW 9i*, London: Routledge.

Jung, C G 1947, *Letter to Mr. O. 2 May 1947, Letters Vol. II*, London: Routledge.

Jung, C G 1960/1972, *Spirit and Life, CW 8*, London: Routledge.

Jung, C G 1961, *Memories, Dreams, Reflections* (Ed. Jaffe, A), London: Random House.

Jung, C G 1971/1985, *Der gefühlsbetonte Komplex und seine allgemeinen Wirkungen auf die Psyche, CW 3*, London: Routledge.

Jung, C G 2009, *The Red Book = Liber Novus. A Reader's Edition*, (Ed.) Sonu Shamdasani, New York: Norton.

Kast, V 1991, *Joy, Inspiration, Hope*, College Station: Texas A&M University Press.

Kast, V 2010, *Was wirklich zählt, ist das gelebte Leben. Die Kraft des Lebensrückblbicks*, Freiburg im Breisgau: Kreuz in Herder.

Kast, V 2012, *Imagination. Zugänge zu inneren Ressourcen finden*, Ostfildern: Patmosverlag im Schwabenverlag.

Kast, V 2014, Complexes and imagination, *Journal of Analytical Psychology*, 59, 5, 680–694.

Kast, V 2019, *Träumend imaginieren. Einblicke in die Traumwerkstatt*, Göttingen: Vandenhoeck & Ruprecht.

Kast, V 2021, Complexes and their compensation. Impulses from neuroscience, (Ed.) S Carpani, *The New Ancestors, Anthology of Contemporary Theoretical Classics in Analytical Psychology*. London: Routledge.

Langwieler, G 2014, Blicke hinter den Vorhang der sinnlichen Wahrnehmung: philosophische und psychologische Merkmale, *Analytische Psycholgie*, 177, 3/2014, 262.

Markowitsch, H-J 2002, *Dem Gedächtnis auf der Spur. Vom Erinnern und Vergessen*. Darmstadt: Wissenschaftliche Buchhandlung.

Schacter, D L, Buckner, R L 2007, Remembering the past to imagine the future: The prospective brain, *Nature Reviews, Neuroscience*, 8, 657–661.

Schaverien, J 2008, Gegenübertragung als Aktive Imagination, *Analytische Psychologie. Imagination und Phantasie*, 152, 148–166.

Tusche, A, Bernhardt, B C, Smallwood, J 2014, Classifying the wandering mind: Revealing the affective content of thoughts during task-free rest periods, *Neuroimage*, 97, 107–116.

Zedelius, Claire M, Broadway, J, Protzko, J, Schooler, J 2020, What types of daydreaming predict creativity? Laboratory and experience sampling evidence, *Psychology of Aesthetics, Creativity and the Arts*, http://dx.doi.org/10.1037/aca0 0000342.

Chapter 7

On the Therapeutic Relationship

Marianne Müller

Introduction

The central importance of the therapeutic relationship – that is, the relationship and the process between analyst and analysand – is undisputed. The effectiveness of a therapy depends on it, which has been proven time and again.

This chapter is first of all about analytic psychology and its view of what happens within the therapeutic relationship. Regarding this, Jung created a new understanding and distanced himself from Freud's restrictive method. Jung sees the "analytical method is unassailable (...) in the relationship between doctor and patient" (Jung 1921, para. 276). In pointing to its importance, he anticipates in a sense the outcome of more recent psychotherapy research. Some of his statements in early writings on this subject are remarkably modern. Later, in "The Psychology of the Transference" (1946) Jung outlines the fundamental principles for his way of looking at the relationship in therapy and between the conscious and unconscious of the participants. However, Jung's statements are meant as various perspectives and not as differentiated or extensive explanations of the therapeutic relationship. Similarly, the relational aspect generally occupies only a small place in his theory. Jung left this to his successors. Since then, various authors have dealt with this topic in more depth. This chapter will also make a contribution to the significance of the relational aspect.

In the beginning, it was mainly the terms "transference" and "countertransference" that defined the processes in the therapeutic relationship. According to different interpretations of the unconscious in psychoanalysis and analytical psychology, and also the different application of a certain analytic technique, these terms were understood and used differently. Further contributing to a more differentiated understanding have been the insights from developmental psychology into the importance of relationship and attachment in childhood, as well as the contributions from infant research, which have been applied to the therapeutic relationship.

DOI: 10.4324/9781003219910-11

New insights into the therapeutic relationship were later gained by representatives of the theory of intersubjectivity (Stolorow et al. 1987/1996) with their special focus on what happens between patient and therapist. For them, inner-psychic differentiation and development emerge from relational experiences.

One can speak of a paradigm shift in psychoanalysis, from relational psychology to a paradigm of relatedness. According to this, human beings are born into human relationships, gain a relationship to themselves and to the world through social relationships, and remain dependent on such relationships throughout their lives. As human beings, we become unique, distinctive individuals precisely because we internalize our "relational fates" and use them to build our psychic structure (Altmeyer and Thomä 2010, p. 8).

Intersubjectivity theory has supplemented one-person psychology with a two-person perspective. It has become more and more clear that analysts decisively shape the unfolding analytic relationship with their subjectivity, which includes their personalities, emotional histories, theories, and more. These insights, in turn, challenged several areas of earlier psychoanalytic theory and technique, such as the notion of the analysts' objectivity and neutrality, with respect to their interpretations and to the transference (Orange et al. 2015). Analytical psychology had freed itself from this earlier and can therefore be more directly compared to the new approach of intersubjectivity.

In terms of understanding the unconscious, Jung is known to assume that, in addition to the so-called personal unconscious, it also includes a collective layer with creative forces from which a person's specific individuality develops. Therapy is about grasping the intentions of the unconscious as well as making conscious the attitudes, which block the relationship of the conscious ego to the dynamic unconscious. In order to understand these connections and to communicate them, the therapeutic relationship with its possible entanglements now plays a central role. Further exploration of this topic is the focus of this chapter.

The Analytical Approach to the Therapeutic Relationship: The Transference

Already by the end of the ninteenth century, Freud had redefined the relationship between doctor and patient with his psychoanalytic method and given it central importance in the healing process, especially through his insights into the phenomenon of the transference. He was the first to introduce the concept of transference in his *Studies on Hysteria* in 1895 and to harness the effectiveness of this unconscious process for therapy. Freud found his clients transferred embarrassing ideas arising from the content of the analysis to the person of the analyst (doctor). This happens through a false association, he writes (Freud 1895, p. 308ff). What is meant is that unfulfilled or repressed desires from the past tend to resurface in the transference onto a new "object", namely the person of the analyst. In this way the hidden and forgotten drives emerge and it is possible to work on the neurosis, in this case the so-called hysteria, and hopefully resolve it (Jacoby 1993, p. 26). For Freud, transference was virtually a condition for the successful course of therapy.

Further findings later prompted Freud to refine his initial position and to introduce new rules for therapy. These included strict rules of abstinence, which were intended to prevent the analysand from becoming too comfortable in his dependence on the analyst:

> the analyst must show no emotional reactions and be present only with free-floating attention. His activity is limited to interpreting connections between the feelings expressed to the clinician and the corresponding desires and conflicts from childhood.
>
> (ibid., p. 27)

Personal questions to the analyst are never answered. It is known, however, that Freud himself did not always adhere to these rather rigid instructions, which from today's perspective was certainly intuitively correct. Indeed, a too rigid application of the abstinence rule can lead to unnecessary uncertainty, if not to blockages, in clients.

Jung recast the theory of transference and expanded and deepened it according to his understanding of the unconscious. Above all, it was always his concern to formulate theoretical statements as broadly and generally as possible, so that theories and techniques do not obstruct individual access to the unconscious. This openness offers analysts a great degree of freedom and does not lead them into the temptation of being confined by a particular technique, although young colleagues at the beginning of their therapeutic practice may also feel this as a lack of more precise guidance.

According to Jung, transference is primarily a projection. Unconscious parts are transferred onto another person and experienced in him. Such entanglements play a role in all interpersonal relationships. In therapy, this means above all the transfer of unconscious psychic dimensions of the patient onto the analyst. The projection, or transference, creates a bond between the analyst and analysand with a very specific quality and nuanced tone. It can often create "an atmosphere of illusion which leads to continual misinterpretations and misunderstandings, or else produces a most disconcerting impression of harmony" (Jung 1946, para. 383). This specific coloring is therapeutically of great importance, which is why analysts cannot and should not distance themselves from it, as Freud continued to do with his technique (ibid., para. 358). For better or worse, analysts must expose themselves to the influences of the analysands and to the inner-psychic entanglement created by them. Under certain circumstances this is the only possible way to experience the unconscious of the analysand, in order to understand and work on their specific disturbances. Dealing with the transference is part of the analysts' craft. They must not only recognize the contents, they must also understand how to deal with them and make them more conscious to the analysand.

This requires not only good empathy but also a deeper understanding and knowledge of the processes of the human psyche from the perspective of developmental psychology as well as psychopathology. Insights from recent psychoanalytic research, such as attachment theory, infant research, and self-psychology, among others, have contributed much to a more sophisticated understanding of transference.

Concerning the study of the unconscious, including the understanding of dreams or imaginations, Jung's research provides a wealth of valuable insights. It is the task of the analyst to understand the symbolic language of the unconscious as comprehensively as possible. For the therapeutic relationship however, it is essential to know how the analyst is perceived by the analysand when conveying their interpretations. This is not just a question of the analyst's knowledge, but rather includes their personality as well as their handling of the transference and countertransference.

Jung's References to Alchemy: The Coniunctio

In 1946, Jung put the understanding of transference on a new basis with his article, "The Psychology of the Transference" (Jung 1946). He again referred to Freud's findings and acknowledged their great importance for analytic work. However, he also emphasized their complexity and multilayeredness, which also had to be taken into account in their concrete application. He wanted to provide a new orientation for the understanding of transference from the point of view of analytical psychology. To this end he made use of the symbolism of alchemy, to which he also referred on other occasions when it was a question of explaining and better understanding the psychology of the unconscious.

Jung refers to the idea of the "mystic marriage" (ibid., para. 353). Originally, in mysticism, it denoted the union of God and man. Later, this was understood philosophically as the union of polar opposites, such as the union of spirit and matter or of the masculine and the feminine. Jung then introduced the concept of the "coniunctio", a kind of "chemical" connection, which unites what was formerly separated and thus becomes a unification of opposites. Psychologically understood, these are symbolic expressions of unconscious dynamics also reflected in interpersonal processes.

If this image is transferred to the relationship between analyst and analysand, it makes clear the complexity of their interactions on the different levels: on the one hand the conscious exchange, then the interactions between the conscious on the one hand and the unconscious on the other of each participant. Also important are the inner-psychic processes between the conscious and unconscious of each individual. This schema derived from the image, which captures the different connections between the conscious and unconscious of analyst and analysand, can be an important guide to better understanding the complexity of the transference dynamic.

How can these different processes of exchange between analyst and analysand be understood dynamically? On the conscious level, first of all, it is about the "working alliance" between the two, their exchange about the concerns of the analysand, his suffering, his reasons for wanting therapy, and, on the other hand, the analyst's consent to work with the analysand and agreement on the conditions. At this level, a first contact is established, which should help to build mutual trust. From the beginning, emotions, fears, blockages, and fantasies are present on both sides and are experienced in the therapeutic interaction. Unconscious parts resonate and projections come into play. It is the analyst's task to recognize these as far as possible and to make them useful for the therapy. On the one hand, he must examine to what extent these feelings have to do with himself, with his own complexes or fears. However, he is particularly interested in the unconscious of the analysand, which he experiences through the transference and perceives through empathy. It often takes a great deal of sensitive observation and of experience to even recognize certain transference phenomena, for the analysand often wards these off. In Jungian analysis, the analyst tries to establish a relationship with the conscious as well as the unconscious parts of the analysand, in the hope that this will also foster the analysand's relationship with the unconscious in his soul (Jacoby 1993, p. 48f.). This is not only about unconscious parts from the personal unconscious, which have arisen from personal experiences, but also about parts of the collective unconscious with their drive for development and individualization. It must also be taken into account that an exchange between the unconscious of the analyst and that of the analysand always resonates in a certain way. This results in a common unconscious that can have a self-regulating effect on both sides. Among other things, the theory of intersubjectivity, which I will discuss later, refers to this interactive field.

The central theme of coniunctio is the unification of opposites. The analytic process is about bringing conscious and unconscious, which are in conflict with each other, into contact and trying to reconcile these opposites (Jung 1946, para. 375). It is a matter of making conscious those tendencies and attitudes which obstruct the relationship of the ego consciousness to the active unconscious. Jung calls for great caution in this regard, since for him the weakness of the conscious attitude is proportional to the strength of the resistance. One must therefore continue to support the conscious standpoint until the patient can let the "repressed" contents rise up spontaneously (ibid., para. 381). In many cases therefore, the analyst also has the delicate task of supporting the analysand in accepting and enduring his conflict for the time being, and thus also his suffering. This is all the more important because the analysand himself is often embarrassed to acknowledge the inner-psychic conflict. And finally, the attempt to suppress the other side always leads to an aggravation of the suffering (ibid., para. 392). Supporting enduring oppositional tensions is one of the central tasks of the analyst. Inexperienced analysts may be at risk here of reaching too quickly for a harmonizing solution.

Despite the admitted importance of transference, Jung rightly warned against understanding it too one-sidedly as a necessary factor for an effective therapeutic process, especially since it cannot be produced on demand. He saw a danger in not understanding the complexity of transference, in simplifying it at best, but also in overestimating its effectiveness compared to other factors. This openness towards the whole field of interpersonal interaction in therapy is very modern and deserves to be specifically emphasized here.

Countertransference

Countertransference, already recognized and named by Freud, is about what arises in the analyst through "the influence of the patient on the unconscious feeling of the doctor" (Freud 1910, p. 108). Until the 1950s, psychoanalysis saw a danger for therapy in this involvement of the analyst since the analyst could lose his neutrality towards the client. Therefore, one strove to avoid countertransference feelings as much as possible.

Jung soon distanced himself from this view of the therapeutic situation because according to his experience: "By no device can the treatment be anything but the product of mutual influence, in which the whole being of the doctor as well as that of his patent plays its part" (Jung 1929, para. 163). In Jung's view, then, it is not at all possible for the analyst to distance himself completely from the emotional turmoil of his patient. Nor, contrary to the view of early psychoanalysis, is this at all desirable.

Jung was the first to see the therapeutic potential in the countertransference. What the therapists themselves experience, feel, perceive, can be related to the patient in various ways, but need not be. It is the task of analysts to recognize the nature of the influence and to make it useful for the analytic work, as well as to ascertain and ponder their own contributions.

> We could say, without too much exaggeration, that a good half of every treatment that probes at all deeply consists in the doctor's examining himself, for only what he can put right in himself can he hope to put right in the patient. It is no loss, either, if he feels that the patient is hitting him, or even scoring off him: it is his own hurt that gives the measure of his power to heal. This, and nothing else, is the meaning of the Greek myth of the wounded physician.
>
> (Jung 1951, para. 239)

Jung makes clear here how central the inner process of the analyst is for therapy and the therapeutic relationship. Only openness and honesty about one's own wounding can deepen the relationship with the analysand. This is the reason why it is part of the professional training of analysts to undergo a thorough analysis, which hopefully also enables them to reflect on their own unconscious parts in their later work.

The handling of countertransference is complex, but as a working tool of the analyst it has become increasingly important in modern psychoanalysis. It is a matter of understanding psychic processes that are often unconscious on both sides. To clarify the interaction, distinctions such as that of Michal Fordham between syntonic and illusionary countertransference or that between concordant and complementary countertransference are helpful (Jacoby 1998, p. 67ff.). The latter refers to psychic phenomena that the analysand experiences himself, but which he is often not aware of. A distinction is made between unconscious, internalized relational experiences of the analysand, which he now triggers in the analyst and to which the analyst unconsciously reacts. For example, the analyst behaves as the mother once did. In this complementary countertransference reaction, the analyst does not primarily identify with the experience of the analysand but with the inner-psychic parts projected onto him (Lesmeister 2009, p. 272). However, in order for the understanding gained in this way to become therapeutically fruitful and effective, an empathetic attitude is again required on the part of the analyst.

This process is also known as projective identification. Jung speaks in this context of "induction" (Jung 1946, para. 399) or of "infection" (ibid., para. 365), in the sense of the therapist more or less taking over the patient's suffering. Thus, for a deeper understanding of the other, it is basically inevitable in psychotherapy that the "therapist allows the patient to live in him or herself" (Lesmeister, p. 273f). The degree to which such empathic alignment is necessary depends on various factors, often including the severity of the patient's disorder.

The task of an analyst is undoubtedly multifaceted and complex. Optimal empathy and the perception and differentiation of countertransference feelings are as much a basic professional requirement as the professional analysis of and reflection on disorders present in the analysand and the handling of adequate interventions.

Beyond Transference and Countertransference

In the relationship, the psychoanalytic approach focuses in particular on the unconscious processes of exchange as they are revealed in transference and countertransference, where inner-emotional patterns and complexes emerge and can be made useful for the therapeutic process.

Of central importance for the effectiveness of therapy is also and above all the ability of the analyst to establish a genuine I-Thou relationship with the analysand, which presupposes that the analyst can regulate closeness and distance. The analyst must be able to understand the analysand in their as-is state and to see and accept them as Other. Through empathy, the analyst tries to empathize as much as possible with the analysand and their suffering. At the same time however, the analyst must be able to withhold themself and not identify completely with the analysand. To use an image of Jung, this means "to be inside with one foot and to keep one foot outside". One of the central skills of analysts must therefore be to resonate empathically and, at the same time, to perceive themselves through introspection and also to reflect psychological knowledge (Jacoby 1993).

Modern psychotherapy researchers also emphasize the necessary competence of therapists to be present both cognitively and empathically, to grasp the patient's disorder from both perspectives and to adapt their interventions accordingly. Furthermore, commitment, positive regard, and honesty (congruence) are important attitudes of the analyst and prerequisites for establishing a trusting, affective relationship in which the analysand feels motivated and empowered to actively participate in the therapeutic process (Wampold 2018).

The distinction between a genuine I-Thou relationship and the transference countertransference is also crucial because these can be confused in a therapeutic process and thus contribute to a disruption of the therapeutic relationship. Thus it can happen that the analyst transfers his own unconscious parts onto the analysand, e.g. by not knowing how to deal with a justified criticism on the part of the analysand because it hurts him too much in his unconscious grandiosity. Or he does not recognize in the pleasant, perhaps also adapted, behavior of the analysand the defense of his resistances and fears, whereby the therapeutic process can stagnate and get caught in a repetition of old patterns of the analysand. This problem has already been mentioned in the preceding section on countertransference but deserves repetition in this context.

We know from practice that each processed transference and thus withdrawal of projection can advance the therapeutic relationship. This also means a "certain liberation to form real relationships, which constitutes one of the goals of psychotherapy or analysis" (Jacoby 2005, p. 22). Such developments bring relief and relaxation to the interpersonal relationship and the therapeutic process.

It should not be forgotten that every therapy is bound to a certain framework, which is accompanied by a mission and an objective. A sustainable working alliance also includes agreement between client and therapist regarding goals and objectives of therapy (Wampold 2018). It is always about the therapy and the analytic process of the analysand. And so it is the responsibility of analysts to make their skills, expertise, and life experience available for this purpose.

Intersubjectivity

The understanding of the therapeutic relationship has experienced a significant expansion in the last 40 years thanks to the theory of intersubjectivity,

often referred to as the intersubjective turn. This is not a new psychotherapeutic theory, but rather a meta-theory that is applied to different psychotherapeutic approaches. It describes the shift from relational psychology to a
paradigm of relatedness. Relatedness is the original, while the individual only
emerges and is formed in the relationship. According to this paradigm, the
analyst and analysand are in a mutual exchange and from the first moment of
their encounter in a process of reciprocal influence. The common experience
in the here and now is the focus of consideration (Ermann 2017, p. 11). Every
feeling, thought, and act is embedded in intersubjective fields or systems.

Intersubjectivity theory has various roots. Philosophical approaches come
from Edmund Husserl, Hans-Georg Gadamer, and also Martin Buber, among
others. Major psychoanalytic contributions come from Sandor Ferenczi,
Michael Balint, Donald W. Winnicott, and also Heinz Kohut, among others.
They all put the human need for relationship at the center of their theory, each
with a different starting point. The developmental psychologist Daniel Stern
was one of the first to present an intersubjective theory of self-development,
which is empirically supported by findings from infant research. What is
really new is how self-experience is interwoven with the other at all stages of
development. He distinguishes several levels or domains of self-experience
and social relatedness (Stern 1992).

Intersubjectivity theory as such is also understood as a response to the multitude of Freudian-psychoanalytic metapsychologies. Robert Stolorow et al.
(1987), in examining psychoanalytic metatheories, found that they all arose
from the subjective view of those who designed them. They were personal
attempts at solutions to the central crises and dilemmas in the personal development of their founders (Atwood and Stolorow 2013; Jaenicke 2014, p. 64).
Thus subjective truths had become universal truths. According to Stolorow
and Atwood, psychoanalysis therefore needed its own theory of subjectivity
and thus a frame of reference that makes the theories themselves the subject.

The intersubjective perspective, which Orange, Stolorow and Atwood now
adopt, does not stem from a clinical metatheory of its own, but rather raises
a series of questions to be asked of a theory. With "intersubjective perspective" they describe a particular sensibility that guides their clinical thought
and action. What is meant is a particular attitude that is connected with the
" fallibilistic " awareness that one can also be mistaken. The analyst does not
see himself as an initiate with a certain method but is involved in the process
through dialogue. This kind of understanding requires a special sensitivity,
which Orange has called "intersubjective clinical sensitivity" (Orange et al.
2010, p. 174).

Intersubjectivity theory has liberated psychoanalysis from a claim to universal truths and defined it as a science of personal encounters. Basically, it
is a recognition that each person's truth is highly subjective and that psychoanalysis is a method that attempts to help the individual find their way back
to their authentic experience and give them a voice while maintaining their

connectedness to others and the world (Jaenicke 2014, p. 67). Jung, after all, had also substantially distanced himself from classical psychoanalysis and shown an astonishing openness to the individual experiences between analyst and analysand in his statements about the therapeutic relationship.

Stolorow et al. have questioned various basic assumptions of classical psychoanalysis, such as the neutrality of the analyst, the demand for abstinence and anonymity, or the possibility of interpretation without suggestion (Stolorow and Atwood 2002). As an alternative, they offer the stance of the "Empathic-Introspective Inquiry". This method is intended to illuminate the following three principles: principles that unconsciously organize the patient's experience (empathy); principles that unconsciously organize the experiences of the analyst (introspection); the principle of the oscillating psychological field, which is created by the interaction of the above two principles (p. 197f.).

Such a research attitude requires the analyst to constantly reflect on the inevitable entanglement of the personal–subjective and the more objective–theoretical assumptions that affect the ongoing processes (ibid., p. 198; Orange et al. 2015, p. 66). Furthermore, these authors emphasize that the "empathic-introspective stance" is in no way intended to deny or obscure the asymmetry of the patient–analyst relationship.

The asymmetry refers to the role of the analyst and his therapeutic task. The significance of this asymmetry should be examined and should not be obscured. Analysts should also assess, to the best of their ability in each situation, the extent to which self-revelations promote or interfere with the analytic process, i.e., "whether they support the unfolding, exploration, illumination, and transformation of the patient's subjective world" (Stolorow et al. 2002, p. 198).

The relationship between the patient and the analyst as real persons, as well as the analyst's active participation in the processes in the treatment, is much more emphasized in this approach than in earlier times.

This does not mean, however, that the theoretical insights are thereby obsolete. On the contrary, the analyst is required to incorporate into their considerations all their knowledge about the development of the psyche, psychopathology, in analytical psychology also their symbolic understanding. This knowledge is now also to be understood much more rigorously as part of the interaction between the participants.

Analytical Psychology and Intersubjectivity

A number of Jungian analysts in recent years have referred to the theory of intersubjectivity and connected it to analytic psychology (Jacoby, Knox, Lesmeister, Braun, Otscheret, Wiener, and others). I, too, see in these references a valuable addition to and concretization of Jung's open but still poorly differentiated understanding of the therapeutic relationship and the relational aspects of his theory.

Many formulations of the intersubjectivity theorists are reminiscent of passages in Jung, with comparable meaning in relation to the therapeutic relationship. Some aspects will be summarized and compared here. They confirm the recognition that the analytic relationship needs to be more flexible than the classical psychoanalytic interpretive model or the classical Jungian archetypal model would allow (Knox 2011, p. 407).

Mutual Influence: Co-transference

Already in one of his early writings Jung emphasizes the reciprocal influence of doctor and patient. He points out the primary confusion of patient and therapist, which in the final analysis means nothing other than that the physician is as much "in analysis" as the patient.

> He is equally a part of the psychic process of treatment and therefore equally exposed to the transforming influences. Indeed, to the extent that the doctor shows himself impervious to this influence, he forfeits influence over the patient; and if he is influenced only unconsciously, there is a gap in his field of consciousness which makes it impossible for him to see the patient in true perspective.
>
> (Jung 1929, para. 166)

The meeting of two personalities is similar to the mixture of two different chemical substances: "if there is any combination at all, both are transformed" (ibid., para. 163).

In this sense, the mutuality of the analytic process is also the basic principle of intersubjectivity. Donna M. Orange has chosen the term co-transference. What this means is that there are always two differently organized subjectivities participating in the exchange. Two subjective worlds, that of the patient as well as that of the analyst are involved in the process and mutually influence one another, so that there is no difference between the participation of the analyst and the patient in the analytic process. However, this central principle does not absolve the analyst from their special role and corresponding task of being committed to the best interests of the analysand (Orange 2004, p. 92f.).

With her statements, Orange has once again recast the understanding of transference and countertransference, which Jung had already substantially reformed, opened up and expanded with a focus on the personal encounter.

Coniunctio: The Intersubjective Field

As already mentioned, in his article, "The Psychology of the Transference", Jung presented his view on the subject by means of a symbolic, alchemical text on coniunctio. Therapeutic, i.e., psychological, experiences or processes are compared with chemical processes. Ultimately, this is a guide to Jung's understanding of the different levels of encounters within the therapeutic relationship, an approach that focuses on a multilayered dynamic in space and time between the two participants.

Intersubjectivity theory views psychological phenomena as a product of the meeting of two subjective worlds. Accordingly, an analytic therapy deals with the whole field that emerges from the reciprocal interplay between the patient and the analyst. Therefore, the latter cannot work within the inter-subjective field and at the same time try to describe it from the outside. This also means it is impossible not to be involved, not even through passivity or abstinence. For even this behavior affects the patient as an action.

The intersubjective field is used to refer to an intermediate and transi-tional space, as Winnicott so helpfully and aptly described and illustrated. It is the growing security throughout the intersubjective field that allows for the exploration, play, and development of a new or reworked psychological organization in a therapeutic process (Orange et al. 2015, p. 50). The analyst is not an observer of what is happening; he or she is part of it and is drawn into the process in a variety of ways.

The level of the shared unconscious within the relationship is ultimately the starting point of the analytic process and thus of the individual develop-ment with its processes of differentiation and growth (Lesmeister 2005, p. 49). From this shared unconscious can also emerge those experiences that Daniel Stern has called the Now-Moment (Stern 2005).

The Dialectical Process: The Empathic–Introspective Stance

We know that Jung criticized the narrow technique relationship advocated by psychoanalysis and contrasted it with an alternative treatment model. He characterized analytic psychotherapy as a "dialectical procedure," by which he also meant a particular therapeutic attitude that is fundamental to everything that follows from it. In his article, "Principles of Practical Psychotherapy", Jung elaborates on this dialectical procedure. He understands it as a "dia-logue or discussion between two persons" (Jung 1935, para. 1). He goes on to write: "A person is a psychic system which, when it affects another person, enters into reciprocal reaction with another psychic system" (ibid., para.1). This refers to the person of the patient and of the therapist and includes them in their totality. The conscious and unconscious from both sides are involved. He then continues:

> This, perhaps the most modern formulation of the psychotherapeutic relation between physician and patient, is clearly very far removed from the original view that psychotherapy was a method which anybody could apply in stereotyped fashion in order to reach the desired result.
>
> (ibid., para. 1)

Above all, Jung distanced himself from a rigid application of a method. These statements confirm again the proximity to intersubjectivity with a context-oriented, individualized analytic method, which does better justice to the subjectivity and intersubjectivity than a rule-based technique (Lesmeister 2005, p. 52).

Jung's case for individual treatment also has consequences with regard to the application of a technique: "Since individuality ... is absolutely unique, unpredictable, and uninterpretable, in these cases the therapist must abandon all his preconceptions and techniques and confine himself to a purely dialectical procedure, adopting the attitude that shuns all methods" (ibid., para. 6).

Today we know that the therapeutic effect does not depend primarily on a certain technique or the correctness of an interpretation but above all on the quality of the therapeutic relationship. For analysts, the ability to tune in emotionally to the patient's inner state plays a central role. The presence of the analyst is conveyed by their personality. However, this also includes their professional knowledge and attachment to a method, as well as their ability to empathically contribute an interpretation and modify it if necessary (Wampold 2018).

There is a direct connection to the empathic–introspective research method of intersubjectivity theory mentioned earlier. Constant reflection and the best possible empathic receptiveness are the basic attitudes of the analyst. It is all about an attitude of ongoing empathic research.

The Therapeutic Relationship in the Light of Current Psychotherapy Research

I would like for a moment to step back from the considerations of what takes place in the relationship between analyst and analysand and how this relationship can be made useful for the therapeutic process. In connection with the question of the core competencies, I would like to take the liberty of looking at the therapeutic process from the outside and consult current psychotherapy research.

According to Wampold (2001), the multifaceted concept of the therapeutic relationship includes the following:

> (a) the client's affective relationship with the therapist, (b) the client's motivation and ability to accomplish work collaboratively with the therapist, (c) the therapist's empathic responding to and involvement with the client, and (d) client and therapist agreement about the goals and tasks of therapy.
>
> (p. 150)

In the end the quality of the therapeutic relationship is created by the interaction of various factors (Beutler 2020, p. 136). This quality and the extent to which therapists are convinced of their method and their individual competencies are decisive factors in the effectiveness of psychotherapy. The person of the therapist is also in itself one of the important influencing factors in psychotherapy (ibid., p. 137f.). Finally, it is especially the individual personality of the patient, the ability to engage in a therapeutic relationship, and last but not least, the type and severity of the disorder, which predominantly influence the therapy outcome (ibid., p. 139). In general, it can be said that the treatment method used is of secondary importance for the success of the treatment. Other effective factors concerning the patient, the therapist, and their relationship to each other exert a far greater influence (ibid., p. 134f.).

In addition to what has been said so far, I would like to refer here to statements by Jung, which are in line with these more recent research findings. Already in his early writings Jung pointed out the importance of the relationship between patient and therapist, the individuality of this relationship, and the demands placed on the analyst to give up preconceived opinions but at the same time to introduce possible explanatory hypotheses. These would give the analysand a picture of the analyst's way of working and of his reaction to the case (Jung 1929, para. 163). Further Jung writes:

> Hence the personalities of doctor and patient are often infinitely more important for the outcome of the treatment than what the doctor says and thinks (although what he says and thinks may be a disturbing or a healing factor not to be underestimated).
>
> (ibid., para. 163)

The affective quality of the relationship and the empathic response of the therapist described by current research have been further differentiated by the empathic–introspective stance of intersubjectivity. "Psychoanalysis heals because participation in a conversation in which the emotional life of another is taken so seriously can create a bond that enables personal change" (Orange 2004, p. 10).

Concluding Remarks

It has been important for me to point out the complexity of what happens between analyst and analysand. In therapeutic work, the intrapsychic cannot be considered independently from the interpersonal level. It is therefore up to individual analysts to continue to sharpen their personal senses in order to be as present as possible in the therapeutic field. This is a never-ending process.

For a long time, however, analytical psychology was primarily concerned with the interpretation of material from the unconscious of the patient and the optimal understanding of the symbolic language of the unconscious. As valuable as this knowledge is for therapeutic work and the understanding of the therapeutic relationship, the question of how the unconscious manifests itself in the here and now of therapeutic interaction and its emotional concomitants has remained relatively unaddressed and undifferentiated. With intersubjectivity, a method of approach can be called on that also usefully complements the practice of analytical psychology.

In the end what counts, as Jung has already said, is that the analyst can only facilitate the creation of a space and a conscious attitude "which allows the unconscious to co-operate instead of being driven into opposition" (Jung 1946, para. 366).

References

Altmeyer M, Thomä H (Hrsg.) 2010, *Die vernetzte Seele. Die intersubjective Wendein derPsychoanayse*, Stuttgart: Klett-Cotta.

Atwood, G E, Stolorow, R D 1998, Metapsychologie, Verdinglichung und Vorstellungswelt von C. G. Jung, *Analytische Psychologie, 29*, 212–242.

Atwood, G E, Stolorow, R D 2013, Legacies of the golden age: A memoir of a collaboration, *The Humanistic Psychologist, 41*, 285–300.

Beutel, M E, Doering, S, Leichsenring F, Reich G 2020, *Psychodynamische Psychotherapie*, Göttingen: Hogrefe.

Braun, C 2016, *Die Therapeutische Beziehung*, Stuttgart: W. Kohlhammer.

Ermann, M 2017, *Der Andere in der Psychoanalyse*, Stuttgart: W. Kohlhammer.

Freud, S 1895, Studien über Hysterie, *Ges. Werke I*, Frankfurt: Fischer.

Freud, S 1910, Die zukünftige Chance der Psychoanalyse, *Ges. Werke VIII*, Frankfurt: Fischer.

Jacoby, M 1985, *Individuation und Narzissmus. Psychologie des Selbst bei C. G. Jung und H. Kohut*, München: Pfeiffer.

Jacoby, M,1993, *Übertragung und Beziehung in der Jungschen Praxis*, Olten: Walter.

Jacoby, M,1998, *Grundformen seelischer Austauschprozesse*, Zürich und Düsseldorf: Walter.

Jacoby, M 2005, Zu den Wurzeln intersubjektiver Bedürfnisse. Von derKleinkindforschung zur psychotherapeutischen Praxis, L. Otscheret & C. Braun (Hrsg.), *Im Dialog mit dem Anderen. Intersubjektivität in PsychoanalyseundPsychotherapie* (S. 14 – 56), Frankfurt/M.: Grandes & Apsel.

Jaenicke, C 2002, Einführung in die Intersubjektivitätstheorie, *Selbstpsychologie, 8, 3. Jg.*, Heft 2, 174–188.

Jaenicke, C 2006, *Das Risiko der Verbundenheit – Intersubjektivitätstheorie in der Praxis*, Stuttgart: Klett-Cotta.

Jaenicke, C 2014, Die Entstehung und Entwicklung der Intersubjektivitätstheorie, P Potthoff, S Wollnik (Hg.), *Die Begegnung der Subjekte. Die intersubjektivrelationale Perspektive in Psychoanalyse und Psychotherapie* (pp. 63–78), Giessen: Psychosozial-Verlag.

Jung, C G 1921, *The Therapeutic Value of Abreaction, CW 16*, Princeton, NJ: Princeton University Press.

Jung, C G 1929, *Problems of Modern Psychotherapy, CW 16*, Princeton, NJ: Princeton University Press.

Jung, C G 1935, *Principles of Practical Psychotherapy, CW 16*, Princeton, NJ: Princeton University Press.

Jung, C G 1939, *Conscious, Unconscious and Individuation, CW 9i*, Princeton, NJ: Princeton University Press.

Jung, C G 1946, *The Psychology of the Transference, CW 16*, Princeton, NJ: Princeton University Press.

Jung, C G 1951, *Fundamental Questions of Psychotherapy, CW 16*, Princeton, NJ: Princeton University Press.

Knox, J 2011, Die analytische Beziehung: eine Zusammenführung jungianischer, bindungstheoretischer und entwicklungspsychologischer Perspektiven, *Analytische Psychologie, 166*, 403–426.

Lesmeister, R 2005, Technik und Beziehung. Erkundung eines Widerstreits, in L Otscheret, C Braun (Eds.), *Im Dialog mit dem Anderen. Intersubjektivität in Psychoanalyse und Psychotherapie* (S. 29–56), Frankfurt/M.: Brandes & Apsel.

Lesmeister, R 2009, *Selbst und Individuation. Facetten von Subjektivität und Intersubejktivität in der Psychoanalyse*, Frankfurt/M.: Brandes & Apsel.

Orange, D M 2004, *Emotionales Verständnis und Intersubjektivität.* Frankfurt/M.: Brandes & Apsel.

Orange, D M, Stolorow, R D, Atwood G E 2010, Zugehörigkeit, Verbundenheit, Betroffenheit. Ein intersubjektiver Zugang zur traumatischen Erfahrung, (Eds.) M Altmeyer, H Thomä, *Die vernetzte Seele. Die intersubjective Wende in der Psychoanayse* (pp. 160–177), Stuttgart: Klett-Cotta.

Orange, D M, Atwood G E, Stolorow R D 2015, *Intersubjektivität in der Psychoanalyse*, Frankfurt/M.: Brandes & Aspel.

Otscheret, L, Braun, C (Eds.) 2005, *Im Dialog mit dem Anderen. Intersubjektivität in Psychoanalyse und Psychotherapie*, Frankfurt/M.: Brandes & Apsel.

Stern, D N 1992, *Die Lebenserfahrung des Säugling*, Stuttgart: Klett-Cotta.

Stern, D N 2005, *Der Gegenwartsmoment. Veränderungsprozesse in Psychoanalyse. Psychotherapie und Alltag*, Frankfurt/M.: Brandes & Apsel.

Stolorow, R D, Brandschaft B, Atwood G E 1987, *Psychoanalytic Treatment: An Intersubjective Approach*, Hilsdale, NJ: Analytic Press.

Stolorow, R D, Atwood G E 2002, Der Neutralitätsmythus in der Psychoanalyse, *Selbstpsychologie* 8, 3.Jg., Heft 2, 189–209.

Wampold, B E 2001, *The Great Psychotherapy Debate; Models, Methods, and Findings*, Mahwah, NJ: Lawrence Erlbaum.

Wampold, B E, Imel, Z E, Flückiger, C 2018, *Die Psychotherapie-Debatte. Was Psychotherapie wirksam macht*, Bern: Hogrefe.

Wiener, J 2009, *The Therapeutic Relationship*, College Station, TX: A&M University Press.

Chapter 8

Analytic Interpretation

An Illustration of Core Competencies in Jungian Psychoanalysis

Mark Winborn

Introduction

This chapter addresses the subject of analytic interpretation as a core competency in Jungian psychoanalysis. The focus moves from a broader perspective to a narrower perspective. It opens with a discussion of core competencies: what core competencies are, how they are developed, how they are utilized, and why they are central to the development of any field of practice. To illustrate this section, a case study is offered that describes the development and implementation of a comprehensive set of psychoanalytic core competencies by the American Board for Accreditation in Psychoanalysis, a professional organization in the United States providing independent accreditation of both psychoanalytic and Jungian institutes. The second portion of the chapter discusses the need for the development of core competencies in Jungian psychoanalysis and some of the challenges that will likely be encountered in that process. Finally, the core competency of analytic interpretation illustrates the development of a core competency that applies across all schools of psychoanalysis. The illustration provides an operational definition of interpretation, a discussion of how the core competency would be integrated into the analytic curriculum and supervision, and how competency in analytic interpretation can be evaluated.

What Are Core Competencies?

Core competencies are created from areas of fundamental knowledge and ability that qualify a professional in a specific subject area. In terms of analytic instruction and supervision, the question moves from "what does the candidate need to be taught?" to "how well is the candidate able to utilize what they have been taught?" Therefore, a core competency is not an articulation of a theory, concept, technique, or a method, although core competencies are connected to these elements of analytic education. Core competencies describe a person's capacity to utilize knowledge and skills in an effective manner that supports the overall process of an analysis. For example, one

DOI: 10.4324/9781003219910-12

of the ABAP (2017) core competencies is, "Facilitate the exploration of unconscious experience" (p. 3). The existence of unconscious experience is common to all forms of psychoanalysis and therefore any candidate who is training to become an analyst must understand unconscious experience from a theoretical and experiential perspective but must also know how to facilitate the exploration of the patient's unconscious experience. It is the integration of theoretical and experiential knowledge with methodological skills that constitutes core competency. How the unconscious is conceptualized and engaged will vary significantly between the various schools of thought, but the underlying core competency remains the same.

In higher education there has been a recent movement toward competency-based education; in other words, a movement away from what does the professional "know" to how effectively is the professional able to apply what they have learned. This trend has been accompanied by a shift toward direct assessment of core competencies, particularly with the accreditation of professional training, such as psychoanalysis (Lemma, Roth, and Pilling 2008; Parth and Loefler-Stastka 2015; ABAP 2017; Barsness 2018).

In terms of accreditation of psychoanalytic and Jungian training institutes, a focus on core competencies represents a shift from a model of accreditation that evaluates how an institution is organized and what it is teaching, towards a model that evaluates whether an institute's curriculum is designed to produce competent psychoanalysts, how well that curriculum is being taught and how well the institute's candidates are integrating that instruction. Psychoanalytic core competencies represent the areas of knowledge, skill, and attitude that, taken together, represent the ability to engage in effective analytic practice. Another way of thinking about core competencies in Jungian analysis is that core competencies articulate the underlying building blocks by which an analysis is conducted. Therefore, core competencies can be thought of as functioning, in analytic practice, in an analogous fashion as the *archetype-as-such*, that is, providing a universal underpinning for experience without determining the specific form that experience will take.

To integrate core competencies into analytic training, an initial task for any accrediting organization or training institute will involve the identification of the essential core competencies, across theoretical orientations, that are required by a practitioner to effectively foster an analytic process. We might think of this task as an extension of what Wallerstein identified as "the common ground of psychoanalysis," which rests "in our shared clinical enterprise in our consulting rooms where we relate comparably to the immediacy of the transference-countertransference interplay with our patients" (Wallerstein 1990, p. 19).

Because core competencies should reflect the field as a whole rather than the individual patterns of one person, they are developed through consensus, usually by a group of experienced practitioners of a profession who are acknowledged as "experts" within their field. Once the consensus group arrives at a statement of core competencies for their profession, the statement is then shared with a larger group of experienced practitioners within the field to obtain feedback, and the statement of core competencies is modified as needed based on the feedback of the larger group. Core competencies are formulated as a group of statements, each representing a single ability or area of knowledge. Ideally, a set of Jungian core competencies would be conceived at a sufficiently high level of abstraction that they would apply across the various approaches to Jungian analysis: classical, developmental, archetypal, or Giegerichian. The group of competencies developed would represent a comprehensive overview of the knowledge and abilities required to success-fully be trained as a Jungian analyst and to work psychoanalytically from a Jungian perspective.

In addition to the set of core competencies developed by the ABAP, a number of other prominent psychoanalytic organizations have incorporated core competencies into accreditation and program development: The European Psychoanalytical Federation, European Association of Psychotherapy, American Psychoanalytic Association, The American Board of Examiners in Clinical Social Work specialty certification in psychoanalysis, The Academy of Psychoanalysis of the American Board for Professional Psychology. Being accredited members of ABAP, the C. G. Jung Institutes of New York, Boston, and Chicago are now integrating the ABAP core competencies into their training programs.

Conceivably, a project to develop a comprehensive set of core competen-cies for Jungian analysis could be initiated by the IAAP and then passed on to each training group to be used as a guide in setting program objectives for their specific training programs, just as minimum standards have been established for IAAP training programs in terms of outlining educational content areas to be taught, minimum number of faculty, minimum number hours of coursework, personal analysis, and supervision required for each candidate. Core competencies and associated program objectives could be tailored to the specific needs of each training group. Alternatively, each training group could undertake the task of developing their own set of core competencies based on their approach to Jungian analysis. In either case, the core competencies would then become integrated into learning, course, and program objectives for candidates, objectives that would then guide program implementation.

Practically speaking, the integration of core competencies, accompanied by associated learning and course objectives, are useful at the program level in evaluating effectiveness of course design, teaching and supervision, and in evaluating candidate proficiency in the abilities and knowledge neces-sary to become Jungian analysts. In turn this helps candidates understand what is expected of them and assists the training programs in focusing their curriculum, teaching, and supervision on the primary objective of developing new analysts. These tools, the competencies, and objectives generated during the implementation of core competencies, also assist training programs in evaluating whether their overall training has issues that need be addressed.

Why Do We Need Core Competencies?

As we know, enrollment is down substantially in most Jungian and psychoanalytic institutes across the North America and Europe. Applicants from the traditional mental health disciplines (such as psychiatry, psychology, clinical social work, and counseling) have less and less exposure to any psychoanalytic theory or depth psychology in their undergraduate and graduate programs. Additionally, through the marketing of shorter-term therapies, the public is becoming more and more conditioned to expect treatment, and by extension training, to be "evidence based" or "empirically validated," even though the public often does not fully understand what these terms imply. These trends have consequences for the public reputation of our field. If Jungian analysts can agree upon and articulate what constitutes minimal competence to engage in Jungian analysis, across theoretical differences, we potentially establish credibility.

Furthermore, by assessing what works and what does not work, and by developing strong tools for assessing progress in the acquisition of what works, we also gain increased confidence in our educational process. Assessment methods that are overly subjective fail our responsibility to our candidates. While Jungians place high value on the equation of the individual analyst, that should not mean "anything goes." A mutually agreed upon set of core competencies for education in Jungian analysis, built around the outcomes we hope to cultivate in each of our candidates, allows us to diminish some of the political and overly subjective elements involved in the assessment of candidate progress and institute effectiveness (see Junkers, Tuckett, and Zachrisson 2008). It can also facilitate the development of an environment where we can let candidates fail who might need to fail.

As Tuckett (2005) writes, without assessment:

> it will be personal likes, dislikes and preferences that are decisive [in candidate evaluation] with the result that the process of qualification is viewed as personalized, cliquish, opaque and particularistic rather than regarded as transparent and universalistic (i.e., open to anyone who can do it).
>
> (p. 35)

In short, competency-based education allows for the intended outcomes to be more explicitly tied to and integrated with instruction and assessment.

ABAP: A Case Study of the Development and Implementation of Core Competencies

In January 2015, I was serving as the Chair for the Committee on Accreditation for the American Board for Accreditation in Psychoanalysis (ABAP). My committee was tasked by the ABAP board to develop a set of psychoanalytic core competencies that could be integrated by all of the institutes accredited by ABAP. ABAP is a pluralistic organization that accredits institutes from a wide variety of theoretical orientations: Jungian, contemporary Freudian, relational, object relations, modern psychoanalytic, self psychology, and eclectic. Therefore, the core competencies we were developing had to be crafted in such a way that each of those theoretical orientations could be appropriately accommodated. Our aim was to craft these competencies to be as free of influence from theoretical orientation as possible. A sub-committee was formed consisting of five psychoanalysts and two non-psychoanalyst experts with experience in higher education accreditation and regulatory issues. For over two years, the sub-committee met several times a month, carefully reviewing the published literature on core competencies, the literature on evaluation in psychoanalytic training, and all of the published examples of core competencies from other psychoanalytic and mental health organizations. Once this initial review was completed, the committee began to draft the initial ABAP core competencies. We utilized the United Kingdom core competency model, developed by Lemma, Roth, and Pilling (2008), as our beginning point and modified those core competencies to fit the circumstances of our member institutes. This involved months of discussion, negotiation, debate, and refinement of the form, content, and wording of each competency. The entire process was a rich opportunity for each of us on the committee to reflect deeply on what we do as analysts and to articulate what we find essential to the analytic process, while at the same time being in dialogue with colleagues from different schools of thought. Ultimately, the committee arrived at 40 core competencies, divided into four broad categories of competence (see Figure 8.1).

While the ABAP core competencies were in development, the sub-committee also began to educate our member institutes regarding core competencies. The educational process with our member institutes took place during the bi-annual ABAP meetings, which occur in the fall and spring of each year. In the initial meeting, we introduced the ABAP member institutes to the core competency development project and explained what core competencies are.

Six months later, the accredited members of ABAP were given a presentation explaining how core competencies would potentially be integrated into their training programs. As our illustration, we chose the following competency: "the ability to be aware of, process, and engage the transference effectively in the psychoanalytic encounter." The implementation of this core competency was described from both Jungian and self psychology

General Psychotherapeutic Competencies for Psychoanalysts	Foundational Psychoanalytic Competencies	Psychoanalytic Assessment and Intervention Competencies	Competencies that Integrate the Practice of Psychoanalysis
Operate within legal and ethical guidelines	Understand development from one or more psychoanalytic perspectives	Evaluate whether the patient's needs are appropriately served by psychoanalysis	Maintain an analytic attitude – a set of guiding psychoanalytic stances and values that focus the analyst's attention and intention
Engage interpersonally in a professional manner	Understand motivation from one or more psychoanalytic perspectives	Conduct psychoanalytic assessment	Recognize various domains of patient experience in prioritizing interventions
Be sensitive to and willing to work with diverse identities of individuals and groups	Understand psychopathology from one or more psychoanalytic perspectives	Formulate a psychoanalytic diagnosis	Apply psychoanalytic models flexibly in response to the patient's individual context and conscious and unconscious needs
Recognize the importance of socio-cultural influences on behavior, cognition, and emotion	Understand core concepts of psychoanalysis according to one or more theoretical orientations	Establish and maintain a psychoanalytic frame	Make use of the psychoanalytic relationship as a vehicle for change
Understand lifespan development	Understand therapeutic action from one or more psychoanalytic perspectives	Work with both a patient's internal and external realities	Capacity to create and defend a comprehensive psychoanalytic case formulation
Understand biological contributors to behavior, cognition, and emotion		Facilitate the exploration of unconscious experience	Make appropriate use of psychoanalytic supervision and consultation
Be aware of non-psychoanalytic models of psychotherapy		Employ a range of psychoanalytic interventions	Evaluate and incorporate research on psychoanalysis and ancillary fields
Conduct global patient assessment		Be aware of, process, and effectively engage the transference	Make use of the personal training analysis to work through personal and emotional issues that may interfere with psychoanalytic treatment
Make diagnostic formulations		Be aware of, process, and effectively engage counter-transference	

General Psychotherapeutic Competencies for Psychoanalysts	Foundational Psychoanalytic Competencies	Psychoanalytic Assessment and Intervention Competencies	Competencies that Integrate the Practice of Psychoanalysis
Understand the interaction of affects and psychopathology		Identify and respond to enactments within the psychoanalytic relationship	
Identify appropriate interventions		Recognize and work with the patient's defenses and resistance	
Respect the patient's socio-environmental and intrapsychic realities		Recognize psychoanalytic indicators of therapeutic change	
Navigate the emotional content of sessions, includingshifts and endings		Maintain a consistent focus on core analytic aspects of treatment	
Understand empirical research			

Figure 8.1 ABAP core competencies for psychoanalysis

perspectives to illustrate how the theoretical orientation of the institute would influence the implementation of the competency. We then guided the institute representatives through the various steps involved: developing learning objectives, processes for evaluation competence, the integration of the core competency into a curriculum and the supervision process, and how to utilize core competencies to improve program and faculty evaluation.

Once the preliminary set of ABAP core competencies were developed, they were distributed to the Directors of Training and Training Committees for each ABAP accredited institutes. They served as our expert group outside of our committee. In a structured survey, we asked the Directors of Training and the institute Training Committees to provide feedback on our preliminary core competencies. The core competencies sub-committee then collated the feedback from the institutes and made further refinements to the ABAP core competencies. These became the provisional core competencies. The provisional core competencies were then published on the ABAP website for a 90-day period of public commentary.

Finally, after nearly three years in process, the final version of the ABAP Core Competencies in Psychoanalysis was presented to the member institutes during our meeting in November 2017. The accredited member institutes of ABAP voted to ratify and adopt the final competencies for implementation in all ABAP institutes. Following ratification, the core competencies sub-committee provided guidance to the institutes on the timeline for implementation in terms of the periodic re-accreditation process, and described the ongoing support and education they could expect from the Committee on Accreditation regarding core competencies.

Implementation of Core Competencies in Jungian Training Programs

I believe there are hurdles to overcome in the Jungian community in terms of adopting core competencies. Often there is active objection to the suggestion of any standardization of training, whether it involves core curriculum, core competencies, or core readings. My observations come from my work in accreditation (involving both psychoanalytic and Jungian institutes), over 20 years of teaching in a wide variety of institutes in the United States and internationally, as well as having served on the Training Committee of the Inter-Regional Society of Jungian Analysts.

In many Jungian institutes, a clearly outlined curriculum of courses each candidate must complete does not exist. For example, the I-RSJA (my home institute) has eight different locations (I-RSJA training seminars) where training is provided, but there is little educational coordination between the eight seminars. Instead, as in many Jungian institutes, there are broadly defined areas of recommended content and a minimum number of hours of coursework that must be completed. But the content and focus of those course hours is primarily determined by the instructors, and the selection of those courses is often largely left up to the candidate. It would not be a stretch to say that Jungian training is often presented in an à la carte style. While this potentially creates opportunities for exploration by the candidates, it does not ensure that they possess the requisite competencies for the independent practice of Jungian analysis at the time of graduation.

In terms of implementing core competencies in Jungian analytic training, perhaps one of the largest obstacles to overcome is the lasting impact of Jung's negative stance towards technique and the establishment of a prescribed curriculum, an attitude that has carried over to many in the generations that have followed. Adler (1967) summarizes the traditional Jungian position as follows:

> One of the main differences between Analytical Psychology and other schools lies in the undogmatic approach of Analytical Psychology to each individual case. The basic presupposition from which Analytical Psychology starts is that each patient has his own particular and "personal" psychology necessitating an approach which varies with each individual case ... Such a conception must obviously involve a considerable limitation on general technique, since the whole point of a technique is to provide certain universally applicable rules.

(p. 23)

In examining Jung's relationship with technique, it is important to hold in mind that one of Jung's principal agendas, particularly throughout much of his early post-Freudian writing, was to highlight the contrast between Freud's approach and the position he was advocating (Zinkin 1969). Any examination of Jung's views on the practice of analysis is complicated and fraught with ambiguity. As Dehing (1992) puts it, "Unfortunately, C. G. Jung is rarely explicit with regard to his analytical practice; he always refused to lay down technical rules and little is known of his actual psychotherapeutic interventions" (p. 31). In most instances, Jung utilized his published case studies to support theoretical constructs he was developing or to elaborate on the archetypal themes present in the material of his patients. Only infrequently does he provide glimmers of how he worked with his patients. In fact, according to Astor (1998), "Jung often sounded hostile to close discussion of technique that he feared might turn the individual relationship between therapist and patient into the application of a method" (p. 698).

Typologically, Jung was an intuitive (like many who have been drawn to his ideas) who had an aversion to methodological approaches. Dehing (1992, p. 42) indicates that Jung detested any sort of systemization. Kirsch (2000) indicates that, "Jung eschewed the word technique" (p. 247). Additionally, Jung felt that the pursuit of analytical psychology was so unique to the individual personality of the practitioner that he did not believe one should provide specific guidelines as to the practice of analytical psychology.

While Jung's adoption of an anti-methodological position may have been useful in differentiating analytical psychology from Freudian psychoanalysis, the adoption of this attitude by the generations following Jung undermined the emergence of an effective and consistent approach to training new generations of Jungian analysts. In contrast, in my book on interpretation (Winborn 2018), I maintain that analysis is rather like the creative process in jazz improvisation. In jazz, having an adequate knowledge of melodic structure, underlying chord structures, and proficiency with one's instrument is what frees the jazz musician to improvise most creatively and freely. The establishment of core curriculum, core readings, and core competencies in analytic training does not limit the candidate; rather it frees the candidate to explore from a firm foundation. Connolly (2008) also highlights the intimate relationship between technique, theory, and the creative art of analysis:

> Technique ... derives from Aristotle's notion of *techne* or *ars*, the name given to that skillful activity (*poesis*) that accomplishes its purpose in the production of a particular work that is never already given but which can or cannot appear and in which the certainty of success is always in doubt. In *techne*, method and theory emerge from the thoughtful examination of the way in which the production of the work is carried out.
>
> (p. 482)

Analytic Interpretation: An Application of Core Competencies in Jungian Psychoanalysis

Interpretation Stated as a Core Competency: "Ability to effectively utilize dynamic interpretations."

As a core competency, interpretation falls under the broad category of competencies related to analytic techniques, methods, and interventions. As such, interpretation is involved with other core competencies falling under the same category. For example, in the ABAP (2017) core competencies, the ability to effectively utilize interpretations would also be interwoven with the following core competencies: (1) establish and maintain a psychoanalytic frame, (2) work with both a patient's internal and external realities, (3) facilitate the exploration of unconscious experience, (4) employ a range of psychoanalytic interventions, (5) be aware of, process, and effectively engage transference, (6) be aware of, process, and effectively engage counter-transference, (7) identify and respond to enactments within the psychoanalytic relationship, and (8) recognize and work with the patient's defenses and resistance (p. 3). To some extent, all of these core competencies rely upon the analyst's competency in interpretation.

What is an interpretation? Before proceeding further, I will articulate what I mean by interpretation. Contrary to some perceptions, an interpretation is not everything that is presented verbally to a patient in sessions. It is a specific type of verbal interaction, which sets it apart from other types of therapeutic utterances. In this context, I am not referring to the process of interpreting dreams but rather the technique of interpreting what is occurring throughout the analytic session – i.e., what the analyst and patient are saying, feeling, and sensing, as well as how they are behaving and responding physiologically. For me, interpretation is the verbal expression of what is experienced with and understood about the patient's psychological situation, including the field constellated by the analytic dyad.

Fordham offers two useful definitions of analytic interpretation. He (Fordham 1978) indicates that an interpretation, "connects together statements of the patient that have a common source unknown to the patient. So, when the analyst tells the patient about the source, he makes an inference that goes beyond the actual material at hand" (p. 113). This definition highlights the element of surprise essential for effective interpretation and the necessary movement beyond the immediate concrete meaning of the patient's verbalizations. Therefore, analytic interpretation treats all patient interactions as potentially symbolic. Elsewhere, Fordham (1991) elaborates further:

> An interpretation is composed of that part of the patient's unconscious digested and thought about by the analyst. The result is then communicated to the patient in such a way as to give meaning to the patient's material. To do this it must have a clear structure and contain a verb.
>
> (p. 209)

This definition highlights the creation of meaning, the importance of the analyst's reflective capacities, and the need for clarity in the interpretive process. In the simplest terms, an interpretation functions as an invitation for the patient to see their world in a new way.

The establishment of a core competency around interpretation is not meant to suggest there is a "right" or "correct" interpretation for every analytic situation. There are always multiple, potentially transformative interpretations available for any situation. However, the establishment of a core competency for interpretation helps the candidate to learn and utilize interpretation more effectively. As Sullivan (2009) frames the issue, "While there is certainly no right way, there are ways that are, if not simply wrong, deeply problematic" (p. 11). Ideally, the establishment of core competencies in Jungian analysis reduces the likelihood that candidates will adopt problematic ways of conducting analysis.

Small differences in wording often have significant impact on the effectiveness of an interpretation. An example of this can be found in the following exchange in which the patient is pressuring me to provide more direct instruction on how to proceed at this point in the session:

P: Okay. So, the question is how to get past the block and get back in touch with where I need to be in this hour.
[analyst's thought: *another attempt to get me to become responsible for getting her to feel*].
A: Um hum.
P: (*laughes*) No, see that's the question that you're supposed to answer. See how this works? (*laughs*)
A: So, you want me to take it over for you
[analyst's thought: *I am feeling seduced here, but I choose to respond out of my countertransference reaction to her efforts to force me to be responsible for making something happen affectively*].
P: No, I want you to explain to me how to do it.
A: By talking about the things that you don't want to talk about.
P: Like what?
A: Well, unfortunately I am not a mind reader, so I don't know in this moment what it is you don't want to talk about.

My intervention was intended as a mild confrontation of the magical thinking implied in her communication, i.e., that I should know what she does not want to talk about. However, my intervention sounds somewhat irritated or chastising. A better phrasing would have involved focusing my intervention on what she wants from me, "I often have the sense that you want me to be a mind reader but unfortunately, in this moment, I don't know what it is that you don't want to talk about." It is a small shift in focus and words, but the change would have made the interpretation much less accusatory and therefore more available for the patient to take in.

Delineating the interpretation core competency: Once a core competency has been identified, it needs to be operationalized so that those utilizing the core competency (the candidates, faculty, and supervisors) have a mutual starting point in terms of learning, teaching, and supervision. While it is impossible to provide exact instructions to a candidate in how to form an interpretation and utilize it, a guiding framework can be established to assist the candidate in navigating through unfamiliar territory and find their own "voice" for interpretation. For example, working from a psychoanalytic model, Lemma, Roth, and Pilling (2008) have deconstructed the core competency of interpretation into smaller elements, grouping the various aspects of interpretation under two broad categories of knowledge and application:

Knowledge

- An ability to draw on knowledge of unconscious processes to help the client become aware of aspects of emotional and interpersonal experience that lie outside their immediate awareness and that are a source of conflict.
- An ability to draw on knowledge that the process of interpretation is collaborative.
- An ability to draw on knowledge that interpretation is best seen as a process (i.e., based on a series of interventions over time, rather than on a single comment.
- An ability to draw on knowledge that the aims of interpreting are manifold (p. 1).

Application

- **Focus of Interpretation**
  - An ability to maintain the primary focus of interpretations on: 1) dynamically unconscious content; and, 2) the client's interpersonal and affective experiences.
  - An ability to communicate to the client an interpretation that captures multiple levels of meaning (i.e., it goes beyond what the client consciously reports feeling). (p. 2)
- **Process of Interpretation**
  - An ability to integrate information gathered from various sources (e.g., accounts of external events, relationship with the therapist, or countertransference reactions) to arrive at hypotheses regarding unconscious processes.
  - An ability to help the client explore and become more aware of painful conflicts by pointing out unacceptable or uncomfortable feelings (that are otherwise managed by being kept out of the client's conscious awareness).

- An ability to draw the client's attention to communication that is unclear, vague, puzzling or contradictory, with the aim of encouraging the client to elaborate on these elements.
- An ability to help the client become aware of incongruent elements in their communication.
- An ability to consider the potential latent content in the client's communications.
- An ability to share with the client an interpretation in a manner that is clear, appropriately timed, appropriate to the amount of time left in a session, of appropriate depth, and pertinent to the affective and/or interpersonal focus of the session. (p. 2)

- **Client's Experience of Interpretations**
  - An ability to assess the client's capacity to make use of an interpretation.
  - An ability to critically appraise the helpfulness and accuracy of an interpretation. (p. 3)

While not every core competency must be or can be operationalized in such a detailed manner, this operationalization of interpretation serves as a useful example of how it is possible to define a competency while still leaving ample room for the individual personality and style of the candidate or analyst to emerge and develop. In the next few paragraphs, I provide a few illustrations of the application of analytic interpretation in the clinical context.

One model for the interpretation of unconscious dynamics is a triangular connection between past relationships, current relationships, and the analytic relationship (see Winborn 2018, pp. 87–88). For example, a patient, with an overbearing and critical father, would frequently withhold negative reactions she was experiencing toward me out of fear I would become angry and judgmental of her. This pattern became more apparent as the analysis progressed. Relying on the triangle of relationship as a template, I made the following interpretation:

I have the sense that your difficult experiences with your father have influenced the sort of interactions you anticipate with men, including me. You've come to anticipate that I will easily become angry and critical, like he was. However, you seem to protect against that possibility by never expressing your reservations about things that I say and do. In making that choice you feel momentarily safer but, because your negative feelings are not expressed, you never have the opportunity to discover whether I will respond like your father as you anticipate. As a result, your short-term fear diminishes but your long term-fears of conflict, anger, and criticism remain intact in our relationship.

In this interpretation, I focused primarily on the dynamics of her past relationship with her father and how that shaped her perceptions and behavior in her interactions with me specifically but also more generally in her current relationships with other men.

Another important aspect in the competency with analytic interpretation is to be able to effectively distinguish between interpretation and other types of interventions, such as supportive interventions that are useful and necessary to the fostering of the analytic relationship and that often contribute to stabilization of the ego but which do not increase insight or consciousness in terms of the patient's understanding of the functioning of their psyche. The following exchange is an example of an intervention that could have remained primarily supportive but shifted to an interpretive intervention as the exchange progressed. The exchange takes place at the conclusion of a session. The patient, John, was a student in his late thirties. He manifested sociopathic tendencies and a previous history of drug and alcohol abuse. John had lived a marginal existence for much of his life but seemed to have arrived at a frame of mind where he could begin focusing on lasting transformation. In the session, we had been focused on John's anxiety regarding interactions with his mother. He had recently received a letter and check from his mother and was experiencing anxiety and ambivalence about feeling he should write her back. I made an observation about the level of anxiety she constellated in him and made reference to something he had said, during our previous session, about having to drink two beers before returning a call to his mother. The patient responded, "Oh you remembered." John was moved that I remembered what he had said in the previous session. From a supportive perspective, I could have concluded the session, or I could have said "Of course, I remembered," but neither of those interventional options would have helped John know anything about himself or how he utilizes me. Instead, I choose to continue with an observation and interpretation of his surprise:

A: You seem surprised that I remembered.
P: I didn't mean any offense. I just meant that none of my therapists before have ever remembered what I've said from week to week.
A: I didn't think you were making a derogatory comment about me.
P: Good because I wasn't. This therapy is really important to me.

At this point I made an interpretation focused on his self-experience, i.e., of not feeling memorable and his transferential expectation of me. The interpretation was offered in two parts with space for him to respond between the two elements of the interpretation.

A: I think you were telling me that you don't feel memorable so it surprises you that I could hold you in my mind.
P: (*he grins somewhat sheepishly but mixed with some expression of pleasure*) Well I know that you see a lot of patients and it must be hard to keep all of this stuff straight.

A: You seem to be wondering whether you're important enough to me for me to remember you as an individual among the other people who come into my office.

P: (*patient becomes tearful*) I know I'm important to you and it's really important that I stay with this and finish therapy this time. I've gotten started and quit so many times. I can't do that again.

The patient's internal narrative manifested in his belief that he was not memorable and in his anticipation that I would confirm this by not remembering him as a unique individual among my other patients. This exchange highlights the difference between supportive and interpretive interventions. While a supportive intervention would have been well received by the patient, it would not have deepened his understanding of himself or the role I play in his interior landscape (see Winborn 2018, pp. 10–14 for more on supportive versus interpretive interventions).

Evaluation of Competency in Interpretation

There are many possible approaches to evaluating competence in interpretation. For example, is the candidate/supervisee able to articulate why they made a specific interpretation? One model for this area of competence involves being able to articulate the what, where, when, and why behind an interpretation: what is being interpreted (e.g., a complex, defense, process, affect, transference, or archetypal pattern), where is the interpretation focused (e.g., in the patient, in the analytic relationship, towards the analyst, or in the patient's outer world relationships), when is the interpretation offered in terms of the timing of the interpretation and the patient's readiness to take in the new information the interpretation carries, and why the interpretation is being offered in terms of how the interpretation fits into the overall course of the analysis and the patient's individuation process (see Winborn 2018, pp. 90–93 for more on formulating interpretations use the *what, where, when, why* focus).

From a more specifically Jungian perspective, core competency in interpretation would involve the capacity to offer interpretations that facilitate and deepen the *circumambulation* of the complex. In other words, is the candidate/supervisee able to create interpretations that foster the patient's understanding of their complexes, including insights into how the complex originated, how it functions in the present psychic landscape, and where the complex is leading the psyche (i.e., the teleological thrust of the complex)? Core competency in interpretation from a Jungian perspective would also involve the capacity to formulate interpretations that are directed towards the various autonomous complexes rather than just directed towards the concerns of the ego position. Naturally, there are several other aspects of interpretation from a Jungian perspective that could also be incorporated, including being able to incorporate archetypal themes into analytic interpretation (for more on interpretation from a Jungian perspective see Winborn 2018, pp. 107–133).

Based on my experience as an evaluator and supervisor, it is not possible to determine a candidate's competency in the utilization of interpretation based on the candidate's verbal summary of what transpired in a session or sessions. Optimally, evaluating competence in interpretation is best assessed through direct access to the candidate's sessions with several of their patients, i.e., through the review of verbatim transcripts of sessions or audio/video recordings of sessions. Naturally, some may have concerns about the disruption of the analytic vessel in terms of transcriptions and recordings. However, the research on this issue indicates that disruption of the analytic process is minimal or non-existent (see Gill et al. 1968; Simon et al. 1970; Karp et al. 1993; Firestein 2001). However, if local regulatory guidelines or sentiment preclude direct review of the candidate's interpretive interactions with patients, there are alternative ways to evaluate interpretive competence. The evaluator(s) could select clinical exchanges from anonymized or published sources and ask the candidate what interpretation they would make at different junctures of the exchange. Also, role-playing of analyst–patient interactions could be employed in evaluating the candidate's interpretive competence, with the evaluator, or a stand-in volunteer, playing the role of the patient for the candidate. Case reports, if they include examples of the candidate's significant interpretations that served as transitional points during the analysis, can also provide insight into the candidate's interpretive competence. The existence of a well-delineated statement of core competency in analytic interpretation serves to reduce the influence of the evaluator's personalistic–subjective perspective on interpretation during the evaluation.

Conclusion

I hope this chapter gives the reader a greater appreciation for the value of integrating core competencies into analytic training. Core competencies are guidelines for the effective practice of analysis, which facilitate learning, instruction, and supervision, without infringing on freedom, creativity, and individuality in the practice of Jungian analysis.

Additional Resources on Analytic Interpretation

For additional background on analytic interpretation, I refer the reader to Levy (1990), Blue and Harrang (2016), Rubovits-Seitz (2002), and Winborn (2018). Each of these texts can be thought of as an extended operationalization of the core competency of interpretation.

References

ABAP (American Board for Accreditation in Psychoanalysis) 2017, *ABAP Core Competencies in Psychoanalysis*, Core Competencies Sub-Committee of the Committee on Accreditation. www.abapinc.org/core-competencies/
Adler, G 1967, *Studies in Analytical Psychology*, New York: Putnam.

Astor, J 1998, Some Jungian and Freudian perspectives on the Oedipus myth and beyond, *International Journal of Psycho-Analysis*, 79: 697–712.

Barsness, R E 2018, *Core Competencies of Relational Psychoanalysis*, London: Routledge.

Blue, D, Harrang, C (Eds.) 2016, *From Reverie to Interpretation: Transforming Thought into the Action of Psychoanalysis*, London: Karnac.

Connolly, A 2008, Some brief considerations on the relationship between theory and practice, *Journal of Analytical Psychology*, 53(4): 481–499.

Dehing, J 1992, The therapist's interventions in Jungian analysis, *Journal of Analytical Psychology*, 37(1): 29–47.

Firestein, S K 2001, Teaching with tape-recorded psychoanalysis, *Psychoanalytic Quarterly*, 70(3): 655–663.

Fordham, M 1978, *Jungian Psychotherapy*, London: Karnac.

Fordham, M 1991, The supposed limits of interpretation, *Journal of Analytical Psychology*, 36(2): 165–175.

Gill, M M, Simon, J, Fink, G, Endicott, N A, Paul, I H 1968, Studies in audio-recorded psychoanalysis—I. General considerations, *Journal of American Psychoanalytic Association*, 16: 230–244.

Junkers, G, Tuckett, D, Zachrisson, A 2008, To be or not to be a psychoanalyst – How do we know when a candidate is ready to quality? Difficulties and controversies in evaluating psychoanalytic competence, *Psychoanalytic Inquiry*, 28(3): 288–308.

Karp, J G, Hyler, I, Wald, M, Whitman, L, Herschkowitz, S, Goldberger, M 1993, The use of an audiotaped analysis in a continuous case seminar, *Psychoanalytic Quarterly*, 62: 263–269.

Kirsch, T 2000, *The Jungians: A Comparative and Historical Perspective*, Routledge: London.

Lemma, A, Roth, A, Pilling, S 2008, *The Competencies Required to Deliver Effective Psychoanalytic/Psychodynamic Therapy*, London: Research Dept. of Clinical, Educational and Health Psychology, University College, London. www.ucl.ac.uk/pals/research/clinical-educational-and-health-psychology/research-groups/core/competence-frameworks-6

Levy, S 1990, *Principles of Interpretation*, Northvale, NJ: Aronson.

Parth, K & Loefler-Stastka, H 2015, Psychoanalytic core competencies, *Frontiers in Psychology*, 6, Article 356 (open access online journal).

Rubovits-Seitz, P 2002, *A Primer of Clinical Interpretation*, Northvale, NJ: Aronson.

Simon, J, Fink, G, Gill, M M, Endicott, N A, Paul, I H 1970, Studies in audio-recorded psychoanalysis—Ii. the effect of recording upon the analyst, *Journal of American Psychoanalytic Association*, 18:86–101.

Sullivan, B S 2009, *The Mystery of Analytical work: Weavings from Jung and Bion*, London: Routledge.

Tuckett, D 2005, Does anything go? Towards a framework for the more transparent assessment of psychoanalytic competence, *International Journal of Psycho-Analysis*, Vol. 86(1): 31–49.

Wallerstein, R 1990, Psychoanalysis: The common ground, *International Journal of Psycho-Analysis*, 71: 3–20.

Winborn, M 2018, *Interpretation in Jungian Analysis: Art and Technique*, London: Routledge.

Zinkin, L 1969, Flexibility in analytic technique, *Journal of Analytical Psychology*, 14(2): 119–132.

Chapter 9

The Relevance of Reflective Practice in the Training of Jungian Analysts

Astrid Berg

Introduction

When a seasoned Jungian analyst, X, was asked about his conduct during a past interaction that was distressing to a colleague, he said: "For me the work is to focus on myself, to know and understand what the interaction meant to me, and not so much on what it meant to the other person." The colleague, Y, who made the approach, felt somewhat shattered by this answer, felt 'objectified' and dismissed as it seemed that all the mattered to X was his personal growth and nothing else.

On the face of it, it could be seen as laudable that the "work is to focus on myself"; it is after all, the basis of Jungian analysis to get to know one's shadow – that part of the self of which one is not aware. However, what is so strikingly absent in the statement is the acknowledgement of the 'real outer other', the acknowledgement that what I do has an effect on the other person, and that I need to take responsibility not only for my personal growth but for what effect I have on the other.

Psychoanalysis, and in particular Jungian analytical psychology, is by its very nature focused on the self – it is often a largely introverted, self-absorbed process, which tends to eclipse the other who disappears as a person.

Why this may be particularly so in those with a Jungian orientation is an interesting question. Current infant research may provide a signpost in the other direction, namely that there can be no 'self' without the recognition of an 'other', as Stern so amply demonstrates in his work *The Interpersonal World of the Infant* (Stern 1985). The more recent concepts of mentalization and reflective functioning could be seen as the extensions of this core notion into adulthood. After all, the most valuable gift for humanity may lie in its ability to be reflective – reflective about the self and the other. Before turning to definitions and contemporary research, let us start with our ancestor, C. G. Jung.

DOI: 10.4324/9781003219910-13

Jung and the 'Other'

Jung was a lonely child who from very early on had learnt to 'hold' himself through sensations and images. The memories of his infancy and early childhood contain only two where a caring adult was with him when he was distressed: one where his father sang to him when he was ill and the other one where he was held by the female helper, whose hair and complexion he recalled vividly in his *Memories, Dreams and Reflections* (Jung 1967). He was shown things in the world – the Alps by his aunt, the evening sky by his father, stuffed animals at the Basel museum – but it is less evident that he was 'held' in a continuous, consistent manner by a significant other in his childhood.

Jung grew up in an unhappy home; he was a solitary child who was frightened by his fantasies but who also found solace in his imagination. Not surprising then that, in the words of his grandson, "Carl the younger was an introverted intuitive type, a gifted thinker and writer. His life was an 'inner experience' with only few external upsets. He researched the human soul and his goal was the Self" (Jung 2001, p. 663). Jung turned inwards, focused on himself – the unconscious with its primary processes provided him with the 'holding' that he, like every human being needed, and that to him might have seemed more satisfying and reliable than an outer human relationship. His subsequent theory was to a large extent built around this 'focus on myself' notion.

For many individuals this turning inward has offered a way of connecting with libidinal energies that have helped them find meaning. However, the downside to this introspection is that the 'other', the real, outside other person may get lost and literally overshadowed. The importance of the other is often regarded only in terms of what he/she may bring to consciousness about one's self. This may at certain times be a necessary stance, but it could be regarded as egocentric. If we aspire to be 'whole' human beings, we need to bestow on the other the same importance as we do onto ourselves. This is not merely an idealistic stance but is one that arises from our very beginnings as human beings. It is infant development that helps us shed light on the importance of the living other for the self.

The Development of the Reflective Self

The mind is interpersonal: self-understanding and understanding the other are intertwined. I cannot truly know myself without also knowing or getting to know the other. Consciousness of the self is also consciousness of the outer, real person. This consciousness evolves in the context of the first relationships.

It we try, in our imagination, to go back to the first hominid mother with her baby, we might wonder at what point she may have realized that this little creature that has come out of her has feelings and has a mind? If we follow Damasio's 'Levels of Life Regulation' (Damasio 2000), the mother may have reached some level of 'high reason', that is, neo-cortical responses that allow for conscious images and behaviour. The cry of the baby may have evoked feelings of hunger and pain that she would have experienced in her life. Instinctively, and from a species survival point of view, she would feed the infant in order to stop the crying, but at what point would she go beyond the physical, feeding behaviour to also respond with thinking? Perhaps, it is at the point where the baby first smiles, and she makes eye contact with the baby that is meaningful. The baby's smile acts as a 'social releaser' (Bowlby 1978), evoking pleasure and thus enabling and encouraging the mother to respond in a loving way, thereby increasing the interaction between them.

It may be that in those early days, the primary caregiver realized that behind the behaviours of the infant there is a mind and this mind in turn influenced the way in which the young child was handled and reared. If this way of handling and rearing then ensures survival and makes for a robust individual, it would have been perpetuated and become 'hard-wired' in the human species. In Jungian terms this hard-wiring could be called an arche-typal predisposition.

Thus it could be imagined how human infants are born into relationships – they cannot survive alone – neither physically nor psychically. As the parent–child relationships evolved over the centuries, parents increasingly were able to see their children as separate individuals (de Mause 1974). This further evolved to more recent times where it can be said that most parents are able to convey to their infants the sense of personhood from the very beginning of their lives.

However, this early relationship is not equal. During infancy this 'being reflected upon' comes from the adult caregivers, that is, it is the adult's task to think about what the child might be experiencing. It is not yet expected for the infant to reciprocate and to have this kind of awareness for the people in its life. But as the child develops and matures, there is an increasing sen-tience of the inner life of the other, an awareness of what might go on in the mother or father's mind. By the time adulthood is reached, a sense of equality between the importance of self and other should be possible. There is ample evidence in the research literature that having been understood and reflected upon in the early years, ensures that this is carried over into the next gener-ation (Rosso & Airaldi 2016). However, for some individuals this ability to reflect upon self and other has been impeded or is not sufficiently developed. If a care-giver is preoccupied with worries, is feeling depressed, or frightened, as would be with domestic violence or trauma, then they are not able to be aware of their child's inner needs or state of mind. At best all they can do is to keep the child safe. But the reflective process, as will be described below, cannot occur.

Children whose parents have been traumatized or who are mentally ill are affected by not having their perspective, their inner life validated; they may present with behaviour or emotional problems. It is therefore not surprising that parenting interventions that focus on parental reflective functioning have gained ascendancy.

For example, a study that was done on a reflective parenting intervention for high-risk mothers in the Western Cape of South Africa (Suchman et al. 2019) serves as an example of how facilitating a reflective attitude improved the mother–child interactions. This particular mentalization-based intervention, called "Mothering from the Inside Out", has demonstrated efficacy in other clinical trials in the US (Suchman, DeCoste, Castiglioni, et al. 2010; Suchman, DeCoste, Leigh, & Borelli 2010).

While reflective parenting interventions are increasingly used in clinical practice, the term 'reflective practice' has found its way into broader areas in the mental health field. Before turning to the broader processes, let us examine more closely how reflective functioning in the parent–child relationship is operationalized.

Defining and Differentiating between Mentalization, Reflective Functioning and Reflective Practice

While these three terms are often used interchangeably, there are subtle differences between them. Mentalization could be regarded as the umbrella term that has been defined as the human capacity to make meaning of one's own or an other's behaviour through understanding the states of mind that underlie that behaviour (Jurist 2008). The terms reflective function and reflective practice could be seen as a refinement or further development of mentalization in that there is a specific focus on the effects that one's actions have on the other. Most people have the ability to mentalize – it's not that we are born with it, but it develops naturally within the parent–child relationship along the lines that were imagined earlier in this chapter. The meaning making is what differentiates us from the animal world. It is to be noted that the definition includes to make meaning of one's own OR of the other's behaviour, so the focus could be only on the meaning of one's own behaviour with little or no regard of the other – neither of the effect one has on the other, nor of the meaning of the other's behaviour.

The term reflective functioning is a construct that was borne out of the research done on adults' narratives of their childhood memories (Fonagy et al. 1991). Reflective functioning is the "overt manifestation, in narrative, of an individual's mentalizing capacity" (Slade 2005, p. 269). A measurement has been developed – the Parent Development Interview (PDI) – which sets out to assess the reflective processes as they show themselves in the current parent–child relationship, moving from the inner past parent–child memories, as measured by the Adult Attachment Interview (AAI) to the present parent–child relationship. Besides being a concept that has been operationalized via the PDI, it specifically also focuses on the 'other'.

Reflective functioning, as opposed to mentalization, is a circular process between self and outer other. The following steps could be seen to occur: I am able to make the link between what I am feeling and how that is determining or influencing my behaviour; I become aware of how my behaviour is affecting the other person and I wonder how that makes the person feel and how that person in turn then behaves towards me. Phrased differently it means that I am conscious of myself as well as of the effect or impact I am having on the other person. It ultimately implies taking responsibility for one's behaviour in the world.

Reflective practice takes relational processes beyond the 'me and you' to the level of the professional conduct, organizations and larger human ecosystems (Sparrow 2016). It is to this we turn in the next section.

Reflective Practice

Simply stated: reflective practice places the relationships between human beings and the quality thereof at the centre of its endeavours. It starts with the first relationship – between infant and caregiver. From there reflective practice grows in concentric circles to family relationships, relationships within the work place and community and ultimately with relationships in larger organizations.

Placing relationships at the centre is a process that contains several core elements. Only a few of these will be highlighted here.

1. Multidirectional interactions means that all partners have equal value and an equal say and that there is an openness to hear the other person.
2. Reparative processes: the ability to acknowledge mistakes and errors of judgment, and to use these as an opportunity for learning through experience.
3. Cultural self-understanding and humility – knowing that we are all immersed in our culture and view the world through particular cultural lenses, and that each person has an equal right to be informed and act according to his and her culture. This includes valuing the diversity and complexity of human nature (ibid., p. 609).

These three elements may be of particular importance to psychoanalytic practice – not only in terms of relationships with analysands but also in terms of professional, collegial relationships and functioning of groups and associations. It may not be too far-fetched to speculate that many a fractious institutional battle could be avoided if there was more awareness of reflective practice. If relationships embracing equality and openness, acknowledgement of mistakes, and an awareness that we all have cultural lenses through which we see the world, could be moved to centre stage, we might find constructive ways in solving systemic problems.

Reflective practice is increasingly being included in a variety of fields. A simple literature search reveals over 13,000 items using the term in various disciplines – from pharmacy education to physical therapy.[1] Even the World Bank reflected on itself in a study that examined how its staff interpreted evidence and how this influenced policy. The recommendation coming out of this study is to adopt a 'reflective practice' approach to inform policy and practice (McKee & Stuckler 2016). If 'concrete' disciplines are embracing reflective practice, how much more is it not our task, as analytical psychologists, to include the term in our thinking, teaching, and clinical practice so that we hopefully come to integrate its essence into our very being?

How Can Reflective Practice Be Taught?

Fundamental to reflective functioning is the awareness of the other and how I affect the other. It is this relational process that needs to be experienced – it cannot be taught. It can be thought about, it can be theorized about, but it also has to be 'felt' in a real life way. How this could be incorporated in a conscious way into a training programme is a challenge. One possibility is offered here. In many academic and training programmes Infant Observation is a required module. The model followed is that of the Tavistock, as it was developed by Ester Bick (1964). It means observing an infant from birth to the age of one or two years, on a weekly basis. The student is required to write process notes after the observation in as much detail as can be remembered. The group of students then meets with a seminar leader once a week and during this meeting one of the observations is discussed. A central part of the discussion is reflecting on what the observer felt, what they thought the baby might have experienced, and on what in turn, the student group is feeling. This to and fro sharing of thoughts and feelings across these different layers is a nuanced and multifaceted process. It acts as a container for the primitive anxieties that invariably get stirred up when witnessing a young infant with his/her mother, perhaps struggling with hunger, or pain, or whatever discomfort might be present. The process helps to 'hold' the observer not to act out, or, if there is an ethical dilemma as often happens (Berg 2016) it serves as a 'think tank' about what action, if any, could or should be taken. The circular process that defines reflective functioning is then experienced by the students at the level of feeling contained, of being kept in mind, and of seeing and experiencing the effects that actions of the 'self' have on the 'other'. This learning through experience is something that becomes part of the students and they take with them into their various professional fields.

Is This Model Translatable into Jungian Practice?

It could well be that there are analytical psychology associations and societies who, as part of their training programme, have a module of Infant Observation as a requirement. However, if this is not the case, how could one envision replicating some of what is embedded in the Infant Observation process? Perhaps one way would be for analyst trainees to have regular peer supervision groups in which turns get taken in presenting material from a patient. In the group format the circular, horizontal process would be more readily activated than in individual supervision which might follow a more vertical process – by that is meant, more on the Conscious–Unconscious axis in the trainee and his/her patient. A group process with members all participating would by its very nature provide more opportunity to reflect on dynamics that occur between individuals. These dynamics would, of course, also include individual and group unconscious processes, as so well described by Fuller (Fuller 2003).

The Relevance of Reflective Practice for Jungian Analysts

Traditional Jungian analysis has at its heart the aim to bring the ego into relationship with the Self. This is an intensely inner process that requires the kind of devotion and attention that the alchemists had in their pursuit of gold or the philosopher's stone. Jung's life took him from his lonely childhood into the realms of his inner world, where he found solace in the rich symbolic material that emerged. The theories that emanated from his experiences have served to broaden and deepen the concept of the unconscious.

However, the other side of this could be the relative neglect of the relationship to the outer other person. The outer other could end up only serving to develop the self, as analyst X in the introduction so clearly articulates. What happens to Y in the process is then of less importance. It is at this juncture that a correction or re-calibration is needed – the real other person is as important as the self, and "I carry responsibility for you" is something that we may have to consider more.

The African proverb "Umtnu ngumntu ngabantu" – "I am because you are" (Berg 2012, p. 93) – is profound in its humanity and is an ideal that should be heeded. In today's world this is not only a noble goal to have, it is a necessity if we are to survive as the human race.

Note

1 www.ncbi.nlm.nih.gov/pm c/?term=Reflective+practice+overview

References

Berg, A 2016, Reflective practice in infant mental health – a South African perspective, *Infant Mental Health Journal*, *37*(6), 684–691.

Berg, A 2012, *Connecting with South Africa – Cultural Comunication and Understanding*, College Station, TX: Texas A & M University Press.

Bick, E 1964, Notes on infant observations in psychoanlaytic training, in *Collected Papers of Martha Harris and Esther Bick* (pp. 240–256), Perthshire: The Clunie Press.

Bowlby, J 1978, *Attachment and Loss Vol 1*. Harmondsworth, UK: Penguin Books.

Damasio, A 2000, *The Feeling of What Happens*, London: Vintage.

de Mause, L 1974, *The History of Childhooe – the Evolution of Parent-Child Relationships as a Factor in History*, London: The Psychohistory Press.

Fonagy, P; Steele, M; Steele, H. M. G. S.. H. A. C. 1991, The capacity for understanding mental states: The reflective self in parent and child and its significance for security of attachment, *Infant Mental Health Journal*, *12*(3), 201–218.

Fuller, V C 2003, Supervision in groups, in J. Wiener, J; Mizen, R; Duckham (Ed.), *Supervising and Being Supervised – A Practice in Search of a Theory* (First Edit, pp. 118–131), Bristol: Palgrave MacMillan.

Jung, A 2011, The grandfather, *Journal of Analytical Psychology, 56*, 653–673.

Jung, C G 1967, *Memories, Dreams, Reflections*, London and Glasgow: Random House.

Jurist, E L 2008, Minds and yours – new directions for mentalization theory, in S. Jurist, E. L.; Slade, A.; Bergner, S. (Ed.), *Mind to Mind: Infant Research, Neuroscience and Psychoanalysis* (pp. 88–114), New York: Other Press.

McKee, M, Stuckler, D 2016, Reflective practice: How the world bank explored its own biases?, *International Journal of Health Policy and Management*, *5*(2), 79–82. https://doi.org/10.15171/ijhpm.2015.216

Rosso, A M, Airaldi, C 2016, Intergenerational transmission of reflective functioning, *Frontiers in Psychology, 7*, 1–11. https://doi.org/10.3389/fpsyg.2016.01903

Slade, A 2005, Parental reflective functioning: An introduction, *Attachment & Human Development*, *7*(3), 269–281. https://doi.org/10.1080/14616730500245906

Sparrow, J 2016, Reflective practice in organizational learning, cultural self-understanding, and community self-strengthening, *Infant Mental Health Journal*, *37*(6), 605–616.

Stern, D 1985, *The interpersonal world of the infant*. New York: Basic Books.

Suchman, N, Berg, A, Abrahams, L, Abrahams, T, Adams, A, Cowley, B, Decoste, C, Hawa, W, Lachman, A, Mpinda, B, Cader-Mokoa,N, Nama, N, Voges, J 2019, Mothering from the Inside Out: Adapting an evidence-based intervention for high-risk mothers in the Western Cape of South Africa, *Development and Psychopathology,* 1–18. https://doi.org/10.1017/S0954579418001451

Suchman, N E, DeCoste, C, Castiglioni, N, McMahon, T J, Rounsaville, B, Mayes, L 2010 The Mothers and Toddlers Program, an attachment-based parenting intervention for substance using women: Post-treatment results from a randomized clinical pilot, *Attachment & Human Development*, *12*(5), 483–504. https://doi.org/10.1080/14616734.2010.501983

Suchman, N E, DeCoste, C, Leigh, D, Borelli, J 2010, Reflective functioning in mothers with drug use disorders: Implications for dyadic interactions with infants and toddlers, *Attachment and Human Development*, *12*(6), 567–585. https://doi.org/10.1080/14616734.2010.501988

The Analytical Training

Integrative View and Assistance to Individuation

Part IV

The Analytical Training
Integrative View and Assistance
to Individuation

Chapter 10

Training in Thirdness and Thirdness in Training

August Cwik

Introduction

The Third and Thirdness

What Is It?

Jung's notion of the *third* and *thirdness* is a central proposition in analytical psychology as it describes an innate function of psyche, most prominently demonstrated in, "The Transcendent Function":

> The confrontation of the two positions generates a tension charged with energy and creates a living, *third* thing – not a logical still birth in accordance with the principle *tertium non datur* [the *third* is not given], but a movement out of the suspension between opposites, a living birth that leads to a new level of being, a new situation.
>
> (Jung 1916, para. 189)

It is this generative space that results in the formation of a symbol that unites the two opposing positions accounting for change in analysis and individuation in general. In the "Psychology of the Transference" (1946), Jung described it as a mercurial content that "possesses the patient like a demon flits about from patient to doctor, as the *third* party in the alliance" (ibid., para. 186, italics added). He also said, "Psychological induction inevitably causes the two parties to get involved *in the transformation of the third* and to be themselves transformed in the process" (ibid., para 399, italics added).

These ideas of *thirdness* led to the analytic encounter being conceived as mutual in nature. *Thirdness*, as envisioned by Jung is a rich, fertile, emergent space that allows the potentiality of the reconciliation of opposites through a new symbol, stance, or attitude. Unfortunately, Jung never elaborated the specifics of how this *third* space operated in the clinical situation. Drawing on a reinterpretation of the alchemical series, *The Rosarium Philosophorum*, and the clinical literature of the intersubjective and relational schools, I (Cwik

DOI: 10.4324/9781003219910-15

1991, 1995, 2006a, 2006b, 2010, 2011, 2017) have discussed the operation of *thirdness* from a Jungian standpoint.

Benjamin's (2017) focus on *thirdness* has been through recognition theory. Her theorizing saw the *third* as a process, function, or a particular kind of relating rather than as a thing in itself.

> The Third refers to a position constituted through holding the tension of recognition between difference and sameness, taking the other to be a separate but equivalent center of initiative in consciousness with whom nonetheless feelings and intentions can be shared.
>
> (ibid., p. 4)

Her emphasis has been on moving out of a state of what she calls "complementarity" where there exists a separateness of other into a "twoness", which results in "doer or done to" dynamics—or, at worst, an "only one can live", attitude. As the complex struggle for liberation from these complementary doer–done to positions evolves, it becomes apparent how necessary it is to think in terms of a *third*.

Ogden (1997, 1999, 2005) has developed a body of work clearly demonstrating how *thirdness* is apprehended, experienced, and used to inform what is said to the patient in the clinical situation. His use of reveries to elaborate the working of the *third*, which is unconscious and can never be known with certainty, is unparalleled in clinical literature. There is no longer any attempt to keep the fantasy of a neutral observer, but that one is also in and co-creating the experience with the patient. The analyst must acknowledge that reality and take responsibility for his/her part in it. Every transference is a counter-countertransference. You can never tell with certainty what belongs to whom, or who started what.

What has begun to evolve in considering interpersonal interaction through *thirdness* is the defining uniqueness of each dyad—and in training, any grouping with the candidate whether it be supervision or monitoring and evaluation committees. Any aspect of assessing the suitability of a candidate has to take into account that each evaluative conclusion is best understood in the context of the candidate and the evaluating member/group.

The Absence of *Thirdness*

Now that the *third* and *thirdness* have been described, what is the state defined by an "absence of *thirdness*" (Gentile 2001)? It is the absence of *thirdness* that permeates most, if not all, of our training institutions. Gentile stated that an absence of *thirdness* leads to a "collapsed state of twoness, fusion-based dynamics, power relations, and brute force yield[ing] a relatedness that looks like, but actually precludes, psychological intimacy" (ibid., p. 624). It is this "brute force" quality that is the sequelae of a breakdown of *thirdness*—the analyst, or committee, ends up polarized into an authoritative stance. This often leads to enactment. The term enactment is used to describe the acting out of a mental state with little or no reflection. It is a "jointly created" inter-action, fueled by unconscious psychic forces in both therapist and patient. It differs from other strong transference/countertransference interplays in that it is unconsciously motivated by the mutual stimulation of strong affect, with both persons feeling out of control—compelled by something mysterious and powerful (Maroda 1998).

Sounding almost Jungian, Benjamin (2017) said it this way: "In my model of the intersubjectivity, breakdown is understood as twoness – the comple-mentarity of 'doer and done to' with its ball-in-socket interlocking depend-ency of opposites" (p. 49). The way out of this breakdown of *thirdness* is through repair; the therapist carries the responsibility to acknowledge failure and bear the shame involved. The notion of *red flags* will be used to note a potential absence of *thirdness*.

The Ethics of *Thirdness*

Related to the ethical nature of analysis Jung (1958) stated:

> The concept and phenomenon of conscience thus contains, when seen in a psychological light, two different factors: on the one hand a recollection of, and admonition by, the mores; on the other, a conflict of duty and its solution *through the creation of a third standpoint*. The first is the moral, and the second the ethical, aspect of conscience.
>
> (para. 857, italics added)

If the dynamics of *thirdness* are constituted in the manner described above, the practitioner and training committees must acknowledge a certain eth-ical requirement in the stance taken towards interpretation, and particu-larly enactments. If we do not know with any kind of certainty who started what, or who caused something to happen, then our participation in such interactions needs to be owned and responsibility taken. Benjamin (2017) was quite clear in naming the "moral *third*", "the orientation to a larger principle of lawfulness, necessity, rightness or goodness" (p. 37).

> In calling this the moral *third*, I am suggesting that clinical practice may ultimately be founded in certain values, such as the acceptance of uncer-tainty, humility, and compassion that form the basis of a democratic or egalitarian view of psychoanalytic process.
>
> (Benjamin 2004, p. 34, italics added)

Jung's (1958) essay on the psychological nature of conscience distinguished between ethics, the collective customs and conventions akin to traditional superego functioning and what we think of as morals, a personal standpoint that is subjective and evaluated by the rightness of our own total personality. Conscience, he says, emerges out of these two standpoints held in tension. We may often feel morally correct in an interaction of the rightness of our viewpoint, but this can be affected by unconscious bias and complexes.

Training in Thirdness

I (Cwik 2010, 2011, 2017) have outlined in several papers how *thirdness* may be imagined from a Jungian perspective and how to work with it in the clinical situation. In the now familiar *quaternio* diagram showing all the possible levels of communication (Jung 1946) between the conscious and unconscious of the therapist and patient, the unconscious-to-unconscious connection can best be thought of as the *analytic third*. By definition it is unconscious and cannot be known with any certainty, but hints of its operation can be accessed through the analyst's reverie and somatic reactions while in session (Ogden 1994, 1997, 1999). Extending traditional reverie, the seemingly random thoughts that arise in the analyst (Ogden 1997) to more organized forms such as: images, books, movies, dreams; to more traditional Jungian fare as myths and fairytales; and, finally to theoretical cognition, I have coined the term "associative dreaming" (Cwik 2010).

In order to access this split consciousness, one listening to what the patient says, and the other facing inward to the contents of mind and body, a slight altering of consciousness is necessary—an *abaissement du niveau mental* (Jung 1916). The best way to teach the candidate this lowered state-of-consciousness is for the candidate to be well practiced in formal active imagination (Cwik 1995).

What is being described here is expanding the idea of active imagination into a broader sense of the therapist's own discourse with his/her imaginal contents during the analytic session. Active imagination becomes the paradigm for approaching countertransference contents (Cwik 2006, pp. 215–217).

> The therapist enters into a receptive or altered-state to elicit imaginal material assumed to be arising from the *analytic third*. The therapist then engages these images/reveries while staying consciously attuned to the patient. The therapist speaks *from* what is extracted from the active imaginal engagement or shares the actual content of the material. Active imagination becomes no longer just a Jungian technique, but a way of 'being with' material emerging from the unconscious in therapeutic sessions.
>
> (Cwik 2010, p. 20–21)

The art of working in *thirdness* is using what is extracted to formulate an intervention with the patient at this *from* or *about* level. I (Cwik 2011) gave an example of speaking at the *from* level in which I repeatedly was having an image of seeing the patient across a deep abyss in the form of Munch's print, "The Scream". Speaking *from* this associative dream I said, "It seems to me that there is some kind of gulf between us that feels unbridgeable. And that you are on the other side trying to express something unspeakable". The patient had been hypomanic up to this point, but at this intervention she quieted, sat down, and burst into tears. It would make no sense to speak to her at the *about* level, sharing the image with her, as she would just be confused as to why I was telling her this.

The *about* level is sharing the analyst's thoughts or body reactions directly with the patient usually not done in traditional psychoanalytic work. Ogden (1999, 2004) makes a distinction of generally two types of patients: those with what he calls "undreamt or undreamable dreams", and those demonstrating "interrupted cries". The category of patients who are unable to dream, not meant literally as they can have a dream experience, but meaning that they are unable to do psychological work, or as Jungians might say they are unable to be symbolic. The analyst must be able to dream for the patient as in the example I gave above. Patients who are in the interrupted cries category means that they are capable of dreaming, that is doing psychological work, but the affect becomes too great for them to handle so the analyst's role is that of helping the patient to contain the affect (Cwik 2011).

I suggested (ibid.) that the analyst can speak to the patients in the interrupted cries category either from or about level, but can only use the from level to speak to the patient in the undreamt dream category. Helping candidates to understand these distinctions is important to training in the nature of *thirdness*. Likewise, for candidates to learn when amplification is clinically appropriate.

Amplification is using myth, fairytales, and historical and cultural parallels to clarify and "amplify" clinical material. Amplification is clearly speaking at the *about* level—a myth comes to mind and it is shared directly with the patient. Helping him/her to place the patient's material in a larger collective understanding helps the patient take a more objective stance to their emotional dilemma. Cambray (2001) reminded:

> The authentic striving for amplification arises not from a need in the analyst or analysand only but originates in the *analytic third*. This emergent need is often discovered through comparing strands of associative processes of both partners of the dyad (again, to be explored silently by the analyst until the timing is correct for intervention). By continuing to analyze the subjective contributions of each partner the analyst is

assisted in avoiding the dangers of using amplification for supportive or defensive purposes.

(p. 285, italics added)

A *red flag* appears when a candidate makes the statement that they are sure the material coming up in them is their own—maybe a preoccupation with something going on in their life. I consider this type of statement a possible indicator of defensiveness to acknowledging *thirdness*. One dictum of *thirdness* is that if you, the candidate, is experiencing something the patient may have or be struggling with it too.

Benjamin (2004, 2017) also pointed out two other elements of *thirdness* of which candidates need to be aware: the *rhythmic third*, or the *one in the third*; and, the *differentiating third*, or the *third in the one*. The *rhythmic third* is the analyst accommodating to the needs of the patient, it is like a dance where the patient takes the lead and analyst follows—it is the basis for empathic rapport primarily focused on the patient.

> This ability to maintain internal awareness, to sustain the tension of difference between my needs in yours while still being attuned to you, forms the basis of the *differentiating* Third—the interactive principle that incarnates recognition and respect for the other's common humanity without submission or control.
>
> (Benjamin 2017, p. 27)

The therapist's needs actually begin to predominate and begin to guide the dyad.

I have worked with supervisees who took on severely disturbed individuals demonstrating "borderline" symptomatology requiring multiple sessions, emails, and texts. Many therapists might never take on such individuals and/ or would work with them for a while and then unconsciously get them to quit before needing to terminate themselves. We usually uncover deep developmental woundings in the therapist that fit "hand-in-glove" with the patient's pathology. Due to these early deficits the therapist was able to constellate the *rhythmic third* when many others would have given up. But since the "relentless hope" (Stark 2006) of the patient to find perfect *thirdness* can never be completely met, they eventually reach an impasse. Here is a *red flag* of an impending loss of *thirdness* as the therapist is "burned out" and ready to terminate the patient. If the supervisor can help the supervisee to navigate his/her way to a *differentiating third* and find a way of saying to the patient that things cannot keep going the way they have been, then the enactment might be prevented and both individuals able to move on in the work. But I would emphasize it emanates first from the therapist's need and not from the patient's needs being met. This working of the material emanating from the *analytic third* provides an "analytic compass" (Cwik 2011, 2017) for the analytic work to progress.

Thirdness in Training

Overview

When it comes to training, Jung's reluctance even to establish a training institute must be remembered. Beautifully stated by Astor (1991):

> Jung, who had many theories, did not want to start a school or a movement for Jungian analysis ... Schools can develop bodies of knowledge, theories, which can become orthodoxies, and so destroy the spirit behind their inception. Perhaps one reason why Jung distrusted setting up institutions for analytical psychology was that, like theories, they can be used to restrict the revolutionary nature of the discoveries of the work group. This is because theories tend to reduce experience and observation to conscious knowledge. Jung, as we know, valued uncertainty, the irrational, and the struggle that accompanies individuation.
>
> (p. 178)

Having been reluctantly established, Jungian training organizations immediately began to operate from old binary and complementary positions, in spite of Jung's insight into the importance of *thirdness* in the analytic situation. We tend to end up in "doer and done to" dynamics and processes—analysts and committees imposing guidelines and evaluations of what is right and wrong on candidates (an authoritarian) model—just what Jung sought to avoid.

A "training attitude" needs to be developed and held by all of the analytic community members emphasizing that, "The trainee ... is first and foremost a responsible independent clinician loyal to patients' needs; being an analytic trainee supplements this primary identity, never replaces it" (Berman 2013, p. 230). While certainly there is and always will be an asymmetry, this should never be used as an excuse not to attempt mutuality between trainees and analysts. Most societies quickly fall into complementary and authoritarian ways of being. The overall effect is of promoting submissiveness as a characteristic of analytic candidates (Kernberg 2006).

The concept of initiation is often used as a paradigm for training. And certainly training is a type of initiation, a rite of passage from psychotherapist to analyst, but when a trainer consciously engages the archetype of initiation in order to make things difficult or even painful, it risks becoming rationalized sadomasochism. This type of dynamic is an indicator, *red flag*, of the absence of *thirdness*—there is a lack of mutuality in a process that expects/demands submission on the part of the candidate.

As early as 1948, Balint attempted to address this shadow of initiation:

> The whole atmosphere [of training] is strongly reminiscent of the primitive initiation ceremonies. On the part of the initiators—the training committee and the training analysts—we observe secretiveness about our esoteric knowledge, dogmatic announcements of our demands and the use of authoritative techniques. On the part of the candidates, i.e., those to be initiated, we observe the willing acceptance of the exoteric fables, submissiveness to dogmatic and authoritative treatment without much protest and too respectful behaviour. We know that the general aim of all initiation rites is to force the candidate to identify himself with his initiator, to introject the initiator and his ideals, and to build up from these identifications a strong super-ego which will influence him all his life.
>
> (p. 167)

Operating from a *thirdness* perspective takes time and effort to implement. The first dictum is to always approach candidates whenever there is a concern or a change in training requirements. Statements that "it is better not to include candidates in a discussion because their viewpoints might not be included in the final decision" is a *red flag* to an absence of *thirdness* about to occur, rationalized as "for their own good". Report writing after an evaluative meeting often includes understandings and interpretations that were never actually made to the candidate—thus never giving him/her a chance to respond—another *red flag*. Decision-making falls back to an authoritarian model because it is quicker and easier. It takes time to have the candidate return and hear the concerns and understandings of a committee, and allowing them to respond. Slavin (2007) decried:

> In my view, the situation in psychoanalytic training represents a picture of a systemic absence of 'thirdness', of an 'is what it is' reality, of binary distinctions, and categorical ideas: for example, one's way of working is or is not psychoanalysis ... one is or is not analyzable; a theory is or is not truly psychoanalytic; a clinical approach is or is not a depth psychology; one is or is not dealing with transference or the unconscious. Where in these assertions is the third space we can come to in order to help us look at and disembed ourselves from fixed positions?
>
> (p. 605)

The next sections will review the application of a *thirdness* model to several familiar training situations. Again, *red flag* designations will highlight the need for increased awareness.

Supervision

"The notion of the intersubjectivity [*thirdness*] has enormous implications for the analytic relationship and, I believe, for psychoanalytic supervision as well. If taken seriously, intersubjectivity points the way to potential radical changes both in the content and in the style of supervision" (Berman 2013, p. 185).

In, "The art of the tincture: analytical supervision", I (Cwik 2006b) put forward a model of supervision based on *thirdness* principles. The *quaternio* diagram, discussed earlier, between analyst and patient was extended into a triadic model, now envisioned equally between supervisor, supervisee, and patient (and back to the supervisor so that there indicates a direct unconscious connection between supervisor and patient—the supervisor is imagined as not solely impacting the patient by influencing the supervisee).

The goal of analytical supervision is to promote the fullest expression of the professional-self of the supervisee. The professional-self of the supervisee is that aspect of the true self that operates through a developed persona in a therapeutic situation. This learned persona is informed by what has proven to be effective therapeutic practice garnered over the last 100 years (ibid., p. 2009).

In the supervisory process the supervisee is seen as making the best possible presentation of the *analytic third* to the supervisor. We are working with the supervisee's perceptions of what is happening in the analytic process. The best *prima materia* for supervision is actually the therapist's self-presentation to give the freest expression of the unconscious. This is best done without notes so that verbatim reports are not privileged over free discussion of the material. The supervisor engages the supervises presentation in a state of mind similar to the one described in the analytic situation—open to reverie and associative dreams which are thought to be reactive to and provocative of the clinical material. A parallel process is created in supervision. We can think of this as providing a *supervisory fourth* in the process as the supervisor presents his/her inner process. The fourth signifies a type of completion of the process by providing missing or blind spots. The supervisor can present more freely from the *about* side of the material as the supervisee is learning how the supervisor is operating in relation to the material.

Some potential *red flags* in working in a thirdness model in supervision is that the supervisor's reveries and associative dreams begin to carry much more weight than the supervisee's. Balint (1948) warned:

> the control analyst is a real person with strong convictions, theoretical likes and dis-likes, preoccupations, and personal limitations. He is not bound by the analytical situation, he can—and often does—represent his views and convictions, with all his weight; moreover, the candidate has a much weaker stand in this situation, he has not the privilege of using his free associations—his strongest defence—any more, he is taught and controlled or ' supervized ' not analysed.
>
> (p. 171)

In supervision and control we are ultimately working to help the supervisee find his/her own personal stance in relation to what arises in the analytic situation. Benjamin (2017) emphasized, "As a supervisor, I often find myself helping the analyst create a space in which it is possible to accept the inevitability of causing or suffering pain, being 'bad', without destroying the Third" (p. 38).

This way of working highlights exactly where the complexes of both patient and therapist dovetail in a hand-in-glove manner—this is the place of mutual transformation. Personal material of the supervisee is necessarily evoked and needs to be brought into the supervisory vessel to be understood. The boundary between analysis and supervision becomes blurred.

It is important to remember that following our notion that both members in the analytic encounter are changed in and by the process, mutual transformation, that a similar parallel process occurs in the supervisory situation. Solomon (2004) said:

> I wish to put forward the view that the provision of ongoing supervision, a *third* area of the analytic discourse, offers the possibility that both patient and analyst are helped to emerge from out of the *masa confusa* of the analytic dyad and that, following Jung's dictum, both are helped to change individuation progresses.
>
> (p. 59)

A word on evaluation is necessary as all institutes require evaluative reports from supervisors. This is a "necessary evil" as I would prefer that supervision be safeguarded by legal confidentiality as in analysis itself as this would allow for a strong container. I encourage evaluations be done through first seeking a self-report from the candidate, followed by the supervisor's reaction to the self-report with the ability to add to it if important material and dynamics are missing. This way the evaluation itself is co-created. The candidate remains more in control of what material is released to committees. I have found using this method over decades that the candidates provide excellent and honest reports often saying much more than I ever would. In this manner both members emerge as agents of the evaluation.

Case Groups and Colloquium

As we extend a *thirdness* model into clinical work performed in and with groups, we first need to note how Jung's negative evaluation of groups and group process has influenced analytical psychology.

> A group experience takes place on a lower level of consciousness than the experience of an individual. This is due to the fact that, when many people gather together to share one common emotion, the total psyche emerging from the group is below the level of the individual psyche. If it is a very large group, the collective psyche will be more like the psyche of an

animal, which is the reason why the ethical attitude of large organizations is always doubtful. The psychology of large crowd inevitably sinks to the level of mob psychology.

(Jung 1939, para. 225)

But Jung also said, "For in a group we see operating all those psychic events which are never constellated by an individual, or may even be unintentionally suppressed" (Jung 1959, para. 889). Following this notion, I would encourage analysts facilitating group work in case groups and colloquia, to use the resources of having a number of psyches in the group to process the clinical material. This opens up the work to *thirdness* and allows for a pool of reveries and associative dreams to be created from which the presenting candidate can draw from in the presentation of the clinical material.

Following similar guidelines of the last section regarding supervision, the candidate speaks freely from memory rather than read the case. Each individual in the group then seeks their own reveries and associative dreams by entering into a slightly altered-stated and "inviting" this type of material rather than just staying "focused" on the presentation itself. As inner material is collected you interact with it as one might in an active imagination—how might it reflect something of the interactive field, what might it be "saying"? The facilitator's role is to halt the presentation when appropriate—when some inner disruption of consciousness occurs, when a reverie becomes prominent and insistent. A collection of the associative dreams of the participants happens encouraging the use of "I" statements by participants rather than focusing on the presenter. The presenter is then free to respond to the material produced by the group. The presentation proceeds—often changing course by what has been elicited in group. I have found that within a few of these breaks in presentation the presenter ends up in a place where his/her own complexes dovetail with those of the patient—the place of mutual transformation. The presenter is allowed freedom to go into personal material if they so wish— they are in control of how much to reveal.

I think it important that the facilitator also contributes his/her own reveries and associative dreams so as to allow the group to see his/her inner process. This also reveals and promotes the learning of the supervisory process. The facilitator may work with the presenter more one-on-one, especially towards the end of the session to sum up the group's content and process.

Red flags in this process are when the group either moves toward the material and presenter or when it backs away. The excessive movement towards the material is often called "feeding frenzy" when there is a critical response either to the person of the presenter or it is overly erotic or aggressive in nature. The facilitator needs to make a process comment and then attempt to unpack what happened. Another *red flag* is when the facilitator's reveries and associative dreams are clearly being given preference by the presenter or group. This is the biggest danger of having the facilitator also be a participant.

This way of working allows the presenter an affective deepening of the work, development of the professional-self (Cwik 2006), containment, mirroring, and, most importantly, illuminating his/her blind spots, since the wealth of associations of the group brings forward missed affect and dynamics. It also allows for further development of the group itself as members witness one another's associations and inner process. The idea is that a parallel process with the patient's material is created in the group and this process provides a group supervisory *fourth* to the *third* being presented.

Monitoring and Exam Committees

Any process that entails evaluation and a determination as to whether one can progress in training is asymmetrical by definition—the evaluators have the power. Most processes in training go relatively well as both trainers and candidates have the best intentions and try to approach things in a conscious and attuned manner. But when they go badly, they tend to go very badly. From a *thirdness* model it is the unique grouping that must be held responsible. I recall a candidate discussing that a member of a monitoring committee made the comment in the heat of a conflict, "I sense that there is a hungry baby in the room". Actually, this is a field comment, or reverie, but taken at face value it becomes a demeaning and infantilizing evaluative comment without its complementary side in the *third* of, "So we must not be feeding or providing very well".

Clear benchmarks are absolutely necessary. Tuckett (2005) noted that, "The personal nature of the work and the use of implicit rather than explicit criteria are also likely to create a tendency to reach judgments on character rather than demonstrated competence' (p. 34). Candidates can be criticized for asking for clarity when negative evaluations are made. For me, training should not be in the business of evaluating character and/or individuation but competency as noted by Tuckett (ibid.). Candidates should be free to discuss personal issues using their own judgement and the role of the committee should be one of helpful containment rather than judgment in how they are handling issues.

Here, as noted earlier, I encourage the use of self-evaluation by the candidate and reaction of the committee so that both emerge as agents of evaluation. Co-creating evaluations is and should be the hallmark of a training centered in *thirdness* principles. This approach is particularly important when questions about cases and whether they are analytic or not, and when (whether?) a candidate is ready to take final exams.

Red flags come into play when an analyst on an evaluative committee has strong negative, or possibly even strong positive, reactions but cannot articulate exactly why. As Jungian practitioners we all seek to have an operational ego/Self axis in order to make important decisions, but when these reactions become characterized as "the voice of God" (Jung 1958, para. 856) one should become weary—there is no infallibility in the ego/Self axis.

Any key evaluation that forecloses on a candidate's progress towards graduation without first engaging that individual has to be a *red flag*. Consensus is a bit of a *red flag* because it reduces the encounter to the lowest possible common denominator—that is not *thirdness*. A better approach would be to include a "minority report", meaning that questionable material or opinions be included in the report as a concern. In this manner the candidate can be aware of concerns rather than neutralizing them as consensus. We might think that unanimous decisions, either negative or positive, might be a *red flag*, as candidates though already well-trained, can neither be totally off-base nor perfect. Sometimes the *third* needs not to be just an attitude but may manifest in actually assigning someone to be a *third* in the process (Solomon 2004). The appointment of an observer by the training committee during committee meetings with a candidate may provide a literal *third* in the process—we all tend to be on better behavior when someone else is watching.

Conclusion

This chapter advocates the implementation of a "training attitude" that emphasizes a *thirdness* approach. What particularly allows if not demands this is that trainees are not neophytes to the therapeutic endeavor and are clinicians in their own right dedicated to their patients. Analytical psychology takes into account the mind, body, and soul of the patient, and that should also be the case with the trainee. But Astor (1991) reminded us that, "The soul cannot be taught in training" (p. 190). Slavin (2007) powerfully reminded us:

> It is not that the analyst possesses some 'healthier' version of psychic capacity that enables this process, but rather the analyst's larger purpose of accomplishing the patient's task through the use of her knowledge, training, and skill that unites with the patient's purpose of changing her life ... Psychoanalytic education and training also needs to be anchored in a larger, *third* space than simply the propagation of its own views to the already initiated.
>
> (p. 607)

We trainers—training analysts, colloquium facilitators, supervisors, and committee members—must keep in mind that we do not possess a necessarily healthier or superior view of what makes a good analyst. We should be striving for our training process to be generative and able to produce "good enough" analysts. Our training attitude should be one of reasonable devotion to and acceptance of *thirdness* principles. A view towards *thirdness* will not produce some sought after utopia in training. In his book, Impossible

Training, Berman (2004) takes to task utopian visions of producing "a new person", considering it part of rescue fantasies in general. Adherence to *thirdness* principles may be necessary, but not sufficient, in creating independently thinking and acting analysts. There will always be conflict.

The role of training should be to enhance and foster candidate initiative, not squash it, in order to produce analysts conforming to some creed. Kernberg (1996) in, "Thirty methods to destroy the creativity of psychoanalytic candidates", reminded us how easily this initiative can be shut down—from shaming candidates who question noted theorists, adding more and more requirements for graduation, implying that one's own institution is somehow better than other analytic places of learning, assigning a large number of readings that candidates cannot possibly keep up with, and that critical or rebellious candidates are subtly held back. Ghent (1989) suggested that all analysts should be able to express their own "credo" on just what they think and feel that analysis is all about. We might ask candidates in preparation for graduation to articulate their own credo (*not to evaluate it*, but to encourage thoughtfulness).

Perhaps we all need to pledge a type of "allegiance" if we are to accept the responsibilities of training (Berman 2013).

- A strong and reasonable commitment to the principles of *thirdness* and attempting to stay conscious when we inevitably fall short—be aware of *red flags*!
- Allow for innovation and democratization of the analytic educational process. Training will always be asymmetrical in its hierarchal organization, but that should not preclude an attempt to be egalitarian and democratic in our process.
- We should strive not only to teach but also encourage engagement with other depth psychological approaches. From Jung's earliest attempts with typology, analytical psychology has always sought to be inclusive of other perspectives and to understand how and where they might fit into a larger wholeness perspective.
- And, particularly as we have more Developing Groups across the world, we must be aware of diversity and cultural issues. This is no small matter. With increasing exposure to different cultures, we are becoming more aware just how ethnocentric our theories are. We need to acknowledge cultural, racial, gender, and national differences.

References

Astor, J 1991, Supervision, training, and the institution as an internal pressure, *Journal of Analytical Psychology*, *36*(2), 177–191.

Balint, M 1948, On the psycho-analytic training system, *International Journal of Psycho-Analysis*, *29*, 163–173.

Benjamin, J 2004, Beyond doer and the being done to: An intersubjective view of thirdness, *The Psychoanalytic Quarterly*, *73*(1), 5–46.

Benjamin, J 2017, *Beyond doer and done to: Recognition theory, intersubjectivity and the third*, Oxfordshire, United Kingdom: Taylor & Francis.

Berman, E 2013, *Impossible training: A relational view of psychoanalytic education*, London: Routledge.

Cambray, J 2001, Enactments and amplification, *Journal of Analytical Psychology*, *46*, 275–303.

Cwik, A J 1991, Active imagination as imaginal play-space, in N Schwartz-Salant and M Stein (Eds.), *Liminality and transitional phenomena*, Wilmette, Illinois: Chiron Publications.

Cwik, A J 1995, Active imagination: Synthesis in analysis, in M Stein (Ed.), *Jungian Analysis* (Vol. 2nd, pp. 137–169), Chicago: Open Court.

Cwik, A J 2006a, Rosarium revisited, *Spring*, *74*, 189–232.

Cwik, A J 2006b, The art of the tincture: Analytical supervision, *Journal of Analytical Psychology*, *51*(2), 209–225.

Cwik, A J 2010, From frame through holding to container, in M Stein (Ed.), *Jungian Psychoanalysis: Working in the spirit of C. G. Jung*, Chicago: Open Court.

Cwik, A J 2011, Associative dreaming: Reverie and active imagination, *Journal of Analytical Psychology*, *156*, 14–36.

Cwik, A J 2017, What is a Jungian analyst dreaming when myth comes to mind? Thirdness as an aspect of the anima media natura, *Journal of Analytical Psychology*, *62*(1), 107–129.

Gentile J 2001, Close but no cigar: The perversion of agency and the absence of thirdness, *Contemporary Psychoanalysis*, *37*(4), 623–654.

Ghent, E 1989, Credo: The dialectics of one-person and two-person psychologies, *Contemporary Psychoanalysis*, *25*(2), 169–211.

Jung, C G 1916/1960, *The transcendent function, CW 8*, Princeton, NJ: Princeton University Press.

Jung, C G 1939, *Concerning rebirth, CW 9i*, Princeton, NJ: Princeton University Press.

Jung, C G 1946, *The psychology of the transference, CW 16*, Princeton, NJ: Princeton University Press.

Jung, C G 1958, *A psychological view of conscience, CW 10*, Princeton, NJ: Princeton University Press.

Jung, C G 1959, *Introduction to Toni Wolff's 'Studies in Jungian psychology'*, *CW 10*, Princeton, NJ: Princeton University Press.

Kernberg, O 1996, Thirty methods to destroy the creativity of psychoanalytic candidates, *International Journal of Psycho-Analysis*, *77*, 1031–1040.

Kernberg, O 2006, Perspectives on psychoanalysis: Impossible training: A relational view of psychoanalytic education by Emanuel Berman, *Journal of the American Psychoanalytic Association*, *54* (1), 281–286.

Maroda, K J 1998, Enactment: When the patient's and the analyst's pasts converge, *Psychoanalytic Psychology*, *15*(4), 517–535.

Ogden, T H 1994, The analytic third: Working with intersubjective clinical facts, *International Journal of Psycho-Analysis*, *75*, 3–19.

Ogden, T H 1997, Reverie and metaphor: Some thoughts on how I work as a psycho-analyst, *International Journal of Psycho-Analysis*, *78*, 719–732.

Ogden, T H 1999, The analytic third: An overview, Fort *Da*, *9*(1), 1–6.

Ogden, T H 2004, The analytic third: Implications for psychoanalytic theory and technique, *The Psychoanalytic Quarterly*, *73*(1), 167–195.

Ogden, T H 2005, *This art of psychoanalysis: Dreaming undreamt dreams and interrupted cries*, London: Routledge.

Slavin, J H 2007, Psychoanalytic training: The absence of thirdness: A review of impossible training: A relational view of psychoanalytic education by Emanuel Berman, *Psychoanalytic Dialogues*, *17*(4), 595–609.

Solomon, H 2004, The ethical attitude in analytic training and practice, in J Cambray and L Carter (Eds.), *Analytical psychology: Contemporary perspectives in Jungian analysis*, London: Brunner-Routledge.

Stark, M 2006, Transformation of relentless hope: A relational approach to sado-masochism, https://aps-tn.wildapricot.org/resources/Documents/Martha Stark-Relentless Hope for APS.pdf.

Tuckett, D 2005, Does anything go? Towards a framework for the more transparent assessment of psychoanalytic competence, *The International Journal of Psychoanalysis*, *86*(1), 31–49.

Chapter 11

How Can the IAAP Router Training Foster the Development of Core Competencies in Future Members of the IAAP?

Misser Berg

Introduction

Many of the training institutions in the Jungian community in the 20th century initially originated from an outstanding Jungian who developed their theoretical notions from Jung's original theories (e.g., Von Franz, Fordham, Neumann, Hillman). These pioneers, who were usually situated in one of the big cities in Western Europe and North America, then founded one of the Schools of Analytical Psychology, be it Classical, Developmental, or Archetypal (Samuels 1985). In contrast to this, the IAAP Router Training was created by the IAAP Administration to fulfil the need of providing training for people often living in remote places without a registered training program to become a Jungian analyst with membership of the IAAP. Since the late 1990s when this process began, a steadily growing number of interested professionals have applied to obtain Individual Membership of the IAAP. The applicants' diversity in terms of culture and professional background, etc. have, in combination with the diverse background of the analysts involved, given rise to some specific challenges in the creation of the Router Training Program regarding fostering the development of core competencies in future members of the IAAP coming from this training.

The first steps towards today's Router Training Program were taken in Eastern Europe during the 1980s and the term 'Developing Group' (DG) was put in place at the end of the 1990s. At the beginning, the primary aim of the DGs was to support an interest in areas where there were no IAAP Group Members, following one of the constitutional aims of the IAAP: "to promote the study of Analytical Psychology" (Art. 5.1) and "to disseminate knowledge of Analytical Psychology" (Art. 5.2). Several persons graduated as Individual Members of the IAAP during this period after having met the requirements for Individual Membership as specified in the IAAP Constitution (Art. 6.3[1], Art. 7.2.c[2] and Art. 7.5, 2013).[3]

The term 'Router' was first used at the beginning of the 2000s, and from then on Router Training was systematized, operationalized, and in 2011 the Education Committee was established as a standing committee, with the aim

DOI: 10.4324/9781003219910-16

to maintain a coherent organizational environment containing the Developing Groups, Routers in training, as well as qualified Individual Members, by providing a coherent and well-thought-out program of teaching, clinical supervision, and personal analysis through the Router Program, underpinned by a thought-through budget (Berg 2017).

The Background of the Applicants for the Router Training

The applicants accepted into the IAAP Router Training Program come, as mentioned, from various backgrounds. Some are psychologists or psychiatrists, some are psychotherapists, and others have non-clinical backgrounds. In addition to the geographic requirement of the applicant living "in a region of the world or a country where there is no IAAP Group Member with Training Status" (RH 2021, p. 5), they must all meet the following criteria for academic qualifications:

Academic Qualifications

> The IAAP requires applicants to become routers to demonstrate that they meet all legal requirements for the clinical practice of psychotherapy in the country in which they live. Clinical experience and a clinical academic degree at a graduate or post-graduate level are the general rule, although there may be exceptions. The Education Committee, in consultation with the Executive Committee, will have the right to grant exceptions.
>
> (ibid., p. 5)

With this variety among the applicants, it is necessary to secure that the basic psychotherapeutic core competencies are met in the Router Training Program. I will come back to this later.

The Background of the Analysts Involved in the Router Training

Over the years, the training has been managed by analysts coming from all over the world with their unique background, often more or less clearly founded in one of the Schools of Analytical Psychology. This means that some of the analysts working in the Router Training come from a training program where the first years up to the intermediate exam are primarily theoretical and where supervised analytical casework with clients starts after these first theoretical years. In contrast to this, other training programs start immediately with the main focus on clinical seminars. Because of the wide variance in the analytic training of the analysts involved in the Router Training Program, it is important to clearly describe the expectations of their work as personal analysts, supervisors, teachers, and/or examiners.

The Specific Challenges for Analysts Working in Different Cultural Settings

Catherine Crowther and Jan Wiener, who were among the first analysts to travel abroad and start a training program for routers in Russia, describe how outreach experiences resulted "in the development of some unique, innovative, and tailor-made training programs in other countries" (Crowther & Wiener 2015, p. xxiii).

The traditional models of training in a Western culture proved to be somewhat limited in meeting the needs of persons interested in Jungian training in remote places in different parts of the world. Examples of the challenges involved in offering this kind of training possibility include the endurance of long flights across different time zones for analysts, supervisors, teachers, and examiners alike; offering multiple hours of analysis to some and supervision to others and then supplementing this with online analysis and supervision between in vivo sessions, and in many cases working with an interpreter when teaching, analysing, supervising, or examining. Added to this is the requirement of working for a local fee, which in most cases means a remarkably reduced fee. These are but some of the concrete challenges for analysts taking part in the Router Training Program. In addition, work in this program requires a heightened sensitivity to cultural differences and values when it comes to cultural identity, cultural complexes, and collective traumas, which need to be respected as an important basis for both theory and practice. Furthermore, awareness of and sensitivity to different mores and practices in the analytic setting are required when it comes to issues related to boundaries and frames such as time, money, confidentiality, and holidays (ibid., p. 279).

Crowther and Wiener state how this work:

> can lead to challenging but fascinating tensions between tried and tested frameworks for learning on the one hand and, on the other, some more inventive and adapted approaches in which the trainers have responded to the specific cultural values, social history, and individual wishes of professionals in each region.
>
> (ibid., p. xxiii)

In her article "The Delivery of Training", another central and significant person in Router Training over the years, Angela Connolly,[4] stresses both the challenges and the fruitful enrichment of having introduced and worked in the Router Training Program:

Adapting our models to different cultural contexts has therefore required considerable effort, much flexibility and patience, and no little capacity to become aware of our own preconceptions and to invent new strategies to resolve unexpected problems. Nevertheless, these experiences have been both enriching and thought-provoking, and, for me, they have been a fruitful source of stimuli for a potential revision of our own more traditional training models.

(ibid., p. 180)

General Requirements for the Router Training

Following the aforementioned diversity in both applicants and involved analysts working in a local culture that is unique and often unfamiliar, it has been important to allow for a broad perspective in the Router Training. This ensures that, in addition to the basic psychotherapeutic core competencies, the specific Jungian core competencies proffered in each of the different Schools of Analytical Psychology are covered and understood, all the while being cognizant of and respectful of the specific cultural influence where the training takes place.

Basic Psychotherapeutic Core Competencies

With the aforementioned described variety among the applicants where some of them do not have a clinical background, it is necessary to ensure that the basic psychotherapeutic core competencies are met in the Router Training Program. Basic psychotherapeutic core competencies are well described by The European Association of Psychotherapy in a comprehensive 32-page document (EAP 2013). Below I briefly mention some of the core competencies important for Jungians:

- Acting according to accepted professional standards (§1.1.3).
- Securing safe boundaries (§1.2) incl. making clear arrangements (§1.2.3).
- Maintaining appropriate Continuing Professional Development (CPD) (§1.4.1).
- Maintaining Personal Development (§1.5).
- Establishing, maintaining, and ending a Psychotherapeutic Relationship (§2.1, 2.2, 2.3, 2.4).
- Taking regular supervision (§9.1).
- Working within an ethical framework (§10.1) and being aware of cultural and social differences (§10.2.1).
- Being aware of and making use of psychotherapy research (§12.1).

Jungian Core Competencies

As written in the introduction to this publication, "most Jungian analysts would recognize the establishment of a living relationship with the unconscious as a core competence and that each training program in analytical psychology focuses on the development of that competence in their own unique way". The variety of articles in this publication shows a broad and diverse understanding of how this is interpreted in any specific training program and by a specific analyst. For some Jungian analysts, the living relationship with the unconscious will be established via the meeting with and interpretation of inner or outer symbols, for others it will be the relational aspects between two persons that pave the way. For some Jungian analysts, the theoretical foundation is the most crucial basis for the analytical profession, while for others it is the clinical experience and understanding that serves as the foundation for the analytical work.

Despite all these differences however, there is a general understanding that a Jungian analyst is an academically educated person who has a solid knowledge of psychological theories as well as a highly developed understanding of symbolic material as it manifests itself in dreams, art, myths, and fairy tales. A Jungian analyst is also a person who through his/her own personal analysis and clinical work with patients has experienced how deep processes in an analysis can lead to personal transformations.

Analytic Talent

In a paper presented at an international conference in Sao Paulo 2021, Jan Wiener, one of the founders of the Router Training Program,[5] described six different but related capacities involved in developing an analytic attitude which, in fact, is an excellent description of some of the important Jungian core competencies:

"a) The capacity for empathy and intuition,
b) The capacity to understand unconscious processes at different levels including the emergence of symbols and the role of dreams,
c) An openness to authentic relationship,
d) The capacity to receive and process countertransference experiences that I view as an aspect of a capacity to be imaginative,
e) The capacity to bear uncertainty and 'not-knowing',
f) Knowing when to hold back and when to move forward" (Wiener 2021).

More than two decades earlier, at the IAAP Congress in Florence in 1998, Adolf Guggenbühl-Craig (1999) presented his view on the necessary basic talent in a Jungian analyst. He wrote: "In the talent to be a good Jungian analyst we are confronted with three dominating archetypes:

1. The Healer. 'When the archetype of the healer is powerful in the analyst, the healer in the patient is constellated'.
2. The Shaman, who is 'able to leave the body, to enter and make contact with demons, with gods, with other dimensions of our human existence'.

For the analyst it is the capacity to put patients in touch with the unconscious, for example by working with dreams.
3.   The alchemist, which 'is usually described or shown in the ability to sym-
bolize, to understand symbols'" (pp. 408–410).

Almost 30 years before the Florence Congress, Guggenbühl-Craig (1971)
wrote: "we choose our profession in order to be able to heal" (pp. 87–88).
But if we split the wounded healer archetype into a wounded, ill patient and
a healthy, healing analyst, the analyst is cut off from his or her inner wound,
and the patient is cut off from his or her healing capacity, and thus the psychic
process becomes blocked.

If, on the contrary, the analyst through the countertransference can recognize his or her own wounds and feel empathy with the patient without identifying with him or her, the patient may get in touch with his own inner healer.
The process can end with an experience of the bipolar archetypal image of the
wounded healer – not separate images of illness and health. (ibid., pp. 92–93).

Both Wiener and Guggenbühl-Craig discuss what needs to be there from
the start and what can be learned. Guggelbühl-Craig (1999) compares the
Jungian analyst with a musician; "to be an excellent musician you must have
a basic musical talent. Then, of course, you can refine that talent by training.
But if somebody has no talent, all the training is lost" (p. 408).

Wiener also recognizes the importance of looking at what must be there
from the start and what can be learned. She writes:

> These capacities involve both the character and the competencies of the
> trainee. When we are required to evaluate our trainees, we need a frame-
> work to contain us when considering the developing relationship between
> character and competence as trainees develop. Such a frame promises to
> help protect us from overvaluing subjectivity and intuition by providing
> the possibility of more objective criteria for evaluation.
>
> (Wiener 2021)

Assessment of Applicants for the Router Training

Assessing applicants for the Router Training requires reflecting upon the suitability of the applicant for beginning Router Training to become a Jungian
Analyst. In other words, does the applicant have a talent, a musicality, a suitable character? Will the applicant be able to develop the necessary competence to become a 'good-enough' Jungian analyst?

The Screening Interview

The first step for the applicant is to pass the screening interview which,
according to the assessment criteria as described in the Router Handbook:

should show whether the applicant possesses good mental abilities, a creative mind, and the capacity for self-reflection. It is necessary for applicants to have a lively interest in people and the motives for their attitudes and behaviour. Further requirements are the capacity for empathy, the relation to the unconscious, personally and professionally, and the aptitude for understanding the symbolic dimension, individually as well as collectively in both cultural and historical perspectives. Moreover, personal integrity and a high ethical standard in applicants are of great importance. Reflections on what the applicant sees as his or her strengths and weaknesses as well as the capacity to bear uncertainty, for holding and containment will be relevant to assess. As routers work in groups it will also be relevant to ask about the applicant's experiences from working in groups.

(RH 2021, p. 9)

Three Pillars: Analysis, Theory, and Supervision

All Jungian training programs worldwide, and thus also the Router Training, base their training on three pillars: Analysis, Theory, and Supervision. But as mentioned earlier, the content, practice, and requirements have great variations. In the following, I will describe each of these pillars with regard to the Router Training.

Analysis

"In all training programs, personal analysis of the candidate is recognized as pivotal to the development of the individual as a person and, especially, as an analyst" (Kelly 2007, p. 161). Personal analysis is an inevitable requirement for all Jungian analysts with membership of the IAAP, and the Router Training Program follows the requirement from the IAAP Constitution of 240 hours of personal analysis. In addition, a router is required to be in continuous analysis throughout his/her training. As in all training programs, because of the future profession as Jungian analyst, it is of great importance that the router gains insight into personal complexes as well as how personal life experiences can influence one's work as analyst. This opens up a:

> fundamental and inherent paradox. While on the one hand we go to great lengths to protect the analytic container in the spirit of fostering the individuation process, on the other we establish norms, standards, expectations, and evaluations in the form of admission interviews, review committees, consultation evaluations and, last but not least, exams.

(ibid., p. 161)

Because of the frequent geographical challenges, both shuttle and online analysis need to be permitted. It is, however, recommended that:

> personal analysis should be conducted in person, face-to-face whenever possible. Personal analysis can be done via Skype, Zoom, or other means of telecommunication preferably with video, in cases where face-to-face meetings are not possible. (There are no upper limits on either face-to-face hours or hours via Skype).
>
> (RH 2021, p. 6)

This means that analysts who want to be personal analysts for routers in training in many cases must be willing to do either shuttle or online analysis. Several factors (e.g., research, improvements in online media, the recent pandemic) have led to a gradual shift towards more online analysis. In 2016, the Research and Evaluation Working Group,[6] chaired by John Merchant, published a review of the use of online media in analysis and training (Merchant 2016). In his conclusion, Merchant writes:

> it would seem possible to argue that a genuine analytic process is not precluded by Skype for the following reasons: Physical proximity of the participants is not necessary because there is a cross-modal communication between the human senses (underpinned by audiovisual mirror neurons), in addition to the instinct for communication and interpersonal understanding. All these can be activated with Skype. Consequently, there is ample and accruing evidence that transference, unconscious communication, countertransference (even of a somatic nature) and synchronicities can occur with Skype.
>
> (ibid., pp. 321–322)

Competencies Fostered Through Personal Analysis

Besides the obvious benefits of learning by doing, Dyane Sherwood (2010) highlights that personal analysis is:

> essential for the future analyst to find a unique personal identity and way of working analytically, a healthy and realistic relationship to the Jungian community, and an ongoing commitment to self-examination and consultation when facing the many challenges in an analytic practice.
>
> (p. 378)

Theory

As already mentioned, an academic degree and successful completion of an analytic training are necessary preconditions for obtaining membership of the IAAP.

A comprehensive Analytic Training Syllabus and an IAAP Reading Resources list, created and maintained by the IAAP Curriculum Working Group, is placed in the IAAP Curriculum Working Group Dropbox archive, which is accessible for all routers as well as for the organizers of the Router Training. A summary of the content is placed in the Router Handbook with the following introduction:

> The lists in the Syllabus as well as the Reading List summarise the various theoretical contributions, both classical as well as contemporary reading within the Jungian field … It is expected that routers have made themselves familiar with both classical and contemporary readings from each module. It is likewise expected that routers generally have read the specified titles by Jung.
>
> The specific readings will be culturally dependent. Basic articles on various subjects in one region will be slightly different from those in another region. But it is important to avoid one-sidedness. Therefore, both classical and contemporary readings as well as a basic knowledge of material from the three schools of Analytical Psychology must be studied.
>
> (RH 2021, p. 34)

Core Competencies Required by the Theoretical Readings

One competence is, of course, to remain informed of the continuous development in the theoretical foundation of our practice. Research and development have dramatically expanded the theories of our profession over time. Although it is not expected that each analyst contributes new ideas within the Jungian theoretical field, we indeed need to be cognizant of and articulate about both the classical perspective as well as more recent and novel developments in order to be able to work as professional Jungian analysts in our modern world.

Assessment of Theoretical Knowledge

During the Router Training there are two exams assessed by the IAAP: the Intermediate and Final Exam. In both exams the router must demonstrate his/ her theoretical knowledge as well as the ability to apply this knowledge to clinical material. Both exams are based on a submitted paper and an oral presentation. Both exam papers must contain relevant theoretical references. The examiners are two experienced Jungian analysts, who will base their assessment on the paper as well as on the oral presentation. The Router Handbook contains guidelines for writing and assessing the exam papers. The following is a résumé of the guidelines for each exam:

Guidelines for writing and assessing the Intermediate Exam paper:

The Intermediate Exam paper (of around 5000 words) should demonstrate the router's theoretical understanding of the common Jungian concepts as well as the ability to apply this understanding to clinical and symbolic material. Examiners are encouraged to explore and evaluate the router's knowledge and grasp of basic Jungian principles and must assess whether the router has not only a classical but also a contemporary understanding of the subject he/she has decided to write about. The paper should contain a shorter case presentation or shorter case-vignettes as well as examples from daily life. Here, the ability to apply the theory to the clinical / practical field is important.

The examiners should during the examination look for the router's general Jungian understanding of personality and psychopathology incl. subjects such as complexes, defence mechanisms, individuation etc., as well as the understanding of psychological processes in the clinic incl. understanding of transference and countertransference, of interpretation of symbolic material etc.

(RH 2021, p. 26)

Guidelines for writing and assessing the Final Exam paper:

The Final Exam paper must be in the form of a case report (between 15,000 and 20,000 words) based on an analytic case which has been under supervision with an IAAP analyst for at least two years, showing the router's grasp and understanding of the analytic process as it has evolved over time. The router is expected to apply theory to practice and to show the integration of the principles of Jungian psychology in the clinical work. In addition, the router should demonstrate the knowledge of the classical as well as contemporary understanding of theory and practice. Although the router may be inspired by and follow one of the Analytical Psychological Schools (Classical, Developmental, Archetypal), he or she is expected to have a basic knowledge of all schools as well as of newer theories.

It is also expected that the router is aware of, and can work with, the interpersonal dynamics as well as intrapsychic dynamics in the clinical work. The router should demonstrate an understanding of a range of analytical approaches to the patient and be able to demonstrate a capability to think critically about theory, so the paper is not just a restatement of what others have already said.

The paper should adhere to strict academic standards. References and footnotes should comply with the standards required for publication.

(RH 2021, pp. 28–29)

Clinical Supervision

In her article "Supervision of the Apprentice", Catherine Crowther (2010) describes how supervision:

> helps to gather in and make 'operational' in the consulting room all the accumulated life experience, theoretical knowledge, instinct, empathy, intuition, and authenticity of the novices in their encounters with their own and their patients' unconscious processes, as well as resonating with archetypal collective images with each individual patient.
>
> (p. 387)

Supervision of routers implies multiple responsibilities for the supervisor. In her article "Reflections on the Therapist-Supervisor Relationship", Barbara Wharton (2003) writes that the supervisor in a training institute:

> has a responsibility to the trainee analyst to make knowledge and experience available, to facilitate learning, and also to contain anxiety. There is concern for the student's patient; that he shall have an adequate, good enough experience of analysis. The supervisor also endeavours to ensure that the work is properly bounded and ethically conducted.
>
> (p. 35)

Requirements for the Supervision

Routers are required to have a minimum of 100 hours of supervision with one or more senior IAAP analysts[7] and they are required to be in regular group and individual supervision[8] for as long as they are in the router program. As with personal analysis, supervision can be done via Skype or other means of telecommunications, but it is recommended that a proportion of the hours are done in face-to-face meetings, especially at the beginning of the supervision.

Core Competencies from Supervision

How does the supervisor facilitate the router's living relationship with the unconscious both in him/herself and in his/her patient?

A solid theoretical foundation and the ability to link theory to practice is paramount, as well as understanding the symbolic material coming from the router's patient and from the relationship. In addition, a grounded understanding of appropriate boundaries and an ethical sense are important factors.

Most beginners start to analyze their patients in the same way they themselves have been analyzed. It is the supervisor's task to help the candidate develop his/her own personal style as an analyst.

What really matters in the long run is whether he (the supervisee) can synthesize his personal knowledge and experience, gained during his life and analysis, with at least some of his reading and knowledge acquired from other sources during his training.

(Plaut 1982, p.107)

The Supervisors' Assessment of the Core Competencies of the Router

Once a year, supervisors are asked to complete an evaluation form, which provides the candidate with important feedback on his/her clinical work. The supervisor is asked to evaluate the candidate in the following areas:

- Theoretical Knowledge,
- Practical Technique,
- Understanding of Symbols/Symbolism,
- Understanding of Transference/Countertransference,
- Understanding and Appropriate Use of Boundaries,
- Ethical Attitude,
- Ability to Use Supervision,
- Willingness to Explore and Work on Areas of Deficit (RH 2021, pp. 22–23).

Supervisors are also invited to comment on areas of strength, resistance, avoidance, recent progress, or any other relevant areas.

In addition to being an important learning tool for the router, the supervisors' reports are also an integral part of the material for the evaluation of the intermediate and final exam.

Research and Evaluation

Continuing evaluation is a fundamental aspect of quality control of any training, and in addition to the Router Training Program's integrated assessments of the routers (screening interview, intermediate- and final exam, assessment of supervision and the router's self-assessment), a comprehensive evaluation of the training as a whole is managed by the Research & Evaluation Working Group. I have already mentioned the review on the use of Skype in analysis (Merchant 2016), which was the first project carried out by the Working Group. This study was followed by a comprehensive study of the general aspects of the Router Training (Kiehl and Klenck 2017, pp. 1487–1512), followed by a research project on Core Competencies by Gražina Gudaitė, whose results are included in this publication and who succeeded John Merchant as chair of the Working Group. The findings of these numerous studies have been presented at several Jungian conferences and congresses.

Concluding Remarks

Securing the quality of a training program spread over many parts of the world requires well-defined procedures and requirements as well as a coherent organizational structure. Extracts of the procedures and requirements for the Router Training have been mentioned in this article. Complete information on the router training and the organizational structure can be found in the Router Handbook.

The Router Training is organized in joint cooperation between the local Developing Groups and the IAAP Education Committee. The IAAP Executive Committee is the approving body, which also decides on an annual budget[9] for each Developing Group.

The organization and administration of the Router Training Program involve many persons, but:

> the final success of the router program depends essentially on the contributions made by a large number of IAAP analysts from many different Group Members who contribute to the Router Program whether as Liaison Persons, … visiting analysts or supervisors, teachers, or examiners as well as chairs and members of Working Groups. The IAAP owes an enormous debt to all these dedicated colleagues from around the world who have spent much time, often for very little money and often under conditions of considerable difficulty.
>
> (Berg 2019, p. 27)

It is through the extensive and dedicated commitment of countless experienced colleagues that the core competencies of the future members of the IAAP who have trained through the Router Training Program can be developed.

Notes

1 There are four categories of membership in the IAAP:
   1. Group Membership (without Training Status)
   2. Group Membership (with Training Status)
   3. Individual Membership
   4. Honorary Membership.
2 Individual Membership
   - Academic or equal qualifications, analytic training, professional status
   - History of all past or present membership in, or rejection by, any IAAP Group Member

- Acceptance of the IAAP Code of Ethics and of the jurisdiction of Association with respect to ethics for Individual Members
  - A finding that an applicant cannot reasonably be expected to become a member of a Group Member.
3 Analytic training is defined as at minimum: 240 hours of personal analysis and 100 hours of case consultation.
4 Angela Connolly, who sadly died in 2020 (https://iaap.org/announcements/obituar ies/angela-mary-connolly-1947-2020/), served, together with Jan Wiener, as co-chair of the Education Committee from 2010 to 2013 and with Misser Berg from 2013 to 2016.
5 In addition to being one of the founders of the Router Training in Russia in the 1990s, Jan Wiener was also involved in establishing the Education Committee and served, together with Angela Connolly as the first co-chair.
6 The IAAP Education Committee is assisted by two Working Groups: Curriculum Working Group and Research & Evaluation Working Group.
7 The supervisor must have at least five years post qualification (or three years and have completed the IAAP Supervision program) – see RH, p. 6.
8 At least 25 percent and not more than 50 percent of the supervision must be as group supervision. At least 50 hours of supervision must be individual. Two hours of group supervision count for one hour of supervision.
9 The budget may be spent on travel expenses, accommodation, interpreters' fees, books, and teaching aids, but not to pay fees to visiting analysts, teachers, supervisors, or secretaries.

References

Berg, M 2017, The IAAP Education Committee, *IAAP News Sheet*, Dec. 2017, No 12. https://iaap.org/news-sheet/

Berg, M 2019, Report from The Education Committee, *IAAP Newsletter*, 2019, Issue #32 https://iaap.org/triennial-newsletters/

Crowther, C 2010, Supervision of the apprentice, (Ed.) Stein, M, *Jungian Psychoanalysis, Working in the Spirit of C. G. Jung,* Chicago and La Salle, Illinois: Open Court.

Crowther, C, Wiener, J (eds.) 2015, *From Tradition to Innovation, Jungian Analysts Working in Different Cultural Settings*, New Orleans, LA: Spring Journal Inc.

EAP 2013, The Core Competencies of a European Psychotherapist (EAP AGM, Moscow, July 2013).

Guggenbühl-Craig, A 1971, *Power in the Helping Professions*, Dallas, TX: Spring Publications Inc.

Guggenbühl-Craig, A 1999, Destruction and creation: Personal and cultural trans-formations (Ed.) Ann Mattoon, Mary, *Proceedings of the Fourteenth International Congress for Analytical Psychology*, Einsiedeln, Switzerland: Daimon.

IAAP Constitution 2003, https://iaap.org, Members Section.

Kelly, T 2007, The making of an analyst: From 'ideal' to 'good-enough', *Journal of Analytical Psychology, 52,* 157–169.

Kiehl E, Klenck, M (Eds.) 2017, Anima *Mundi in Transition: Cultural, Clinical & Professional Challenges, Proceedings of the Twentieth Congress of the International Association for Analytical Psychology,* Einsiedeln, Switzerland: Daimon Verlag.

Merchant, J 2016, The use of Skype in analysis and training: A research and literature review, *Journal of Analytical Psychology, 61,* 3, 309–328.

Plaut, A 1982, Symposium: How do I assess progress in supervision? *Journal of Analytical Psychology*, 27, 105–130.

RH 2021, *The IAAP Router Handbook*, February 2021, iaap.org, Member's Section.

Samuels, A 1985, *Jung and the Post Jungians*, London and Boston: Routledge & Kegan Paul.

Sherwood, D 2010, Training analysis, (Ed.) Stein, M, *Jungian Psychoanalysis, Working in the Spirit of C. G. Jung.* Chicago and La Salle, Illinois: Open Court.

Wharton, B 2003, Reflections on the therapist-supervisor relationship, (Eds) Wiener, J, Mizen, R, Duckham, J, *Supervision and Being Supervised, A Practice in Search of a Theory,* London & New York: Palgrave Macmillan.

Wiener, J 2021, *Supervision as a Modern Discipline: A Practice Evolving a Theory*, Presentation at the Latin American JAP Conference, April 9–11, 2021.

Part V

Relatedness to Culture
in Analytical Practice

Chapter 12

Cultural Otherness

Implications for the Analytic Attitude

Tom Kelly and Jan Wiener

We both have an enduring and passionate interest in training and especially how models of training evolving in one culture may be helpfully used in other socially, politically, and culturally different areas where traditions may require somewhat different theoretical and clinical approaches to training and analysing patients. In our chapter, we will explore two complex and intricately connected aspects of our work as analysts: the analytic attitude, what it is, under what circumstances we might lose it, and also the influences that culture can bring to the analytic attitude.

Development of an Analytic Attitude: Personal Aspects

TK: A number of events led me to Zurich in the early 1980s, that in hindsight, I came to recognize as significant synchronistic events. One of these was reading Jung's *Memories, Dreams, Reflections* while working in Dakar, Senegal. The book had such a powerful impact on me that I decided, in good *puer* fashion and with no financial resources whatsoever, that when my contract there was completed, I would go to Zurich to train.

At the Institute in Zurich, there was a wealth of choice and a wide range of lectures and seminars offered; candidates in training were considered responsible adults and were therefore expected to see to it that they got what they needed in order to prepare for the *propedeuticum*, or theoretical exams. Analysis was usually twice weekly. In the second half of the programme, candidates were expected to work with at least two patients for a minimum of 80 hours each on a once or twice weekly basis. A total of 80 hours of supervision was required, though most candidates did much more. Final exams included a minimum of five case reports, a written thesis, a series of oral exams, including what is called the *clausure* exam.

The training culture in Zurich at that time emphasized that the royal road to the unconscious was the dream and its interpretation. I was fortunate to have an analyst who was also interested in working with

DOI: 10.4324/9781003219910-18

transference. I recall distinctly an experience early on in my analysis of talking about how I felt I was depressed and in a rather dark, inner place. To my surprise and, at the time, to my consternation, my analyst did not say a word and did not make any effort to intervene. I expected him to respond in some way, but he did not. Initially, I experienced a sense of disappointment and then a sense of anguish. Even though I felt disappointed and hurt, paradoxically, I felt that he had understood and that he was totally present with me at a feeling level. In my state of confusion, a little voice in me said, 'this is what you have been looking for'.

This was my first encounter with the essence of an analytic attitude that had emerged naturally within my personal analysis. I realized that I had to find my own answers, because these could only come from inside me and from the development of a firmer and more functional ego-self axis. This was a live learning experience of how to embrace the unknown as one important aspect of the analytic attitude.

Development of an Analytic Attitude: Personal Aspects

JW: The seeds of my analytic attitude were planted young when, as a child, I visited the Anna Freud Clinic in London with my aunt who worked there. Hearing from her about the War Nurseries where many children who lost parents during the Second World War were cared for made a profound impact on me as a second-generation survivor of the Holocaust whose parents and grandparents escaped Hitler's regime of persecution. The children were looked after in houses run by skilled care assistants and therapists, attentive to the painful losses these children had experienced. Many of these children had arrived in the UK on the *Kindertransport*, where their parents, aware of the Nazi regime's extermination of the Jews, decided to save their children's lives and send them out of the country to safety. From a young age, I absorbed unconsciously the effects of what today we would call early relational trauma, inter-generational complexes, separation, and its effects on adult life. These experiences marked the beginning of the development of my analytic attitude, including a painful awareness of the psyche's shadow qualities.

Through a positive identification with my aunt, it also set in motion the idea of training to become an analyst as a career. Recently, I discovered a letter received from the British Institute of Psychoanalysis in London in response to a letter I had sent to them aged just 22 expressing my interest to train with them. In their tactful reply to me, I was advised to go off and have some life experience first. My wish to explore the personal effects on me of these early experiences led me then – more sensibly – to find an analyst who happened to be Jungian. I have written elsewhere (Wiener 2018) about my unconscious journey towards becoming a Jungian analyst.

Later, I trained at the SAP and qualified in 1989. My training was culturally different to Tom's. At that time, the SAP had one training, a four-times weekly intensive training in adult analysis. When I trained, I was required to be in personal analysis four times a week throughout my training until qualification. I used the couch. I needed to see two training patients, each four times a week, each supervised by a different Training Analyst. The shape of the training followed the Eitingon tripartite model of personal analysis, seminars, and clinical supervision. This model takes for granted the need for evaluation of progress within the training. Personal analysis was, and still is, viewed as the foundation stone to training, together with clinical work under supervision. There was less of an academic emphasis during my training in London than in Zurich, and the only written work required of me was a clinical paper presented when I applied for SAP membership.

Perspectives on the Analytic Attitude

TK: While the training we have experienced influences the model we carry with us for training future candidates, the clinical experience accrued over time inevitably challenges us to change and to refine our clinical understanding and acumen. Interestingly, despite the different emphasis in our respective trainings, Jan and I have arrived at rather similar understandings of what we consider to be the essence of an analytic attitude. Our collaboration in writing this chapter has been influenced by our post-training experiences of working with Developing Groups and Router Groups in countries with different cultures that made us aware of the need for new training models, or at the very least some adaptation from those in our respective institutes.

What are the essential components of an analytic attitude? Generally, this comprises the establishment of a clear and safe frame/container/ or *vas bene clausum* (well-sealed vessel), including explicit conditions for the work, such as a clear statement on place and time of sessions, frequency, length of sessions, and payment for sessions including the form of payment (cash, check, direct bank deposits, or transfers).

At a deeper level, the analytic attitude is what sustains and influences how the analyst is during a session, his/her internal frame of reference or inner compass which allows the analyst to arrive at a depth understanding of the patient. This happens, not only through what is said verbally in the session but also through dream images and through what is evoked in the analyst on the affective, somatic, and imaginal level in the presence of that particular individual. How the analyst makes use of the patient's dreams and other unconscious manifestations such as synchronistic events, transference projections, and countertransference reactions to better understand the analysand, all contribute to define the analytic attitude.

Jung's famous 'gate diagram' (1946, para. 422) demonstrates well the complexity and multiple levels of communication taking place simultaneously in an analytic encounter.

In his book, *Interpretation in Jungian Analysis: Art and Technique*, Winborn (2019, p. 65) states eloquently:

> The analytic attitude places the encounter with the unconscious and the unknown at the core of the analytic process, over and above other concerns or considerations. It is reflected in the way the analyst listens, behaves, thinks, feels, and engages during the analytic process. The analytical attitude essentially comprises an ethical attitude adopted towards the analytic process itself.

Jung's instinctive understanding of the analytic attitude is reflected well in his advice about learning to work with dreams: 'Learn as much as you can about symbolism and forget it all when you are analysing a dream'. (Jung 1961, para. 483).

The ultimate paradox is that one of the primary goals of training is to help the candidate get to the point where they recognize the fact that, despite their solid grounding in theory and practice, they simply do not, indeed cannot, know where the process will lead. To be able to sit with a patient and accept what they do not know yet feel securely rooted in the belief that the knowing will reveal itself over time, is in my estimation, the test not only of a candidate's integrity, but also of their readiness to terminate training.

The analytic attitude represents the art of our work and how it is put into practice is of the essence. Just as a chef in his or her kitchen will use four simple ingredients such as eggs, flour, sugar, and butter to create a simple croissant or a spectacular cake, how each analyst will give form to their analytic attitude will be unique to that person and will depend on their approach to symbolic material, to transference projections and to countertransference manifestations.

Perspectives on the Analytic Attitude

JW: I agree with Tom's approach to the general character of the analytic attitude. Without an analytic attitude, it is difficult to imagine that candidates will be able to practise. To this extent, as Tom has outlined, the analytic attitude describes a state of mind or an approach to their work that many candidates find difficult to attain and for sure, it can take a long time to develop. Tom quotes Winborn's perspective on the analytic attitude. I found one from Lemma, Roth, and Pilling (2010, p. 16): 'the receptiveness to the client's unconscious communications and to the unfolding of the transference'.

As a Jungian trained in a London tradition where there is a strong emphasis on the role of transference as one significant royal road to the unconscious, this definition produced by psychoanalysts sits comfortably with me. But in other Jungian societies, it may not hit the spot and for sure, on its own, it seems to me to be insufficient as a definition.

I recall a conference in 2007 on training where both Tom and I presented papers. I (Wiener 2007) presented a paper called 'Character or competence: evaluating progress in training'. Tom's paper at the same conference (Kelly 2007) was called 'The making of an analyst: from ideal to good enough'.

In both our papers, we explored the analytic attitude in terms of a relationship between what I call *character*, how we as teachers, supervisors and personal analysts can help trainees to develop their particular talents through a process of self-discovery, where they gradually find their own style and become the analysts they can be. Alongside this, to protect the public we need to ensure that candidates achieve certain *competencies* during their training. These two aims of personal development/self-awareness and the achievement of comptencies do not necessarily sit well alongside each other. As Kelly highlights (2007, p. 161):

> the paradox of fostering self-knowledge and development, 'know thyself' and establishing minimal standards of accomplishment creates an inherent tension, that we as training analysts, have to own and carry as part of our responsibility in training.

We are talking now about the vision each of us has about the essence of becoming a Jungian analyst. This may vary personally, institutionally and between cultures but for sure, the dimension of character is of the essence.

Is an analytic attitude best fostered through a teacher-centred training or a more candidate-centred training? Parsons (2014, p. 228), a London-based psychoanalyst, puts his cards on the table: 'what matters is to promote not just the acquisition of knowledge but the development of a candidate's internal autonomy'.

Parsons (ibid., p. 205), contrasts a view of the analytic attitude, what he calls 'a development in one's identity', with an approach that is more a matter of learning 'a particular conceptual framework, and to carry out a particular kind of practice'.

He (ibid., p. 205) makes a profound point that made me sit up and think about my approach to working with my own patients in analysis, my role as Director of Training at the SAP, as well as teaching and supervising abroad: 'you cannot teach a child to grow up, and you cannot teach someone to be a psychoanalyst: it is a question of helping them to become one'.

How then can we help our trainees to become Jungian analysts, and might this vary in Jungian institutes where cultural complexes have local as well as personal significance? For Parsons, the developmental aspects of becoming an analyst are more important than didactic teaching.

I was reminded when working on this chapter with Tom, that Jung made it clear that he did not want to create a profession of Jungians. Perhaps we were not listening or maybe we simply could not hear what he said, since Jungian theories and indeed Jung's ways of practising continue to be taught and practiced today, sometimes dogmatically sticking over-closely to his ideas. More personally, I recall how wounded one of my SAP supervisors was when I gave her my qualifying paper to read: 'but you have not quoted Winnicott', she complained! Similarly, when I first telephoned a potential second supervisor to ask if he would supervise me on my work with my second training patient, he asked me first, 'who is your analyst'? So, developing an analytic identity can easily fall foul of the biases, prejudices, and narcissism of our teachers.

I agree with Parsons (ibid., p. 224) that analytic identity is primarily formed through the experience of an analytic encounter, 'to have an analytic identity means that being an analyst makes the analyst feel alive ... being an analyst is in harmony with the analyst's sense of who they really are'.

But of course, we cannot feel alive all the time, and what of the times when our analytic identity feels dented, at a particular time when we are struggling with personal difficulties or illness. Sometimes, we are tired; sometimes we cannot think; sometimes we feel overwhelmed; sometimes we encounter a new situation that needs new perspectives.

Jungian Analysis as a Craft

JW: We can circumnavigate tensions about the relative merits of character and competence in training if we think of the analytic attitude in terms of learning a craft. Richard Sennett's (2008) book, *The Craftsman*, focuses on what it is that we actually do and the skills we need. Sennett (ibid., p. 9) writes about the basic principles underlying all craft work: 'Craftsmanship names an enduring, basic human impulse, the desire to do a job well for its own sake.'

He highlights how many skills are practised intuitively, but this does not mean they cannot be described. He considers that the essence of a craftsperson is: 'the special human condition of being engaged'.

He distinguishes between *embedded learning*, learned from good supervision/teaching and plenty of practice with what he calls *explicit knowledge*, a self-awareness about what we do and what we know, that brings with it a need to put this knowledge into words for others.

Colman (2020, p. 628), in a recent paper called 'Psychotherapy as skilled practice', compares becoming an analyst with becoming a potter. He quotes Pye (1968) the potter: 'good workmanship for a potter is a judicious mixture of care, judgement and dexterity'.

Pye distinguishes between the workmanship of *certainty* and the workmanship of *risk*. Certainty comes through the mechanization of tools and processes to control the work rather than through risk which is what produces unique pots developed in the potter's own style. I agree with Colman when he states that it is the delicate balance between certainty and risk that captures analytic skill.

As a singer, I am drawn of course to musical metaphors. Consider Caruso's (1996, pp. 38–39) ideas about the practice of singing:

> I am told that many people have the impression that my vocal ability is a kind of 'God-given gift', that is, something that has come to me without effort. This is so very absurd that I can hardly believe that sensible people would give it a moment's credence. Every voice is in a sense the result of a development, and this is particularly so in my own case. The marble that comes from the quarries of Carrara may be very beautiful and white and flawless, but it does not shape itself into a work of art without the heart and the hand of the sculptor.

The need for self-scrutiny coming from both heart and hand and especially attention to our own narcissism is as great for analysts as it is for singers, especially as we get older with the possibility of becoming more set in our ways.

Colman (2020, p. 629) draws on the relevance of Aristotle's ideas of *techne* (the kind of knowledge required for the arts and crafts) and *phronesis* (practical wisdom) as of the essence in the making and development of an analyst. He plays down the significance of Aristotle's term *episteme* – scientific knowledge. This leads naturally to a big question: what is the role of theory in the development of an analytic attitude?

The Role of Theory

JW: No longer is the analyst's identity that of an objective scientist. So says Colman (ibid., p. 630) when he tells us that we are not teaching people what to think, but rather, we are teaching people how to think. Of course, candidates need to study theory and there is often a need to know what to think before they can think for themselves. In Pye's language, they need some workmanship of certainty before they can take the risks that come with clinical experience and self-knowledge.

Spurling (2015, p. 53) entitles provocatively one of the chapters in his book 'Why theory does not inform practice?', pointing out how in practice, we simply do not apply a theory or a bit of theory to a piece of clinical work, or if we do, then we should not be doing this! We can make a helpful distinction between *public theory*, the concepts we learn that become a shared language between teachers and trainees, and to some extent in the public sphere, and *implicit, private theory*, the internal working models that affect subtly how we practice in an individual session. These are more difficult to put into words. Both public and private theory are likely to have cultural and institutional biases (e.g. Fordham in London, Neumann in Israel, Hillman in North America and Latin America) within institutes and between institutes. Spurling (ibid., p. 58) talks of his clinical/theoretical repertoire as second nature, to be called upon when needed in the consulting room. He thinks of private theories (ibid., p. 64) as: 'a bank or store of assumptions, models, metaphors, bits of theory etc. that constitute a backcloth to one's practice ... they are held in reserve'.

It is difficult to imagine a training programme where public theory is not taught as it creates a top-down framework and space in which analysts can develop but I think theory, like analytic identity, is more likely to 'live' if we can find ways to fashion it more experientially rather than didactically.

Cultural Otherness and the Analytic Attitude

General Perspectives

JW: I had a patient brought up in India who was looked after by an ayah (Indian nursemaid) as was sometimes the case in colonial families. My patient became very emotional talking about the absence of her mother when she was small. As she cried and curled up on my couch in emotional pain, I found myself unaffected – not usual with this patient. I felt I had lost my analytic attitude, but later realized that this mirrored her internal mother, cold and unaware of the needs of her little daughter. This example showed me how I can lose my analytic attitude but re-find it again. When teaching and supervising in Eastern European countries, I can think of many encounters when I felt that I lost my analytic attitude and did *not* find it again or found it only much later, often after returning home.

I am constantly, surprised, and challenged by such encounters with difference. This takes us to the second part of our paper; how differences in cultural complexes make sustaining an analytical attitude as we know it in our own culture more difficult.

Heyer (2012, p. 630), using a case example from her clinical work with a Muslim, Iranian man makes the point that: 'in our increasingly mobile world, more and more of us are caught between cultures rather than in one culture'.

And later (ibid., p. 640): 'when there is a multiplicity of cultures in the consulting room, awareness of it becomes crucial'.

When teaching, analysing and supervising abroad, we need to acknowledge our own vulnerabilities and awareness as analysts who can remain open to change and growth.

Everett (2016, p. xii), the anthropologist states: 'our unconscious is structured and infused with meaning by our individual experiences and social living'.

Placing emphasis on what he calls 'cultural tacit knowledge', Everett continues (ibid., p. xii):

> anyone who has lived in a different culture, learning to manoeuvre through a different language or alternate set of clues and cues of values, knowledge, food, social interactions, smells, sights, and so on, has been at once exhilarated, exhausted, stymied and challenged by the newness and strangeness of this novel environment.

How true this is.

Jasinski and Kalinowska (2015, p. 152) write thoughtfully about experiences they had during Router training in Poland, highlighting how if transformation is to take place, there needs to be an interactive field that both parties – teachers and candidates – inhabit through mutual understanding: 'using the alchemical metaphor, if transformation is to happen, then both parties need to 'undress' from their own cultural experiences'.

One of these two authors found that in personal analysis, the English language could not contain Polish fragments of experience leading to a 'breakdown of syntax' (ibid., p. 154).

Cultural Complexes: Jungian Perspectives

TK: Until relatively recently, the impact of culture on the analytic process was overlooked in our training programmes. This is an interesting observation, especially in light of the fact that the significance of culture was already highlighted quite early on in psychoanalytic circles. Michael Vannoy Adams (2004, p. 133), in his book *The Fantasy Principle* states:

> Karen Horney was perhaps the first psychoanalyst to emphasize the importance of culture. What interests Horney is 'the problem of normal and neurotic structures within a given culture.' She insists that 'we cannot understand these structures without a detailed

knowledge of the influences that particular culture exerts over the individual (Horney 1937, p. 20)'.

In the Jungian world, Henderson was the first to introduce the notion of the 'cultural unconscious' in a letter written to Jung as early as 1947 (Singer & Kaplinsky 2010, p. 22). This idea was then developed further and expanded by Singer and Kimbles (2004, p.176) who defined cultural complexes as:

> an emotionally charged aggregate of ideas and images that cluster around an archetypal core ... and that exist within the psyche of the collective as a whole and the individual members of that group.

The experience of working with IAAP Router Groups has provided fertile ground for discovering how cultural differences can affect the perspectives we hold consciously and unconsciously about the analytic attitude.

One particular instance that stands out for me was an initial meeting with the members of a Developing Group from a former East European Block country who wanted to train to become IAAP Jungian analysts. In our meeting with them, we had planned to discuss how we could devise a plan together that would help make their dream become a reality. We invited them to begin a conversation with us about this project of mutual interest. To my surprise, no one felt free enough to ask a question or share a reflection. It became apparent that, as IAAP officers, we represented an established authority and that, in their culture, authority figures were not people with whom you could have a dialogue.

In the words of Gudaitė (2015, p. 121): 'Authority was accepted as a dangerous, destructive, and defensive force and was a common theme in the psyche of clients who started psychotherapy.'

What is interesting is the inevitable psychological blindness that operates when a cultural complex is activated. As with our personal complexes, it is only experience that awakens us to how our own culture defines our view of the world.

Bi-directional Learning

TK: It seems obvious that Jan and I are interested in expanding our vision of training so that it is sensitive to the specific cultural context. Our work with Developing Groups has provided us with valuable experiential learning and has made us aware that learning about the texture of an analytic attitude never ceases. Even between the two of us, our respective cultural complexes sometimes get in the way of how we perceive or understand a situation. Despite these cultural differences however, it is clear we have something valuable to offer about the art of our work; like a good chef, we need to try out new recipes.

In an article about bi-directional learning in analytical work across cultures, Cambray (2015, p. 32) states:

> The topic of bi-directionality is timely, perhaps reflective of a shift in focus from exclusive attention on objective knowledge or knowing, to a broader more interactive model of learning. ... Only such an attitude can unshackle us from dogmatic imitation and release the potential for creative empathic contact.

We would like to share with you a few examples of our own bi-directional learning emerging from work with candidates in other cultures.

Examples

JW: I am used to a culture of seminars where clinical and theoretical issues are discussed openly in small groups. I forget how in some countries, educational systems are historically didactic and there are perceived to be 'right' and 'wrong' answers. Teachers are expected to teach and 'to know' and so, trying to create a more interactive learning environment can be complex. In London, we are trained to value 'not knowing' and bearing uncertainty as essential qualities of the analytic attitude. It is worth keeping in mind that not to know in some cultures can generate experiences of profound shame.

TK: Jan and I were called upon to attempt to resolve a difficult misunderstanding with possible ethical undertones that had emerged in a Developing Group. The group was split where one side, mainly women, felt the male leader of the group and his mostly male supporters were behaving like dictators, imposing their opinions and agenda onto the group. They did not feel listened to or appreciated and were consequently angry and uncooperative. Despite our seeming sensitivity to the issues at stake, to the personalities involved and our experience and awareness of group process, we found ourselves embroiled in a dynamic to which we responded in an uncharacteristically autocratic manner. Jan and I met with the two male leaders and, after listening to them, confronted them with what we had heard from the other side. However, the way we did this made it clear we were identified with the other side. In reflecting on this together later, we realized we had become caught in the unconscious dynamics of a cultural authority complex and had not only become identified with one side and taken on an uncharacteristic authoritarian attitude. We had lost our analytic attitude. In so doing, we had also lost sight of the unconscious cultural complex at play. As in our work with our patients, we had to live the transference before we could fully grasp and understand it.

JW: My own training was all face-to-face. Digital technology has expanded out of all proportion since those days, and today, especially in countries without many trained analysts, Skype or its equivalent is the norm. At the time of writing, we remain in the midst of a world-wide pandemic. Whether we like it or not, we are all adapting to seeing patients and supervisees on Skype, Zoom, or on the telephone. There are, however, losses when working online. The analyst is no longer the sole guardian of the setting, relying on their patients and supervisees to play their parts in providing a safe and private work environment. I struggle to sustain my analytic attitude – my internal setting – when working online and I miss face-to-face sessions with two bodies in the room together where my countertransference works so much more effectively. What will be the effect of digital technology on future generations of Jungian analysts? I was amused to hear of an example of a psychoanalyst working on Skype with a number of Chinese candidates in personal analysis. He decided to make a visit to China and offered his patients a number of sessions to meet in person. One of his patients wrote back, respectfully declining his offer, saying that after working on Skype, it would just be too awkward to meet in person!

TK: Usually, the motivation for analysts to become involved in working with Router Groups is founded on a genuine desire to be of service and contribute to the expressed wishes to learn more about Jung in countries where there is no Jungian tradition. In some cases, this motivation has offered refuge for members disgruntled with their own local Society. On the one hand, teaching abroad can provide a frustrated analyst with opportunities to find creativity away from the stressful environment of their own institute. In most cases, visiting analysts find the group members very appreciative. However, admiration from the members of Router Programmes can be quite powerful and it is easy for the analyst to fall prey to their idealizations with which they may identify. While this may temporarily nourish the narcissistic needs of the analyst and fill a void, this idealization can quickly become an *enantiodromic* experience, revealing other underlying feelings of a totally different nature. The fall from grace of the desired object who then becomes the rejected one can feel extremely uncomfortable.

JW: Teaching from the West has helped candidates in other countries develop safer boundaries and this has had universal acceptance in different cultures. Here in the UK, boundary issues will always include discussions about money. At a conference when talking to candidates about how to set their fees, Anna Konstantinova, a Russian analyst stood up and said:

you do not understand Russian attitudes to money. During the communist regime, no cash changed hands; it all came from the state. Now, as psychotherapy grows, the exchange of money is still regarded as a black-market activity, especially by older patients.

Here again is another example of a significant cultural clash that led to mutual learning and transformation.

TK: Visiting analysts inevitably carry with them the knowledge and experience they have developed within their own cultures. None of us can work beyond our level of skill. Ideally, those training in countries without a legacy of Jungian analysis need to have exposure to a variety and broad spectrum of theoretical and clinical perspectives from which they can evolve their own style. They need to discover what resonates more meaningfully in the service of the development of their own analytic identity. There can be more proselytizing, passing on what we value and what is ingrained in our own local organizations, than is helpful. As Jung did not wish to create Jungians, we should be careful about the institutional 'do what you have been done to', creating sub-cultures of for example, Neumann, Fordham, or Hillman loyalists.

Conclusions

TK: What are the implications of our reflections in this chapter for Jungian psychology and our training programmes? Jungian psychology is based on the premise that the confrontation of the ego with the unconscious, of the known with the not-yet-known, will lead to a fuller and more meaningful life. The encounter with the unconscious challenges us to interact with and give serious consideration to the unfamiliar. This is what Jung referred to as the *auseinandersetzung*. While the ultimate goal of this process is self-realization, it is a goal that in reality is constantly in a state of becoming. The process is one that can lead to a sense of meaning and aliveness, of readiness to question and to learn, that leads to flexibility and a willingness to adapt to ever-changing conditions both of the inner and the outer world and to an acceptance of difference, both within oneself and in the other.

Just as psyche is not static, neither should be our guiding principles with respect to training. Exposure to different cultures provides an opportunity to meet 'the other' in its multifaceted forms. We need to recognize that the learning is bi-directional and that we also have a lot to learn. In the words of the American poet Walt Whitman (1955, p. 193): 'the teaching is to the teacher and comes back most to him'.

Whitman's words echo those of Jung (1946, para. 358): 'when two chemical substances combine, both are altered'.

Just as it takes courage and curiosity to meet 'the other within', so too do we need courage and curiosity to meet 'the other' in a different culture.

JW: The concept of the analytic attitude as a helpful embracing idea to describe what candidates need to learn during training, remains as relevant now as in the past. But times have changed, and in a multicultural world, especially when training those from other countries with different cultural complexes and languages, what constitutes the analytic attitude in one institute, may require change and adaptation in another. We need to remain sensitive to cultural bias and prejudice.

Sustaining an analytic attitude all the time is clearly impossible. It is always going to be the case that just as we have found it, we will also sometimes lose it. This may relate to the patient, to the analytic relationship or to factors in ourselves. This is where the analytic attitude requires that we do indeed live with 'not-knowing' in the hope embedded in Jungian psychology that everything happens for a reason that can be grasped if we remain willing to search for meaning.

In a world where we work with patients from different cultures, and where we travel to work in different cultures, we need a bi-directional model of learning and a flexibility to learn from those we are helping to acquire their analytic identity. While we can assume a common language and mutual understanding within our own cultures and our own institutes, this is by no means the case when we are thinking about cultural otherness. Analysts need to be open to adapt what they know, and more importantly the style in which they convey what they know, so that a shared space for meaning can be discovered. We need to work together to develop a programme of training in multicultural approaches to Jungian analysis that upholds the principle that we are learning a craft. The essence of this craft, as with singing or cooking or making a piece of pottery is that it needs an openness to learn the basics together with the flair and individuality that comes with our own imaginativeness.

References

Abramovitch, H 2015, Pioneers or colonialism, in *From Tradition to Innovation: Jungian Analysts Working in Different Cultural Contexts,* Crowther, C and Wiener, J (Eds.), New Orleans: Spring Journal Books.

Cambray, J 2015, Reflections on the bi-directionality of influence, *From Tradition to Innovation: Jungian Analysts Working in Different Cultural Contexts*, Crowther, C and Wiener, J (Eds.), New Orleans: Spring Journal Books.

Caruso, E 1996, Italy, the home of song, in *Great Singers on the Art of Singing*, Mineola, New York: Dover Publications Inc.

Colman, W 2020, Psychotherapy as a skilled practice, *Journal of Analytical Psychology*, 65, 4, 624–645.

Everett, D L 2016, *Dark Matters of the Mind: The Culturally Articulated Unconscious,* Chicago and London: The University of Chicago Press.

Gudaitė, G 2015, Issues of cultural identity and authorship, in *From Tradition to Innovation: Jungian Analysts Working in Different Cultural Settings*, Crowther, C and Wiener, J (Eds.), New Orleans: Spring Journal Books.

Heyer, G 2012, Caught between cultures: Cultural norms in Jungian psychodynamic process, *Journal of Analytical Psychology,* 57, 5, 629–645.

Horney, K 1937, *The Neurotic Personality of Our Time.* New York: W. W. Norton.

Jung, C G 1946, *The Psychology of the Transference, CW 16*, Princeton, NJ: Princeton University Press.

Jung, C G 1961, *Symbols and the Interpretation of Dreams, CW 8*, Princeton, NJ: Princeton University Press.

Kalinowska, M, Jasinski, T J 2015, Influenced, changed or transformed?, in *From Tradition to Innovation: Jungian Analysts Working in Different Cultural Contexts.* New Orleans: Spring Journal Books.

Kelly, T 2007, The making of an analyst: From 'ideal' to 'good enough', *Journal of Analytical Psychology*, 52, 2, 157–171.

Lemma, A, Roth, A, Pilling, S 2010, The competencies required to deliver effective psychoanalysis/psychodynamic therapy, available at, www.ucl.ac.uk/clinicalpsychol ogy/CORE/Psychodynamic_Competences/Backg

Parsons, M 2014, *Living Psychoanalysis: From Theory to Experience.* London: Routledge.

Pye, D 1968, *The Nature and Art of Workmanship*, London: Bloomsbury.

Sennett, R 2008, *The Craftsman*, London: Allen Lane.

Singer, T, Kimbles, S 2004, The emerging theory of cultural complexes, in *Analytical Psychology: Contemporary Perspectives in Jungian Analysis*, Cambray, J and Carter, L (Eds.), Hove and New York: Brunner-Routledge.

Singer, T, Kaplinsky, C 2010, Cultural complexes in analysis, in *Jungian Psychoanalysis –Working in the Spirit of C. G. Jung*, Stein, M (Ed.), Chicago & La Salle, Illinois: Open Court.

Spurling, L 2015, *The Psychoanalytic Craft: How to Develop a Psychoanalytic Practitioner*, London: Palgrave.

Vannoy Adams, M 2004, *The Fantasy Principle: Psychoanalysis of the Imagination*, Hove and New York: Brunner Routledge.

Whitman, W 1955, *Leaves of Grass*, New York: Signet Classics.

Wiener, J 2007, Evaluating progress in training: Character or competence, *Journal of Analytical Psychology*, 52, 2, 171–185.

Wiener, J 2018, Paradoxical affinities: Otherness and ambivalence as creative pathways, *Journal of Analytical Psychology,* 63, 3, 382–393.

Wiener, J 2020, Response to Warren Colman's paper 'Psychotherapy as a skilled practice', *Journal of Analytical Psychology*, 65, 4, 645–653.

Winborn, M 2019, *Interpretation in Jungian Analysis: Art and Technique*, London and New York: Routledge.

Chapter 13

On Relatedness to Cultures

The Struggles with Cultures in the Case of C. G. Jung and H. Kawai

Mari Yoshikawa

Introduction

In recent years, globalization has led to the need for a multicultural approach in the field of psychotherapy. In trying to understand the subjective experience of the clients, the analyst must be aware of the differences between the client's culture and the analyst's own culture. When analysts make an inference about the client's subjective experience, they have to be cognizant of and respectful of the client's cultural frame of reference. In addition, the analyst must avoid unintentionally imposing values from his/her own culture onto the clients. In today's world, not only Jungians but all psychotherapists are required to have "relatedness to cultures" and the basis of a multicultural approach as one of their core competencies.

If we look back at the history of analytical psychology and the development of the Jungian school and its training program, we can see that interest in other cultures and the cultural products of the past played an extremely important role. As a result, Jungian training is particularly cognizant of the importance of culture. From very early on, relatedness to culture was considered a core competence of Jungian analysts.

Jung's Perspective on Non-European Cultures and Cultures from the Past

In 1909 Jung was invited to lecture at Clark University in the US by Dr. Stanley Hall. On the journey there, he had a dream of his house. The impact of this dream inspired Jung to devote himself to the study of ancient myths and other works from diverse cultures.

In the dream, Jung was in a two-story house that, though different from his actual house, nevertheless felt like it was his house. The second floor of the house was decorated in an eighteenth- and nineteenth-century style. When he went downstairs however, he found it was decorated in fifteenth- and sixteenth-century style and furnished in a medieval style. He went further down the stone stairs that led to the basement to find that the walls were Roman. There

DOI: 10.4324/9781003219910-19

he found narrow stone steps that led even deeper down into a cavern littered with dismembered bones and broken pottery, remnants of a primitive culture. There he found two very old decayed human skulls. Jung's own understanding of this dream is as follows: The house in the dream was understood as an image representing his psyche. For Jung, his consciousness was represented by the hall on the second floor, while the first floor represented the first plane of the unconscious. The deeper he descended, the weirder and darker the scene became. In the cave, he found relics of a primitive culture, that is, contents of his own inner primitive psyche. From this dream, Jung got the idea that there is a collective layer of the unconscious that exists a priori beneath the personal unconscious. (Jung 1963, pp. 158–159).

Following this dream, Jung enthusiastically read up on the myths of various cultures and eventually came to believe that the psyche of the ancients was reflected in their myths. He assumed a connection between the material of these myths and the fantasies of Miss Miller, a young American woman. He published 'Symbols of Transformation' in 1911, aiming to elucidate the psycho-historical elements embedded in the personal spontaneous fantasies of Miss Miller.

In this seminal book, Jung highlights the similarity between a variety of images from myths from a wide range of cultures and the fantasies of this American woman. The book refers to a wide range of materials, which consist not only of prehistoric artifacts, Greek and Roman myths and rituals, but also of Biblical stories, European medieval works, as well as myths and works of art from outside Europe, including from Native America, Egypt, Alaska, India, and Bali.

According to Jung, the collective unconscious, the ancient layer of the psyche, is composed of contents that are shared by all human beings, regardless of the epoch or region of the world. Even modern people, who are trained to think logically, can find such contents in their fantasies when their consciousness is weakened and in dreams, as exemplified in Miss Miller's fantasies. Jung came to understand these contents as archetypes. "The concept of the archetype, which is an indispensable correlate of the idea of the collective unconscious, indicates the existence of definite forms in the psyche which seem to be present always and everywhere" (Jung 1936, para. 89).

In the chapter entitled "Definitions" in "Psychological Types" (1921), Jung explains that archetypal images arise in dreams that reflect ancient mythological motifs that have common characteristics beyond the period of time and the region of the world of the dreamer. Jung believed that the material that embodies the archetypes could be found in the dreams, visions, and fantasies of individuals, as well as in the delusions of paranoid patients. When the material found there shows functions similar to those found in myths, religious rituals and fairy tales, then the existence of the archetype can be proven (Jung 1936). Thus, in analytical psychology, when we try to understand archetypes, which are the contents of the collective unconscious, knowledge of the corresponding ancient cultural products, such as myths and rituals, is necessary.

Jung's Encounter and Struggle with Different Cultures

I would like to focus on Jung's own impressive encounters with various different cultures. He travelled to many places with different cultures several times in his life. Each time he had experiences which brought him new ideas that contributed to the development of his ideas that led to what we now call analytical psychology. During his first trip outside of Europe, when in Tunis, North Africa, he wrote:

> At last, I was where I had longed to be: in a non-European country where no European language was spoken and no Christian conceptions prevailed, where a different race lived and a different historical tradition and philosophy had set its stamp upon the face of the crowd. I had often wished to be able for once to see the European from outside, his image reflected back at him by an altogether foreign milieu.
>
> (Jung 1963, p. 238)

On the last night of the North African trip, Jung had the following dream of struggling with a Sultan:

> I was in an Arab city, ... I stood before a wooden bridge leading over the water to a dark, horseshoe-shaped portal, which was open. Eager to see the citadel from the inside also, I stepped out on the bridge. When I was about halfway across it, a handsome, dark Arab of aristocratic, almost royal bearing came toward me from the gate. I knew that this youth in the white burnoose was the resident prince of the citadel. When he came up to me, he attacked me and tried to knock me down. We wrestled. In the struggle we crashed against the railing; it gave way and both of us fell into the moat, where he tried to push my head under water to drown me. No, I thought, this is going too far. And in my turn, I pushed his head under water. I did so although I felt great admiration for him; but I did not want to let myself be killed. I had no intention of killing him; I wanted only to make him unconscious and incapable of fighting.
>
> (ibid., pp. 242–244)

He interpreted the first part of the dream as follows:

> the Arab youth was the double of the proud Arab who had ridden past us without a greeting. As an inhabitant of the casbah he was a figuration of the self, or rather, a messenger or emissary of the self ... His attempt to kill me was an echo of the motif of Jacob's struggle with the angel; he

was—to use the language of the Bible—like an angel of the Lord, a messenger of God who wished to kill men because he did not know them.

(ibid., p. 244)

Jung wrote:

In traveling to Africa to find a psychic observation post outside the sphere of the European, I unconsciously wanted to find that part of my personality which had become invisible under the influence and the pressure of being European. This part stands in unconscious opposition to myself, and indeed I attempt to suppress it. In keeping with its nature, it wishes to make me unconscious (force me under water) so as to kill me; but my aim is, through insight, to make it more conscious, so that we can find a common modus vivendi.

(ibid., p. 244)

His reflection on the dream made clear that:

Obviously, my encounter with Arab culture had struck me with overwhelming force. ... The emotional nature of these unreflective people who are so much closer to life than we are exerts a strong suggestive influence upon those historical layers in ourselves which we have just overcome and left behind, or which we think we have overcome. It is like the paradise of childhood from which we imagine we have emerged, but which at the slightest provocation imposes fresh defeats upon us. Indeed, our cult of progress is in danger of imposing on us even more childish dreams of the future, the harder it presses us to escape from the past.

(ibid., p. 244)

Jung points out that when we encounter the collective psyche of a different culture, a kind of assimilation occurs, but when we find elements in the process that we cannot assimilate; we recognize the heterogeneity of the different culture. This is where we become truly aware of the biases and peculiarities of the culture to which we belong.

The Multicultural Environment of Jungian Analysts' Training in Zurich

After World War II, in 1948, a small institute for the study of Jung's psychology was founded at Gemeindestrasse 27 in Zurich, named the Jung Institute. In the early days, individuals could become analysts by having personal analysis with Jung and receiving a letter of recommendation from him.

"It was only with the founding of the International Association for Analytical Psychology (IAAP) in 1955 that the authority for accreditation was definitively transferred from Jung personally to a professional association" (Kirsch 2001, p. 17 in Kindle Version).

At the time of the founding of the Jung Institute, Jung thought that a non-clinical background could be an appropriate basis for becoming an analyst. Candidates therefore did not need to have a degree in medicine, psychology, or social work. He wrote:

> I have mentioned before that dream-interpretation requires, among other things, specialized knowledge. While I am quite ready to believe that an intelligent layman with some psychological knowledge and experience of life could, with practice, diagnose dream-compensation correctly, I consider it impossible for anyone without knowledge of mythology and folklore and without some understanding of the psychology of primitives and of comparative religion to grasp the essence of the individuation process, which, according to all we know, lies at the base of psychological compensation.
>
> (Jung 1945, para. 553)

In accordance with Jung's idea about training to be an analyst, the Zurich Institute has remained a training center where non-clinically trained people can become analysts. As a result, many mature students from various educational backgrounds and countries come to the Zurich Institute.

Thomas Kirsch wrote, "The Institute was created to be international in character and offered tracks in German, English, French, and Italian" (op. cit., p. 18).

Since those days, the Zurich Institute has a curriculum with subjects that include: Fundamentals of Analytical Psychology, Psychology of Dreams, Word Association Experiments, General History of Religion, Fairy Tales, Mythology, General Psychopathology. Cultural subjects such as General History of Religion, Fairy Tales, and Mythology have also been an important part of the curriculum. In terms of analytical psychology, cultures are products of the collective unconscious. Knowledge of cultural material is necessary to use in the analysis of dreams and active imagination.

It is clear from the above that students from diverse regions were studying at the Jung Institute, and that Zurich was a place that was open to their diverse cultures and allowed them to interact with each other through the diverse framework of their respective cultures. In this multicultural environment, the analyst candidate would first have come to know that his or her own culture is just one of the many diverse cultures worldwide. They would have recognized that their own cultural frame of reference is not absolute, but relative. They would have an opportunity to step out of their own culture and experience another one.

Thus, many multiculturally conscious Jungian analysts were produced and this tradition continues to this day. The Association of Graduates in Analytical

Psychology Zurich (AGAP), an organization of such Jungian graduates, established ISAP, the International School of Analytical Psychology, Zurich, in 2004. ISAP is characterized by its openness to the world and its internationality, accepting students from various countries around the world. I would quote a lively paragraph from "ISAPZURICH: A Journey" (2004):

> At ISAP, the prima materia is made up of the people who learn and participate in the programs – the students and their teachers. Among these, alchemy is at work from the beginning to the end of training and beyond. Students interact with one another, they interact with their teachers and personal analysts and supervisors, and they interact with the unconscious that emerges at many places in the course of their studies. This combination is unique at ISAP because the students and teachers and training analysts come from so many different countries (Some 20 lands are represented in the student body at any given time; the analysts, likewise hail from many countries and cultures and from a wide variety of backgrounds, including the sciences, the arts, business, and other professions). This tremendous variety of cultural and educational backgrounds and ages (from people from 20 to 80) creates a very rich and indeed, a unique prima materia at ISAP. ISAP is multiculturalism realized; it is globalism in action.
>
> (Stein 2004)

In this context, ISAP is a training institution that continues the international and cross-cultural openness originated in the original Jung Institute in Zurich.

Analytical psychology has its roots in the universal depths of culture and psyche. Each culture appears different on the surface, but at its core, it has a common content that transcends differences in culture and time. It is the collective layer of the unconscious where such content exists, which is the subject of deep interest in analytical psychology.

By stepping outside of the cultural sphere in which we lead our daily life, we can enlarge our perspective on different ways of being and realize that the heterogeneity of other cultures resonates with the ancient layers of our mind.

In this sense, the importance for candidates to experience lectures, analysis, casework, and supervision, and interaction among students from different cultural backgrounds in the training process of analytical psychology cannot be overemphasized.

On the First Japanese Jungian Analyst, Hayao Kawai's Struggle with His Own Culture

The Association of Jungian Analysts Japan, AJAJ, was ratified as an association of internationally certified Jungian analysts in Japan by the International Association for Analytical Psychology (IAAP) in August 2001.

In April 2002, the training institute of AJAJ, the Japan Institute of Jungian Psychology, started its own training program whose goals are both to disseminate Jungian psychology and to train Jungian analysts by holding seminars, group supervisions, and symposiums in Tokyo and in Kyoto. AJAJ is officially recognized as a Group Member with Training Status by the IAAP. A person who completes the designated training program will qualify to receive a diploma in Analytical Psychology in Japan. Currently in 2021, AJAJ has 44 qualified Jungian analyst members in Japan. Prior to the recognition of AJAJ training by the IAAP, Japanese who wanted to become certified Jungian analysts had to study abroad for more than four years, usually at the Jung Institute in Zurich, to earn their diploma as a certified Jungian analyst. They had to take on the challenge of living and studying in a different culture, being analyzed by an analyst with a different cultural background, attending lectures, taking exams, and submitting written papers in a foreign language. The initial pioneering analysts from Japan overcame these difficult challenges and applied what they had learned from their experiences with different cultures to their subsequent practice as analysts.

The fact that AJAJ is now able to offer Jungian analyst certification through its own training curriculum facilitates expanding the number of Jungian analysts in Japan. The shadow side of having a domestic course in AJAJ training is the loss of the invaluable opportunities to encounter different cultures in the process of training. To compensate for this loss, AJAJ has a requirement for candidates who have not completed the Propaedeuticum exam in a foreign Jungian Institute to attend group supervision sessions with English-speaking analysts certified by the IAAP and to give presentations in the group sessions.

In this chapter, I would like to focus on Hayao Kawai (1928–2007), a pioneer who was the first Japanese to qualify as a Jungian analyst. He experienced World War II as an adolescent and had a strong aversion to the culture to which he belonged. After the war, he went to study in the US as a Fulbright Scholar to study psychological assessment using the Rorschach method. It was there that, thanks to his advisor, Prof. B. Klopfer, a prominent Jungian analyst, he encountered analytical psychology for the first time. Under the influence of his advisor, he decided to study in Switzerland to get a diploma as a Jungian analyst. There, he began to look at Japanese culture from the perspective of Western culture, and his struggle to rediscover the true value of his own devalued culture started. In this part of my chapter, I would like to describe his struggle with cultures, both Western culture and his own Japanese culture.

In his autobiography, *Memories for the Future: An Attempt at Autobiography*, Kawai (2001/2015) recounted how he spent his sensitive boyhood under the influence of his four elder brothers in the family of a successful and respected dentist in a local city of Japan. On the recommendation of his brothers, he read *The Count of Monte Cristo* and *Sherlock Holmes*, and watched the movie *The Adventures of Robin Hood*. This gave him a taste for stories and a yearning for the European world. On the other hand, he recalled that he was a boy who excelled in rational thinking, perhaps as a result of exposure to the active arguments of his older brothers.

In elementary and junior high schools in Japan at that time, myths were taught to children as objective facts. Education was conducted to make students regard Japan as a divine country and to justify militarism and wars of aggression. He was inwardly repulsed by such education, but at the same time, he also understood that he should never speak out against it.

At the time of World War II, Kawai was in his mid-teens. His second brother had joined the army as a military doctor. At that time, his brother told him, "We will do things like war, but you will never be a soldier " (ibid., p. 63), and went off to war. While some of his friends volunteered for the preliminary course, he was ashamed that he could not bring himself to volunteer in that way. He then told his eldest brother, who was studying at medical school:

> To tell you the truth, I am afraid of dying. I think I have a patriotic spirit, but when I see everyone else going to die, I am the only one who is afraid of it, and I am very sorry about that.
>
> (ibid., p. 66)

His brother wrote back as follows, "It is natural to be afraid of dying, and there is nothing to be ashamed of. You should serve your country by doing what you are meant to do" (ibid., p. 66).

Against his own will, Kawai was recommended by the junior high school to the military academy for prospective officers. He told his father that he didn't want to be a military officer, showing his correspondence with his older brothers. His father accepted his wish and declined the recommendation. This may have been the cause of his failure in the entrance examination for university.

Though he wrote nothing about his feelings and simply related the fact that he entered a technical college, I can imagine it was a huge disappointment for him. Under the conditions of World War II, and as a student of the technical college, he was mobilized to work in a munitions factory. When the war ended in 1945, he witnessed the collapse of the belief shared by many Japanese that the divine nation of Japan would never be defeated in war.

After the war, Japan's school system underwent major changes, and Kawai was able to make a decision to go to university, something he had longed for. He entered the Faculty of Science at Kyoto University in 1948, majoring in mathematics. However, the road to becoming a mathematician was difficult and he spent many days wondering what kind of career he should pursue. He chose to become a math teacher. In parallel with this and in order to improve his skills as a teacher, he decided to enroll in Kyoto University graduate school for educational psychology.

Meanwhile, he became absorbed in research into the application of the Rorschach method in educational settings as an educational psychologist. After spending three years as a high school teacher, Kawai was hired as a lecturer of educational psychology at Tenri University in 1955, where he could continue his research.

In 1959, at the age of 31, Kawai went to the United States as a Fulbright Scholar to study clinical psychology at UCLA under the tutelage of Professor B. Kropfer. There he read *An Introduction to Jungian Psychology* by Frieda Fordham (1953) and was struck by the statement in the book that to be an analyst required the individual to undergo a personal analysis in order to know themselves. Professor Klopfer encouraged his interest in having a personal analysis and referred him to Dr. Spiegelman, who had recently completed his training at the Jung Institute in Zurich. With the recommendation of these two mentors, Kawai decided to enroll at the Jung institute in Zurich to get a diploma as Jungian analyst. When Kawai joined the Jung Institute in 1962, the lectures were given both in English and German. At that time, people studying Jungian psychology were not only from Europe but also from other English-speaking countries and Asia.

In his autobiography Hayao Kawai recounts:

> I always brought a Furoshiki, Japanese wrapping cloth with me to go to the Jung Institute. I took Japanese classics in paperback such as 'Konjaku Monogatari: Anthology of Japanese Tales from the Past' wrapped in Furoshiki and read it on the train [on his way to and from the Jung Institute].
>
> (ibid., p. 264)

While listening to Marie-Louise von Franz's lecture on fairy tales, he recalled the stories in the Konjaku Monogatari, one of the sources of Japanese fairy tales. Many Japanese candidates who followed his path to Zurich tried to learn about their culture while in a different culture and to re-evaluate the culture to which they belonged, reflecting on it from the new viewpoint which they learned there.

When Kawai reached the stage of thinking about the topic for his diploma thesis, he felt a strong resistance to using Japanese mythology as a theme because of his experience of rebelling against the unscientific mythological education in Japan during the war. However, as he discussed his dreams with his analyst, he made up his mind to use Japanese mythology as the theme for the thesis. The following is a quotation about Kawai's cross-cultural experience in the Foreword to his qualifying thesis, "The Figure of the Sun Goddess in Japanese Mythology":

> The longer I stayed in the West, the more I realized 'a Japanese' in me, which, however, does not mean at all that I become against the West.

And my long analytical experience also made me aware of my Japanese psyche. In this journey, to go down deeper into the Japanese psyche, I found Japanese mythology most useful.

(Kawai 1964/2009, p. 112)

Looking back on the life of Kawai, the militaristic education during the war was unacceptable to him, as he had acquired a rational mind from his progressively minded family. Moreover, his refusal to follow through on the recommendation to apply to a military academy almost cost him his dream of going to university. I presume that Kawai may have chosen to major in mathematics, the ultimate in rationality, at university as an opportunity to gain a rational mind and as a compensation for what seemed absent during war time in Japan.

In Japan's militaristic education at that time, myths were treated as objective historical facts. This did not sit well with Kawai, who had developed a rational mind. While Kawai wanted to study Jungian psychology in order to understand the mind rationally, we can imagine he must have felt some resistance to dealing with Japanese myths. Through his experience of dream analysis however, he realized that the myths were deeply related to and rooted in his Japanese psyche. He eventually chose Amaterasu, the goddess of the sun in Japanese mythology, as the subject of his diploma thesis for his Jung Institute certification.

In this diploma thesis, Kawai concludes that the nature of Japanese consciousness is different from that of the West. According to him, Japanese consciousness includes both polarities of masculine and feminine, sun and moon, light and dark, and that the distinction between the two poles is not clear. He calls this consciousness the female-sun consciousness. In addition, his thesis provides a structural analysis of Japanese mythology, referring to several documents. Kawai showed that when Amaterasu, the Sun Goddess and Susano-wo, the Storm God appear, they are then joined by the god of inaction, the Moon God, Tsukuyomi, to form a triad. Kawai further pointed out the repetition of the motif of triads in Japanese mythology, which place the god of inaction (hollow) at the center. The first example of such a triad is the triad of three gods, Ame-no-minaka-nushi, Taka-mi-musubi, and Kami-musubi, who appear in the description of the beginning of the world at the beginning of the Kojiki.

A Jungian Exploration of Japanese Culture after Kawai's Return to Japan

After returning to Japan in 1965 as a certified analyst, Kawai introduced the essence of Jungian psychology with his book entitled, *Introduction to Jungian Psychology* in 1967. This was followed by *Fairytales and the Japanese Mind* (1982), which took up Japanese fairy tales and analyzed them at the collective level of psyche. In addition, his lectures at the Eranos Conferences in 1983, 1984, 1985, 1986, and 1988 took up Japanese stories, the dream diaries of Japanese Zen monks, Japanese mythology, and Japanese fairy tales to discuss the Japanese psyche in ancient and medieval times.

Kawai's lecture "The Hidden Gods in Japanese Mythology" given at the Eranos Conference in 1985, represents the culmination of his continuous research on Japanese mythology since his diploma thesis. In his diploma thesis, Kawai had already pointed out that Amaterasu was by no means the highest deity, and that the triad of three gods, Amaterasu, Susano-Wo, and Tsukuyomi who controlled the balance between the two, was important. He had already mentioned that Hiruko predated these three gods in his diploma thesis. In this 1985 lecture, he focused on Hiruko, who was abandoned because he could not stand on his feet at the age of three. Kawai showed how, with the addition of Hiruko, the triad could shift and transform to become a tetrad. What kind of consciousness would this Hiruko embody? Kawai believed that this discarded Hiruko as the god of the male-Sun consciousness, the counterpart of Amaterasu, and had already presented the following diagram in his diploma thesis in 1964.

In the last chapter of *Mythology and the Japanese Mind* (2003), Kawai argues that the task of the modern Japanese is to reintroduce Hiruko, who was abandoned in the distant past, to the circle of Japanese gods. According to him, this is an almost impossible task that one can venture to take on only at the risk of his/her life. Hiruko was abandoned because he did not fit into

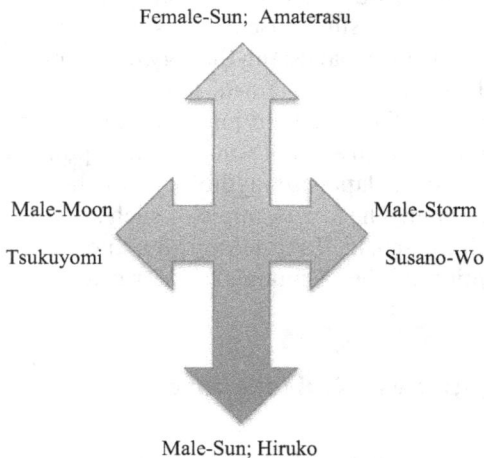

Female-Sun; Amaterasu

Male-Moon

Tsukuyomi

Male-Storm

Susano-Wo

Male-Sun; Hiruko

Figure 13.1 The quaternity in Japanese mythology

Source: Kawai, H. (1964/2009: Copyright 1964)

the hollow equilibrium triad structure and any inadvertent recurrence could destroy the hollow structure.

Even at the age of three, Hiruko was unable to stand on his own legs, which reminds us of the state of consciousness of Japanese people who seem to have difficulty in establishing true centrality and subjectivity in their own psyche. The restoration of Hiruko represents the establishment of a center-integrated structure in one's personal or in the Japanese collective psyche. This is a major paradigm shift in the nature of Japanese consciousness, where it is no longer possible to coexist with the passive hollow equilibrium structure that is adaptive to Japanese culture.

In his book Kawai highlighted the importance of self-determination, and added that in doing so, one must first be able to explain why he/she chose that option at that time; secondly, one must be aware of the responsibility that comes with making a choice; and third, even if one chooses one option, it is important to always remember to consider the perspective from the other side. Kawai goes on to state more specifically that in our age of globalization, in order for Japanese people to be able to get along with people from the West on an equal footing, they must establish themselves as "individuals" who have acquired a solid sense of judgment, expression, and responsibility.

Kawai continued to work at the International research center of Japanese Studies after retiring as professor at Kyoto University, and he spared no effort to establish the qualifications of the Japanese psychologists by engaging with the organizational management for Japanese clinical psychology and certified Clinical Psychologists.

In 2002, Kawai was appointed as the Commissioner of the Agency for Cultural Affairs of the Japanese Government. Despite his busy schedule, he continued his clinical practice. In addition, he managed to continue his research on Japanese culture, mythology, fairy tales, and Buddhism rooted in Japan. Throughout his life, the pioneering Japanese analyst Hayao Kawai continued to study the Japanese culture as an expression of the Japanese collective psyche, not only intellectually but also through the movement of his own soul.

Conclusion

Many Jungian analysts, including C. G. Jung and H. Kawai, encounter other cultures in the process of their training, both assimilating other cultures and deepening their understanding of the culture to which they belong. In the process, they gain a deeper understanding of themselves, as well as a better understanding of the functioning of the collective layers of the psyche. In this sense, understanding of and relatedness to other cultures and to one's own culture should be noted as one of the core competencies of a Jungian analyst.

References

Fordham, F 1953, *An Introduction to Jung's Psychology*, Harmondsworth, Middlesex: Penguin Books.

John Duns Scotus 1969, orig. 1891. *Opera Omnia*, Reprint of the Original Edition, ed. Lucas Wadding (Westmead; origin. Paris: Gregg International; orig. Vivés,1969, vol.9, p.176). Quoted in the seminal work of Harald Walach: *Secular Spirituality. The Next Step Towards Enlightenment* (Springer 2015) p.17.

Jung, C G 1911/1974, *Symbols of Transformation, CW 5*, Princeton, NJ: Princeton University Press.

Jung, C G 1921/1974, *Psychological Types, CW 6*, Princeton, NJ: Princeton University Press.

Jung, C G 1936/1975, *The Concept of the Collective Unconscious, CW 9*, Princeton, NJ: Princeton University Press.

Jung, C G 1945/1972, *On the Nature of Dreams, CW 8*, Princeton, NJ: Princeton University Press.

Jung, C G, Jaffé, A 1963, *Memories, Dreams, Reflections*, New York: Random House.

Kawai, H 1964/2009,『日本神話と心の構造』岩波書店 *Japanese Myths and the Structure of the Psyche*, Tokyo: Iwanami-Shoten.

Kawai, H 1967,『ユング心理学入門』培風館 *Introduction to Jungian Psychology*, Tokyo: Baifu-Kan.

Kawai, H 1982,『昔話と日本人の心』岩波書店 *Fairy Tales and the Japanese Mind*, Tokyo: Iwanami-Shoten, Translated into English: 1996 *The Japanese Psyche-Major Motifs in the Fairly Tales of Japan*, CT: Spring Publications.

Kawai, H 2001/2015,『未来への記憶―自伝の試み』新潮文庫、Memories for the future – a trial of autobiography, Tokyo: Sjoncho-Sya, in Japanese only.

Kirsch, T B 2001, *The Jungians,* London: Routledge. (Kindle Version).

Stein, M 2004, Why ISAP-ZURICH is unique in all the world, (Eds.) Meier, I, Brutsche, T, Egger, D, Stein, M, *ISAPZURICH: A Journey,* Morrisville, North Carolina: Lulu.com.

Index

ABAP 126; core competencies 15; core competencies case study 121–3
'about' level: working in thirdness 149, 153
Abramovitch, H 81
abstinence rule 103
active imagination 5, 32, 48, 66, 67–8, 76, 88–9, 97–8, 148
adaptive systems (complex) 53
Adler, G 124
Adult Attachment Interview (AAI) 138
affective attunement 17, 19
affective fields 53–4
alchemy: Jung's references to 104–6
Amaterasu 204
American Board for Accreditation in Psychoanalysis *see* ABAP
amplification 23, 51, 149–50
analysts: archetypal 165–6; choices 5; experienced 3, 40; role of 1, 22, 38–9; Router Training Program 162–3; *see also* therapeutic relationship
analytic attitude 3–5, 108; core competency study 31–4; cultural otherness and 186–7; development of, personal aspects 179–81; perspectives on 181–4; relevance 192; spiritual dimension 75–6; subjectivity 40; sustaining 192; in terms of learning a craft 184–5
analytic compass 32, 151, 181
analytic identity 168, 183, 184, 186, 191, 192
analytic process 19–20, 21, 182
analytic relationship *see* therapeutic relationship
analytic talent 15, 165–6
analytic third 148, 149, 151, 153

analytic training 7–8; core competencies in 1–2, 118, 124–5; multicultural environment, Zurich 197–9; perceived as offering a healing fiction 77; symbol papers in 69; symbols in 68; thirdness in 8, 151–7, 158; *see also* Router Training Program
anti-methodology 125
Apollo 81
archetypal activation 57
archetypal images: in dreams 195
archetypal predisposition 136
archetype(s): concept of 195; knowledge of 20; of the self 73–4; understanding 195–6
Aristotle 45, 185
The art of the tincture: analytical supervision 153
assessment: Router Training Program 166–7
Association of Jungian Analysts Japan (AJAJ) 199–200
associative dreaming 148, 149, 153, 155
associative methods 51
Astor, J 125, 151, 157
asymmetry of relationships: patient–analyst 110, 151; in training 8, 156, 158
attentive listening 19, 35
attentiveness: to the creative in the psyche 94; to the spiritual dimension 5, 32–3
Atwood, G E 109
auseinandersetzung 191
authenticity 18
authority 8, 188, 189
auto-hypnosis techniques: Jung's use of 48

For Product Safety Concerns and Information please contact our EU
representative GPSR@taylorandfrancis.com
Taylor & Francis Verlag GmbH, Kaufingerstraße 24, 80331 München, Germany

www.ingramcontent.com/pod-product-compliance
Lightning Source LLC
Chambersburg PA
CBHW050353270326
41926CB00016B/3717